DESKTOP PUBLISHING

From Dot Matrix ...... via Lasers ...... to Typesetters

PCTEX
produces
High Quality Output

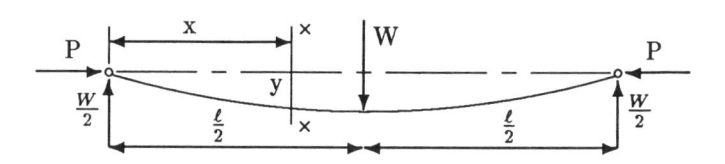

PCTEX automatically handles

- Justification
- Hyphenation
- Tables
- Mathematics
- Diacriticals
- Footnotes
- And much more besides

"sobrietà, al cilicio e all seta?"[a] Certo, Girolamo sosterrà, a giusto titolo, che in molti passaggi non fa che riprendere opinioni espresse da altri autori cristiani; si appella a Tertulliano, Cipriano, Ambrogio, ma la denigrazioni del matrimonio in lui non è più un argomento *ad hominem*, diventerà sistematico. Cerot, Girolamo si rifugerà ...

[a] *Ibid.*, 49, 21, (Labourt, p. 150).

$$\left(\int_{-\infty}^{\infty} e^{-x^2} dx\right)^2 = \int_{-\infty}^{\infty} \int_{-\infty}^{\infty} e^{-(x^2+y^2)} dx\, dy$$
$$= \int_0^{2\pi} \int_0^{\infty} e^{-r^2} r\, dr\, d\theta$$
$$= \pi$$

PCTEX, the best selling PC version of Professor Knuth's typesetting program.
Prices from £229.
UniTEX Systems
12 Daleview Road, Sheffield S8 0EJ Tel: (0742) 351489

This advertisement was created using PCTEX and produced on an HP Laserjet Series II at 300dpi.

DESKTOP PUBLISHING

Second Edition

Kirty Wilson-Davies
Joseph St John Bate
Michael Barnard

KOGAN PAGE

Acknowledgements

We would like to thank all friends, colleagues and organisations who assisted in the preparation and production of this book. In particular: Jo Schurch for her diagrams, her constant enthusiasm and invaluable help at the page make-up stage; Dinesh Vadhia who acted as unofficial technical advisor and organised endless file transfers from one environment to another; and Apple Computer (UK), who generously permitted us to make use of equipment at their Islington Apple Centre.

© Kirty Wilson-Davies, Joseph St John Bate, 1987, 1988

All rights reserved. No part of this book may be reproduced or used in any form or by any means, electronic or mechanical, including photocopying, recording or by an information storage and retrieval system, without permission in writing from the publisher.

First published in Great Britain in 1987 by
Blueprint Publishing Ltd. Second revised edition
published in 1988 by Blueprint Publishing Ltd in
hardback. This paperback edition published in 1988
by Kogan Page Ltd, 120 Pentonville Road, London N1 9JN.

British Library Cataloguing in Publication Data
Wilson-Davies, Kirty
  Desktop publishing. – 2nd ed. –
  1. Desktop publishing. Applications of microcomputers.
  I. Title   II. Bate, Joseph St John   III. Barnard, Michael.
  IV. Series
  070.5'028'5416

ISBN 1-85091-451-6

Typeset on an Apple LaserWriter+, driven by an Apple Macintosh
Introduction to Second Edition typeset by Matrix, London WC2
Printed and bound in Great Britain

Contents

Illustrations   *vi*
Introduction   *vii*
Introduction to the Second Edition:
  Recent Changes in the DTP Scene   *xi*

1. 'Desktop publishing' and 'publishing'   1
2. DTP: where it came from and what it is   13
3. Macintosh the industry standard   31
4. The IBM PC   57
5. Desktop software under MS-DOS   63
6. Enhanced wordprocessing and DTP   85
7. Desktop publishing under networks and UNIX   101
8. Other players in the market   111
9. Peripherals and add-ons   121
10. DTP as a typesetting front-end   145

Appendix 1.   Useful names and addresses   153
Glossary   161
Index   173
Index of advertisers   177

Illustrations

1.	Text output from laser printer and phototypesetter	2
2.	Halftone output from laser printer and camera	4
3.	Constituent parts of a DTP system	16
4.	Typical Macintosh menu	33
5.	Typical MacWrite screen	41
6.	Typical MacDraw document	43
7.	Graph produced under Jazz	46
8.	Typical output from MacAuthor	95
9.	Digitised image from Magic video digitiser	125
10.	Digitised image from the MS300A	126
11.	Linotype distributed system	148

Introduction

The publishing and printing industries, like most other trades with a long history and tradition, have an esoteric craft vocabulary which is jealously guarded by the initiated.

To the publisher, the word 'publishing' itself has a range of subtle nuances, depending on the context in which it is used. It has a legal definition, to do with the point at which a document is considered to be in the public domain. It has a logistical connotation...has a book been 'released' for sale? It is sometimes used as a broad description of a type of career. And so on...

Small wonder that the term 'desktop publishing' initially generated a variety of reactions ranging from puzzlement to amusement or, among the more irascible, something bordering on derision.

It was a contradiction in terms. Publishing - whatever the definition - cannot be contained within the confines of a desk top.

And the one thing it does not mean (to a publisher, at any rate) is 'typesetting' or 'page make-up' or 'printing'.

Yet that is really what desktop publishing is. It is the old business of setting type, making up pages and printing the output, approached from a different direction. As those in the publishing industry all know, that is but a part of the publishing process proper.

The term is therefore a misnomer, but we appear to be stuck with it: the technologists of the microcomputer industry, whence this phenomenon has appeared, have coined a piece of jargon which, however inappropriate, will - in the immediate future at least - describe the processes by which the office automation sector is invading the world of the compositor.

The peculiar problem faced by the publishing and printing industries in trying to get to grips with the situation is that within this new system the conceptual approach to the business of typesetting, composing and 'setting' text and illustrations is so significantly different from the conventional methods of composing and printing that we have to learn completely new methods.

We are presented with a new technique which is at once brilliantly innovative and frustratingly inadequate, stunningly flexible and infuriatingly inhibiting, fascinatingly sophisticated and yet patently down-market.

To understand both its potential and its limitations as a working tool and commercial device we need a guide to its present scope and its probable future development. This book sets out to supply the information which will enable the reader to form a view about desktop publishing in the real 'publishing' environment.

To provide a running visual example of the subject, we have used this book itself as an illustration. The text has been input from a variety of sources: a Hewlett Packard HP110 portable computer with files transferred via 'HP-Link'; a Compaq Deskpro PC running WordStar; an Apricot Single Floppy F1 running Superwriter, an IBM Portable PC (WordStar again) and lastly an Apple Macintosh Plus using MacWrite. The transfer of files from the Compaq and IBM into the Macintosh, was achieved remarkably effectively using PC to Mac and Back, or MacLink. The Apricot files were less simple: we initially transferred using Apricot's 'Asynchronous Communications' software into IBM format. The problem of enabling WordStar to read Superwriter files was overcome by an astute technical advisor' and a small Basic program. The resulting WordStar files were then downloaded to the Macintosh. All editing and a significant amount of text entry was performed on the Macintosh. Fount size and type was specified under MacWrite to minimise additional work at the composition stage.

The pages have been composed on a Macintosh, using PageMaker 1.2. The diagrams have been drawn on an Apple Mac, using MacDraw. Some halftones have been scanned using the Microtek MS 300A, but purely for the purposes of example.

Introduction ix

The pages have been output to camera-ready copy on an Apple LaserWriter printer and then printed from paper plates on a small litho machine.

To avoid giving a false impression of the quality available from such systems we have resisted the temptation to modify the finished artwork photographically, our only concession to strength of impression being to use a reproduction quality paper when outputting from the laserprinter. What you see is what we got.

KWD
JSJB
MB

Introduction to the Second Edition

Recent changes in the DTP scene

When we first discussed the writing of this book, we were obviously aware of the volatility of the content and we agreed with our publisher a method of approach which is not popular with publishers in general but which we all knew was necessary in this instance: we would cheerfully give full exposure to whatever information we thought useful to the reader in 1987, whether or not we believed it would 'date' the book, and we would revise and reprint within a few months, no matter how many copies of the first edition were still gathering dust in the warehouse.

In the event, the first edition sold well, helped on by gaining the 'Best Desktop Published Book' award at the Business Design Centre, and depleted stock levels have for once coincided with the requirements of editorial integrity.

Like all good desktop publishers we kept our magnetic files in reasonable order ready to revise specific text sections but we have been persuaded that it is more interesting and helpful to identify the developments of the past year in a separate section so that those readers labouring under the limitations and deficiencies of the first systems can more readily spot those areas which have advanced.

Departing from the conventions of book publishing, we have positioned this new matter before the main text, where it most logically belongs.

To avoid the charge that we have shirked our responsibility for updating textual comment which has been overtaken by events, we have organised this section into a chapter-by-chapter update. We hope this accommodates both those coming new to the game and those wanting an update on the state of play.

1. 'Desktop publishing' and 'publishing'

Comments on quality and size of output from laser printers, while still relevant and accurate, will almost certainly be overtaken by events in early 1988.

Several laser printers with output resolution in excess of 300 dots per linear inch are on their way from the USA or Japan and initial results look promising for much improved definition of text material. The AM Varityper VT600, at 600 dpi, produces acceptable artwork for many purposes.

A3 size printers are also becoming more readily available (and so is the appropriate software).

Speed of output, except on the highly-priced industrial machines, still shows no signs of reaching printing machine levels and remains unsuitable for long runs.

Automatic page composition systems – referred to on page 11 – are now coming in with some very clever features, although not normally with WYSIWYG so perhaps they are to be considered borderline DTP. In the continuing spirit of experiment, we have put this chapter through such a system – Digital Publications' Telos – and then out to a Linotron 202 typesetter.

It took an hour to set up the parameters for pagination rules and literally seven seconds (on an AT) to paginate the chapter.

2. DTP: where it came from and what it is

The desktop publishing revolution is under examination. The predictions of radical and overnight changes to our working practices have not come about. Nor did we ever advocate that they should. We adhered, rather, to the theory of gradual as opposed to revolutionary change. The former presupposes changes within the structure of a given entity – in this case the publishing industry – the latter, a change to the very structure itself.

We have not witnessed therefore major changes in the organisation of publishing houses or those concerned with publication – in the traditional sense – of written communication. The structures (with a few exceptions) remain firm, the methodology is changing bit by bit. This is the most constructive form of change.

It has been interesting to watch, as we anticipated, so many entrants from the traditional typesetting arena moving in – not only to claim a piece of the action – but to adopt technical enhancements that make sense to vendor and user alike. The fact remains however that the motivation, the driving force and to a greater extent the innovation continue to emanate from the PC end of the market.

The industry professionals are tending to refine and enhance what was started at a low-cost level and in so doing are undoubtedly adding respectability to the concept of desktop publishing.

The perception of DTP

During the early days of DTP there was little or no differentiation made as to the type of user such an application area would attract. Broadly speaking there was a rough and ready breakdown into several types:

The professional publisher addressed by this book

The organisation requiring a considerable amount of typesetting – usually serviced by external agencies

The typical office user who needed to enhance the presentation of written communication.

The solutions for each distinct type were frequently perceived to be the same – the ability to compose pages taking text and graphics from a variety of sources, the facility for high quality output and a WYSIWYG user interface. While this overview remains sound for the purposes of this exercise the perception of DTP for the latter (and perhaps largest) user group requires refinement.

The typical office user has needs other than those of the publisher yet the average user has found himself bombarded by such considerations as winding columns, headings in excess of 200 and in some cases 500 point and finely tuned kerning and leading. The PC industry has done a copy-book marketing exercise . . . but is it providing the ubiquitous PC user with what he wants? He has been told to eat cake, not because it is the only answer available, but because cake is more lucrative – to the vendor – than bread.

In that the raison d'etre of this book is to provide a guide to the publisher, this may seem like an unnecessary soapbox stance against the vendors of DTP systems. The intention is merely to point out that it has become clear in the last year that a great many readers need to assess their needs carefully, and, if the proposal and the company report are the most important documents to emerge from the DTP system, to steer clear of being thrust into the 'we-must-produce-a-newsletter syndrome'.

Key elements

We mention the key elements considered essential components in the DTP system: an operating system with an integral WYSIWYG user interface – as in the case of the Macintosh – or a graphics user interface (GUI) such as Windows or GEM that resides 'on top'; a minimum of three software packages – WP, graphics and page composition – and the facility to support a high resolution output device. We allude to the renaissance of the embedded code approach and a move away from quasi-WYSIWYG (it has never been true).

One of the most striking changes has been a move away from the clear demarcation between WP and page composition. They are increasingly combined (with, admittedly some loss of typographical precision) but serve to address – on the whole – the needs of the less specialised user. We will examine this in more depth in our summary of Chapter Six.

3. Macintosh the industry standard

Despite concerns that the advent of desktop publishing solutions on MS-DOS-based PCs would lead to a demise in the success of the Macintosh, Apple continues to hold a significant market share.

The reasons for this are twofold.

Apple not only led the way in propounding, developing and delivering DTP, but was instrumental in advocating and implementing what have now evolved as industry standards – Postscript support and a WYSIWYG interface. That DTP was at one time synonymous with the Macintosh is a hard conviction to shake. The irony we allude to below – that on the one hand the Macintosh was treated as an up-market toy while the entire PC industry appeared to be dedicated to emulating what they so glibly wrote-off as 'gimmicky' – has latterly been confounded by IBM's intentions to follow suit. The enhanced version of OS/2 with Presentation Manager offers the much-awaited GUI: a Macintosh way of working. The advent of so many Mac-alike environments can only serve to strengthen the case of the original innovator.

Coexistence with DOS

Apple have recently been strengthening the case for coexistence in the DOS world. Not only does the Macintosh SE have a single slot that can accommodate a DOS co-processor board, but the Macintosh II can support both DOS and UNIX applications. A variety of co-processor boards are available including AST's MAC 286 for the Macintosh II and the MAC 86, an Intel 8086-based board, for the SE.

By recognising that the majority of Macintosh users also used IBM PCs or compatibles, Apple successfully overcame the problems of shared data through the AppleTalk PC card. There is no longer any foundation for the 'non-compatible' status of the Macintosh. The irony is thus compounded . . . IBM pursue the Macintosh-type user environment, while Apple is dedicated to addressing the traditional DOS world.

Moreover a concerted campaign in the field of 'desktop communications' has lead to coexistence with the DEC world and has strengthened market perceptions of the Macintosh as a 'power PC'.

Multi-tasking

Multifinder is Apple's answer to the multi-tasking debate. It permits users to view and move between applications and offers significant enhancements over Minifinder. The implications for desktop publishers are considerable. Given a typical scenario where text and graphics are being placed on a page, you can simply move to and amend the graphics image where before you had to exit the page-composition software, load the graphics package, amend, exit and reload the DTP component; only to find that the image still wasn't right!

There have been some significant changes in popular Macintosh software.

Wordprocessing

An increasing number of DTP packages are broadening the brief and incorporating WP into what was previously perceived as dedicated page composition. However, this does not signal the death of stand-alone WP software. Firstly, DTP software is expensive and it would not make commercial sense to replace every WP package. Secondly, it is foolhardy to assume that every user has the need to lay out pages in typographical form.

In this respect the Macintosh environment is unique. Given that all software from the most lowly wordprocessor will permit cut and paste from any other Mac software (and hence integration of text and graphics) and given, moreover, that all will drive a Postscript output device, the user with limited 'publishing' requirements will find that WP will suffice. The standard office requirements for high quality paper-based communication can thus be satisfied.

The same cannot be said of DOS-based software to be examined in more depth below.

MacWrite and Microsoft Word continue to dominate the market and no major contenders have emerged. Software developers appear to be channelling their energies into ever more sophisticated graphics/presentation products and, of course, DTP.

Graphics

MacDraw continues to hold the greatest market share of all Macintosh-based graphics software which no doubt reflects its simplicity of use, flexibility and low purchase price. That is not to detract from innovative software such as Adobe's Illustrator covered below. Our demarcation into freehand, structured and business graphics continues to hold good. Presentation graphics constitute a growing market and it is questionable whether scanning software should not also warrant separate examination. Our contention that the scanning of half tones left much to be desired has altered little, despite the advent of grey scale TIFF. There is evidence that much of the work that was previously carried out using structured or freehand graphics has now been displaced by the scanning of images.

At the end of the day it depends entirely on specific requirements. Freehand drawing still has a role as a creative tool; it is perhaps the typical business user who will use a scanner or indeed symbol sets since he may require company logos and useful (but unoriginal) illustrations. In short nothing new needs to be designed. For those with a requirement for the origination of creative images Illustrator must be recognised as a leading player.

Illustrator emanating as it does from the company that gave us Postscript, makes the language accessible to the user in the form of a graphics package. There is nothing dramatically different about the way you use it, indeed it conforms to the standard mode of working with paint and draw type software. Illustrator can import scanned images or MacPaint files as underlays or bit-map (at less than 300 dpi) templates. Only one can be used at any one time. Several modes are then available to you; 'Artwork and Template' or 'Artwork Only' – depending on whether you wish to work on an existing image or start from scratch. In both modes the drawing will appear only as vectors; shapes can be selected and filled with a shade of grey that will only become visible through the 'Preview' option. The lack of fill patterns may initially confuse the Macintosh user, however, by selecting a precise percentage of grey tone for fills or lines the results are much improved. This is particularly apparent when outputting through a typesetter at high resolution.

Illustrator provides drawing tools for generic creation. A pen for drawing lines and arcs – 'Bezier curves' in Postscript parlance – a rectangle and a circle. Bezier curves can be manipulated with great precision until the required arc is achieved. Various commands are available that serve to provide manipulation and combination of all image elements. A powerful 'zoom' feature permits nine different viewing levels from 1600% to 6.25%.

'Scale', 'rotate', 'mirror' and 'shear' are all tools for transforming the image, if necessary in minute increments (executed through dialogue boxes as opposed to manually). Grouping and ungrouping is a standard feature.

Text can be entered in a text frame or block. Type specs – fount, attributes and point size (from 1 to 1,008 point) – cannot be mixed within one text block. Leading, kerning and alignment are supported within the frame. Text can be transformed – using scale, rotate, reflect and shear – in the same way as images. In addition text can be 'filled' with a shade of grey.

Illustrator files can be exported in Encapsulated Postscript Files – EPS – (Macintosh) or EPS (PC-Windows) or can be saved as 'Postscript only'.

Illustrator provides a powerful graphics solution that could previously only be met with a combination of products. It overcomes the grainy look of so many other graphics packages by abandoning the hatching and fill patterns normally associated with Macintosh software. The potential power of Postscript has been harnessed but in a manageable and easy to use form. Despite this it is questionable how pertinent freehand or illustration graphics are. In order to produce quality results the user must possess more than a modicum of creative design skills. It begs the question whether paper and pencil might not be a preferred medium for such a person. Illustrator retails at £450.

Cricket Draw version 1.1, distributed by Heyden of Quark Xpress fame, epitomises the second generation of draw packages. Primary features include colour support for the Macintosh II, use of shading and 'starburst', to provide a '3D' effect, spiral and curved text, scaling of bit-mapped images and snap-to-grid.

Cricket Draw offers a traditional range of options in the tool box: text, lines, rectangles, squares (with a rounded corner option) circles, oblongs, arcs, diamonds, polygons and pens for freehand drawing. In addition, Bezier curves can be created and manipulated. The option 'Grates' denotes the use of parallel lines in a step and repeat mode or in a mode best described as proportionally increased or decreased repetition.

Illustrator EPS files can be imported and Cricket Draw can export in EPS format. Retail price: £295.

Presentation graphics

Desktop Presentation constitutes a market that meets needs other than those of the publisher. Some interesting graphics products are nonetheless emerging that could sensibly cover the needs of both publisher and presenter alike. While such features as the creation of 35mm slides, OHPs and video or slide shows are not pertinent in this context, presentation software generally encapsulates a little of everything in the graphics sector. A typical example (the Cricket presentation offering) offers some business graphics (pie, bar, column, stacked column, line, area and 3D where applicable). Basic draw functions are provided as is scanned image support and basic text handling. Output in a choice of file formats, PICT and EPS, this could prove of value to the desktop publisher with a desire to kill two birds with one stone.

Business graphics

Probably the area of graphics most used by the non-professional publisher, business graphics software continues to be much in demand by the desktop publisher. We examined in chapter three Lotus' Jazz and Cricket Graph, among others. Significant updates/changes to these products are summarised below.

Modern Jazz constitutes not merely an upgrade to Jazz but effectively a new product. Lotus, the sleeping giant in the Macintosh environment, has reawakened. New functionality includes such features as a unique command language for macro development and greatly enhanced spreadsheet functionality. Users who wish regularly to integrate charts in their publications generally find that a powerful spreadsheet negates the need for re-keying of data. Integrated software also serves to reduce the plethora of products required to deal with specific tasks. The wordprocessing module offers the standard Macintosh functionality plus user-definable rulers and text styles, widow and orphan control, justification and repagination.

The chart types include line, bar, area percentage bar, area, scatter, pie, polar (for trig-related functions) and histograms (statistical distributions). Graphics editing includes fill patterns, line styles, marker arrows and shadow boxes. Modern Jazz supports on-screen colour and takes full advantage of the RAM of the Macintosh II. Up to 8192 points can be supported per plot. Modern Jazz retails at £295 and offers the same components as Jazz.

Yet another product distributed by Heyden, Cricket Graph offers a rudimentary spreadsheet for the purpose of chart production, not for demanding numerical analysis. Eleven chart types are supported, including double Y Polar and 3D options. As with Modern Jazz, legends and labels can be edited and text added using the standard Macintosh fount selection. Multiple charts can be arranged on a page, grouped and imported en mass into the DTP software. On-screen colour is supported on the Macintosh II. Cricket Graph retails at £175.

Page make-up

PageMaker and Ready Set Go continue to dominate the Macintosh market. The former now commands the position of de facto leader in the combined DOS and Apple environment. It is now claimed by Aldus to be the third best-selling software package in the US behind the traditional leaders Lotus' 1-2-3 and Ashton Tate's dBase III Plus. Whilst this claim may hold good for a short period, or a limited sample, recognised market research organisations do not bear this out. The fact remains, nonetheless, that Aldus have consolidated PageMaker's position. PageMaker release 2.00 for the Macintosh now offers all the features of its DOS-based counterpart. Page-based in orientation, and subject to criticism as being unsuitable for long-run documents, the mere fact that this book was composed using PageMaker should prove a point. It's possible, if not the fastest route.

Whilst PageMaker version 2.0 for the Mac offers the functionality of its DOS counterpart it does have one additional feature; support for grey scale TIFF. This is in effect a subformat of the nonproprietary industry standard that we know and love. As yet few scanners support

Recent changes in the DTP scene

the new TIFF subformat, so its value is currently limited. We will expand on this question below.

Letraset have released an enhanced version of their existing Ready Set Go offering. RSG 4 claims to add more than 80 additional features.

RSG4 can cope with any page size up to 99" × 99" providing a 'tiled' output much like MacDraw. Facing pages can be displayed and text and graphics can cross the back margins.

The wordprocessing features of RSG4 have been greatly enhanced. One function in particular will prove extremely useful – indeed has long been demanded by desktop publishers – the ability to search and replace on typeface, point size, fount attribute, case and text. How often has one set headings in, say, 14pt Helvetica bold and wished retrospectively to change the whole lot to 12pt Times roman? Finally it can be done simply.

The spelling dictionary has been expanded from 60,000 to 100,000 words and is intelligent enough to interpret phonetically in some degree.

The existing facility for text flow around irregular graphics is less cumbersome to execute and more precise. Hyphenation features allow controls over minimum letters before hyphen and the number of sequential hyphens appearing on a page. Word spacing is handled in an unusual way. A text area containing unacceptable rivering is highlighted and the spacing between words is altered on a percentage basis. This may entail some trial and error to achieve the correct results, but it can eliminate rivering.

RSG4 can import Pict, TIFF and EPS .Built-in graphics tools include (in addition to the standard lines and rectangles) diagonal lines and a step and repeat facility.

Other RSG documents can be imported into RSG4 and all versions are upwardly compatible. A style sheet facility has been added, and the glossary facility has been improved by 'remembering' key phrases. A facility to print output for colour separations is also included. Lastly, RSG4 is supplied complete with a two hour audio tape to assist users in the learning phase. Retail price £495.

Other vendors have entered the market despite PageMaker's apparent stranglehold. The newcomer to have fared best must undoubtedly be Quark Xpress.

Distributed by Heyden – responsible for introducing Ready Set Go into the UK before losing distribution to Letraset – Xpress has met with a favourable response by the Macintosh desktop publishing fraternity.

Despite our concerted attempts – as an aid to readers and authors alike – to keep each software package neatly compartmentalised, we fear the lines of demarcation are growing ever more nebulous. Xpress is, in a sense, the antithesis of the enhanced WP software we outlined since, like Ready Set Go, Xpress offers wordprocessing functionality. It also uses the frame or block concept for the composition of pages. The software is unique in that it supports colour output, which given the scarcity of colour laser printers may be construed as a long-term strategy or merely a gimmick! The program also supports on-screen colour though currently only an eight-colour palette is supported.

Wordprocessing features include the ubiquitous cut and paste, basic text editing, search-and-replace and a spelling checker. Text files created in the WP mode cannot be exported for use in any other software.

The use of text and graphics frames is enhanced by the Frame Editor which allows the design, editing and subsequent saving of customised frames outlines. This facility can be used to ensure consistency of output in the same way as a style sheet feature. Text can be automatically made to flow around irregular graphics, without any of the laborious manipulation normally associated with the task.

Xpress version 1.04 will accept formatted text files from MacWrite and Microsoft Word 3.0. A variety of unformatted text files can be imported. The package also allows import of other Xpress documents.

Xpress offers automatic or manual kerning in increments of .005 of an em. Three types of leading – automatic, relative and absolute – are supported. Adjustments in increments of .001 of a point are possible depending on the output device in use. Point size control is from 2 to 500! Additional features to assist in the copy-fitting process are horizontal scaling to compress or expand text – a feature which may hold limited appeal to the purist – and tracking. A step and repeat facility is also offered permitting the precise positioning of a duplicated element relative to the original.

Xpress can import standard Pict files, MacPaint and encapsulated Postscript.

The colour support can be used for the purposes of colour separation, since spot colour can be assigned to lines, text and frames. Pages that reflect the separation can then be printed on a Postscript device

Recent changes in the DTP scene *xxiii*

(albeit in monochrome) complete with registration marks.

In common with the Macintosh standard, Xpress employs a WYSIWYG interface and is intuitive to use. On line Help is available though sadly this is not context sensitive.

Quark Xpress offers impressive features which are reflected in its price of £695. It has been criticised for slowness of operation, especially when using the WP functions. yet despite this holds appeal for the user with high expectations of typographical precision and flexibility.

4. The IBM PC

It is in the IBM world that we have witnessed more, heard of more, and await more in terms of radical change. The days of the 640K constraint are nearing their end, the days of MS DOS numbered.

Personal System/2

The PS/2 as it is commonly known is IBM's new PC standard. In essence it is the vehicle for the long awaited but now arrived – at least in part – Operating System/2 (OS/2). The PS/2 has enjoyed considerable success since first shipping in the summer of 1987. So much so that IBM were unable to meet demand on some models and are only now reaching adequate supply levels.

So what are the reasons for the PS/2's success and what are the implications for the desktop publisher?

The PS/2 superseded and replaced all other IBM PCs. Thus the alternatives lay in the purchase of a compatible – in this respect Amstrad has fared well – or to stick with Big Blue and adopt the new standard. Whilst research indicates that users will not be changing over to OS/2 overnight, they perceive a future need for the processing power that the new operating system will release. It would, in practice, be impossible to adopt OS/2 at the time of writing because of a complete lack of OS/2 software.

The hardware is available in four systems: Models 30, 50, 60 and 80. The former will not support OS/2. Specifications are as follows:

Model 30   Either twin 3.5" diskette drives, or 20Mb hard disk and one diskette drive. 640Kb RAM, expandable to 2.64Mb.

Model 50   20Mb hard disk and one 3.5" diskette. 1Mb RAM expandable to 7Mb.

Model 60   Either 44Mb or 70Mb hard disk and one 3.5" diskette drive. 1Mb RAM expandable to 15Mb. Floor standing.

Model 80   Varying hard disk capacities from 44Mb to 230Mb. Single 3.5" diskette drive. Intel 80386 chip. Floor standing.

IBM have adopted 3.5" media for all models – currently causing some confusion since not all popular DOS-based software is available in this format – with 720Kb as standard on the model 30, 1.44Mb on all other models. Optional optical drives and adapter cards are planned for all models which will increase potential storage even more. Removable optical disks can hold up to 200Mb of data.

The PS/2 offers new standards over the existing CGA (Colour Graphics Adaptor) and EGA (Enhanced Graphics Adaptor) in the form of VGA (Video Graphics Array) and the MCGA (Multi-Colour Graphics Array). What this all means in simple terms is that the resolution and clarity of the displays has improved. Graphics are more vivid and precise and on monochrome models text is sharper and easier to read. Moreover, the monochrome models support up to 60 shades of grey. All are supplied with anti-glare screens and tilt and swivel as standard.

Implications for the desktop publisher

A perennial problem in using a DOS-based machine for the publishing function has been the RAM restriction imposed by the operating system itself. In terms of hardware specifications the PS/2 overcomes all the drawbacks and augurs well for the future. The optical disk option also presents interesting opportunities as we see the adoption of CD-ROM in the publishing industry.

The real benefits will emerge, however, with the adoption of OS/2. OS/2 does not have to run on a PS/2. Any 80286 or 80386-based machine will do. Indeed the first PC to be offered with OS/2 is the Zenith, an IBM compatible. Obviously the IBM and Operating System/2 offering will provide the most powerful solution.

OS/2 is currently available in a character-based mode and therefore offers a user-interface not unlike DOS. It does feature multi-tasking allowing several applications to be open and working simultaneously. Only OS/2 software can operate under the system but a 'compatibility box' is provided that permits one DOS program to be run in foreground. The 640K constraint will apply to all software running in compatibility mode.

The next step in the development of OS/2 is a LAN Manager version, due for release in the second quarter of 1988. Of most significance to the desktop publisher is the extended version of OS/2 with Presentation Manager anticipated towards the end of 1988. Presentation Manager will run under a Graphics User Interface – GUI – not unlike Windows. This is not surprising when one bears in mind that the original developers of OS/2 are Microsoft. Windows applications will not run under OS/2 but must be relegated to the compatibility box.

The majority of desktop publishing and graphics software will undoubtedly be adapted to operate under OS/2 with Presentation Manager. This is because GUI will offer the users something more akin to the Macintosh – rather than the DOS – environment, and because ultimately GUI is the direction that IBM wants to go. Given that the market leaders in DOS-based page composition software – Ventura Publisher and PageMaker – both run under a GUI already, it seems unlikely that they would wish to change to a character-based interface.

A distinct advantage of adopting Presentation Manager is that all software running 'inside' has access to the extended graphics application programming interface (API) functions. This, it is anticipated, will provide device independence for graphics software, without having to become a true 'windows-style' product. However, to linger too long on futures is unwise, and until such time as we are able to use fully-fledged DTP software under extended Presentation Manager, any further comment would be premature.

A note for first time purchasers of DTP systems would be to ask what strategy specific software vendors have for their products under OS/2. While the DOS user will be with us for some years to come, it makes sense for the publisher to ensure that the software selected will be upgraded to take advantage of the power and multi-tasking features of OS/2.

5. Desktop software under MS-DOS

The most significant developments in the MS-DOS market are in the WP and graphics sectors. The former will be addressed in the notes on Chapter Six, since all new/improved products fall within the enhanced wordprocessing, if not DTP, category. Once again we see our previous lines of demarcation becoming ever more nebulous.

Graphics software

In our original version we restricted our overview of graphics products to GEM and Windows-based packages. At that time 'aping' of the Macintosh environment was prevelant as was the breakdown into freehand (paint), structured (draw) and business (charts and graphs) graphics.

This is now no longer the case. The product to emerge as leader in the graphics market, Lotus' Freelance Plus (version 2.1) breaks all the rules. Firstly it combines all three disciplines into an integrated solution and secondly it features a character-based interface with mouse support. We examine it below.

Freelance uses a 'Lotus style' interface (users of 1-2-3 will be familiar with the concept) that can be accessed and used with a mouse. As such it requires no user-interface such as Windows or GEM, but resides directly on DOS. An integrated package, Freelance, covers the entire spectrum of uses and performs each one as well as a dedicated package. Thus, freehand drawing is easily accomplished using the mouse (it is possible but cumbersome without) supported by a library of symbols including optional add-ons

Recent changes in the DTP scene   xxvii

such as chemical symbols and maps.

Structured drawing is executed by features that include single point editing, grids, rulers, zoom, rotate, mirror, rescale and a full screen crosshair. Graphic elements are produced in the same manner as architectural drafting or CAD packages. Editing is flexible, and allows greater control than the 'group' and 'ungroup' option offered by most Mac-alike software. Elements can be selected against the following criteria: One, Several, All, Touching and Inside (an area defined by the user). Following selection elements can be moved, resized, deleted, or amended in terms of colour, fount, etc.

Graphs can be produced by importing charts from Lotus' 1-2-3 and Symphony (.PIC format) Graphwriter II in the GMF (Graphic Metafile) format and subsequently enhanced. ASCII and dBase files can also be imported. Freelance offers substantial charting facilities in its own right, and therefore appeals to users who do not wish to utilise spreadsheets. Our dedicated desktop publisher perhaps?

Freelance is ideal for the desktop publisher who may have a variety of graphics requirements but no desire to purchase three software packages. In keeping with other vector-based programs the quality of image is as good as the output device used. Furthermore in addition to a choice of colour fills – which would be of limited value in a desktop published document – Freelance Plus offers half-step grey scale fill options.

Export in the GMF (or CGM as it is sometimes called, just to make life difficult) format is now a standard in the DTP arena and makes Freelance a popular choice for Ventura and other users.

Freelance supports Postscript output devices, non-Postscript laser printers, colour plotters and dot matrix printers. The current output device is always taken into account when working, only the relevant founts and colours supported being made available to the user.

Another contender in the 'Integrated Graphics' stakes, Harvard Graphics offers ease of use at the expense of functionality. Whilst claiming to offer 'a complete graphics solution', closer examination reveals that this is not precisely the case. HG does not offer the full range of graphics components of Freelance Plus; it offers charting and structured drawing without freehand facilities.

HG's charting capabilities are useful. These include quick preview from chart forms, macros to automate tasks in chart production and chart templates. As an aid to the desktop publisher Harvard Graphics is useful but may not satisfy all requirements.

Other products worthy of mention are Ashton Tate's Master series – a combination of what were originally distinct draw and graph packages – GEM Presentation Team and VCN Concorde.

Business graphics

Those with a specific need for business graphics pure and simple should examine the latest generation of products that offer powerful and versatile charting with the option to export to page composition systems.

Lotus' Graphwriter II offers 24 chart types including the less common gantt, bubble, organisation and high-low-open-close. Graphs can be produced from a wide variety of spreadsheet data, dBase or keyed in manually. The product uses a typical Lotus interface and is simple and quick to use. A facility to establish links with a data source allows charts to be updated automatically every time the data changes. Up to 100 charts can be produced on a single command. Graphwriter II can output in GMF format and can be merged with Freelance Plus to provide additional enhancements such as company logo or additional text. The GMF standard ensures that the output can be used in conjunction with page composition systems. Graphwriter II provides the same output device driver set as Freelance Plus.

Soft Image System's Davrelle operates under the GEM environment and makes full use of the GEM/WIMP interface. Davrelle offers only ten chart types but like Graphwriter II provides an autochart facility (picking up data from 1-2-3 and other popular spreadsheets), flexible text positioning and control over colours. The software provides the facility for coloured backdrops and once again, like Graphwriter, for multiple charts per page. Ease of use is undoubtedly its strong point and the package will appeal to existing GEM users. Unfortunately it is precisely as a result of operating under GEM that a limited number of screen founts are available to the user (though output through a Postscript device will offer the standard range of typefaces). Given that it is widely accepted that WYSI never really WYG this does not constitute a major problem.

What might, however, is the limited chart legend and annotation and poor documentation.

Page composition software

Of the three packages we identified as most likely to . . . two are established as de facto market leaders and one has disappeared without trace! Ventura and PageMaker have emerged as winners, and are not only market leaders in their own right but are being bundled with most of the major manufacturers' desktop publishing solutions. Harvard Professional Publisher is no longer being distributed by Software Publishing who have recently shelved plans for a replacement product. Professional Write Plus was to have been launched as an integrated wordprocessor and desktop publishing package. Following a preview the product was put on ice indefinitely.

The main threat to PageMaker and Ventura will not, we feel, emerge from other dedicated page composition systems. Increasingly the trend is to simplify the process and look to an integrated WP/DTP solution. The fact that this approach did not work out for Software Publishing is perhaps indicative of the quality of their product. However it is worth bearing in mind that resistance from dealers may have had a part to play. Selling a WP, a DTP and a graphics package in one fell swoop is more attractive in revenue terms than merely selling two software products.

Other players have emerged in the course of the past nine months, but none appear to be able to shake the pre-eminence of the big two. Migent has recently launched its low cost – £199 – DTP package Page-ability. This product epitomises a range of products at the low end of the market aimed primarily at the Amstrad user. There is no place for further detail since no Postscript support is offered and hence the value to publishers is negligible. Price alone would seem to position the product away from viable DTP solutions.

Digital Research's GEM Desktop Publisher (GEM DP) falls somewhere between stools. What it attempts to offer is an alternative to Ventura at a considerably lower price (£295). GEM DP borrows many Ventura-like features such as the style sheet approach to repetitive formatting and the facility to change the current style sheet in order to alter the document format. Very basic text editing is available but text can be imported from GEM Write, Displaywrite

3 and 4, Multimate Wordperfect and ASCII. Only GEM graphics files can be imported.

No graphics tool box for onscreen rules and borders is supplied and only eight fixed type sizes are supported. The product also lacks the typographical precision of Ventura. Supplied complete with the current version of GEM, it could constitute an appropriate starter system but would be quickly outgrown and holds no appeal for the professional user.

Other entrants in the market include high-level and high cost MS-DOS based page composition systems specifically designed to drive typesetters. These will be noted below.

6. Enhanced wordprocessing and DTP

We pointed out that the generic page composition system would continue to dominate until enhanced WP software was effectively rewritten or dramatically enhanced to address the needs of page composition. We continue to witness a plethora of products laying claim to DTP functionality. Some have fared better than others.

It has also become apparent that the needs of the professional publisher as distinct from the 'business user' are diverging. The average PC user who perceives a need for DTP – for proposals, specifications and perhaps the occasional newsletter – has no absolute need for leading and kerning to an nth degree of an em space. The concern is increasingly with high quality output, integration of text and graphics and rudimentary (in the eyes of the professional) precision. Certainly rivering is not acceptable, H and J is a must (as is column balancing), but certain other facilities are simply not being used.

New features are emerging that reflect this concern with office document production. The most notable is the 'outlining' facility (a feature borrowed from Lotus Manuscript) that provides automatic numbering and multiple levels of headings such as one would expect to find on legal documents.

Recent changes in the DTP scene

Those products that we feel have made the greatest advances in recent months are briefly outlined below.

Despite promises of great things to come, Microsoft's Word 4 (DOS-based) is still firmly in the category of WP and not WP/DTP. Features include the creation of a re-usable style sheet from an existing text file, direct import of 1-2-3, Symphony, Excel and Multiplan spreadsheets, but limited graphics import. A facility exists for converting DCA text files but only ASCII can be exported. A keystroke macro facility has been included since the previous release, as has a redlining option. Naturally an outlining feature has been added from which an automatic table of contents can be generated.

Word is not a Windows-based product (the next release code-named Opus will redress this) and as such is not WYSIWYG. Hence Word does not show proportionally spaced founts or point sizes on the graphics screen, nor can columns be viewed side by side. In order to preview the document an additional program, Pageview, must be purchased.

The spelling checker is subject to criticism since only the entire document can be checked, rather than individual words or lines. Nor is Word considered easy to learn. Were it to offer adequate DTP functionality to negate the need for a separate page composition package, the learning problem would be excusable since only one product would need to be mastered. Currently Word must remain relegated to the status of companion product to PageMaker. Word 4 retails at £425 and Pageview at £35.

We covered Samna in some detail and hence only mention those salient improvements to the product. Samna IV Plus is termed a Document Processor that includes spreadsheet and the wordprocessing features of Samna IV 2.0. Our main criticism of the earlier product was the lack of support for Postscript devices and the fact that the software was pitch rather than point orientated. This has now been rectified and Samna IV offers PS support.

The package has enhanced preview facilities showing specific typefaces, graphs and other images in WYSIWYG mode. File import has been enhanced graphics and software supported including 1-2-3 PIC, Freelance Plus, Samna Decision graphics, PC Paintbrush and TIFF.

In re-positioning the product as a Document Processor designed for use with long reports and technical papers, Samna have followed the lead set by Lotus Manuscript. Certainly improvements have been made over the earlier version and Samna could be said to be moving in the right direction.

In the US market Wordperfect is a market leader and is gaining a considerable following in the UK. As a wordprocessor there seems to be no doubt that it is providing the users with what they want. Wordperfect 5.0 is scheduled for release in March 88 and offers some interesting new features.

Integration of text and graphics with the facility to scale and crop is included. Images can be tied to headers and footers. Graphic file import is extensive and includes Lotus PIC files, Freelance Plus – and other GMF/CGM – files, Windows Paint, HPGL plot files and TIFF. There is an additional utility that allows a graphic screen image to be captured and integrated into the page.

A zoom or preview feature allows a page or facing pages to be viewed in a WYSIWYG mode. The print attributes are selected in terms of fine, small, large, very large and extra large which all sounds terribly easy but not particularly useful. The manufacturers claim that vertical and horizontal spacing are automatically adjusted to match the fount selected. The plot thickens . . . not having access to the software we took a close look at a page of sample output. The most glaring and unaesthetic features were uneven column alignment, poor H & J and quite unacceptable rivering of white space.

While in terms of specification the product looks good, offering additional goodies such as an outline facility, redlining and generation of tables of contents, lists, indexes, etc, the quality of output was sufficient for us to assume that Wordperfect has some way to go before it can lay claim to DTP functionality.

We saw Lotus' Manuscript as 'paving the way for a generation of task specific composition systems'. In the light of the recently announced version 2.0 – due for release in April – we may have to bite back our words.

Manuscript appears to have bridged the gap between WP and DTP most successfully and the pending new version takes the product even further.

Improved memory management will speed up performance, especially preview, printing and document compare (redlining). The facility is there to create keystroke macros and assign them to a specific key. The spelling checker – using an English dictionary – will check individual words, blocks, sections or the entire document. The inclusion of a thesaurus provides definitions as well as synonyms.

Specific WP enhancements include multi-line headers and footers (limited only by the size of the page) that can contain multiple typefaces and images. Autosort is a sort capability that can alphabetise single columns or blocks. Cross reference, outline and indexing have all been enhanced. The notes option has been expanded to encompass not only footnotes but also level and end notes, to allow the build up of appendix material such as a bibliography.

Document formatting features include winding columns. The flow may be interrupted by a graphic or block specifying a different number of columns. The user is given control over gutter widths and column alignment. Named blocks (based on the Ventura 'Tag' principle) can be defined and applied anywhere in the document. Page breaks can be displayed in the editor rather than just in preview mode. Hyphenation is now rule as opposed to algorithm-based, control over subsequent hyphens and number of letters before a hyphen is supported. Word spacing controls are built-in.

Preview features now allow users to preview graphics, equations, blocks or sections from within the editor. Non-printing comments can be included showing initials of the reviewer to enable work groups effectively to review documents. In view of MS 2.0's network support this will prove a useful feature.

It is apparent that whilst not a page composition package the product could be said to provide a credible integrated solution, combining WP and DTP. Manuscript is priced at £395.

7. Desktop publishing under networks and UNIX

The main developments in the UNIX marketplace are factors relating to Interleaf, the leading DTP software package in this market.

There are now available three versions of Interleaf: WPS – workstation publishing system – the original product, RTPS, an implementation for the IBM 6150 or RT PC as it is sometimes known and

TPS, a multi-user version implemented on DEC, Sun and Apollo machines.

WPS is – due to its single-user constraint – frequently used as an input station for users with links to a central unit running TPS.

RTPS is a far more expensive product than WPS despite remaining a single user product, which is strange considering the functionality of the IBM 6150. It addresses and overcomes the areas of weakness in WPS. RTPS can format in multi columns such that graphics can appear adjacent to text. A hyphenation exception dictionary is included as is the automatic generation of indexes and tables of contents.

Graphics import includes CADAM, CIEDS, CATIA and HPGL – provided they conform to certain formats – in addition to bit-map graphics.

TPS is basically a multi-user version of RTPS and offers the same functionality. The recently released version 4.0 will run on 386-based machines, the Macintosh II, DEC minicomputers and the Sun and Apollo workstations mentioned above.

Unixsys Softquad is now being offered by Torch in a bundle referred to as Torch Triple X publishing system. Dealers can bundle their own printer.

Altos Computer systems, vendors of low-end UNIX workstations, have released a DTP system based on Deskset Publisher and complementary WP software. The system currently offers no Postscript support, but claims to support up to 64 users depending on the workstation employed.

Samna Plus IV mentioned above is available in a UNIX version.

8. Other players in the market

Almost every IBM compatible vendor offers a DTP system, including software – normally Ventura and/or PageMaker – PC, laser printer and possibly a scanner of some kind. There is quite frankly very little to differentiate one from another, and it is questionable

Recent changes in the DTP scene xxxv

whether it is beneficial to purchase as a bundle rather than as component parts. With the exception of the Xerox Documenter, very few are task-specific systems. Thus, though you may benefit from the addition of an A4 screen the main selling points seem to be the fact that you can run your other computer applications on the system. This leads us back to the concept of buying component parts.

Entrants in the last nine months include AST, CPT, IBM and Olivetti, Facit and Research machines. Without exception all the systems mentioned employ either PageMaker or Ventura or a choice of both. IBM's system is based around the PS/2 model 30, and offers PageMaker, Windows and the IBM pageprinter – a 300 dpi Postscript device. Obviously IBM do not foresee Aldus jumping on the OS/2 bandwagon too soon!

9. Peripherals and add-ons

Front-end peripherals

Graphical digitisers or scanners have received a boost with the increasing adoption of the TIFF standard. The grey scale subformat will also enhance their usefulness as it becomes more widespread. While the standard 300 dpi scanner continues to be produced in ever increasing numbers, and by ever increasing players, several innovative and interesting products have emerged.

Agfa Gevaert have produced two models the 5600/5800 Focus scanners offering resolutions of 600 and 800 dpi. Maximum image size is 8.8" × 12.1". Obviously with a resolution of this magnitude considerable RAM is required which limits compatible machines to the Macintosh, Sun and Apollo.

A lower resolution scanner (72 to 400 dpi) distributed by CCA Micro Rentals is the Agfa PS Scan 200, which can be used with the Macintosh and IBM's DTP system.

Kurzweil Computer Products have produced a 300 dpi scanner to cope with larger documents – 11" × 14" – but at a much higher price (£20,000). The only hardware requirement is an RS232 interface though one would assume that considerable RAM would be required to hold such a large image.

The CPT Image Scanner is worthy of mention if only for its very reasonable price. This 300 dpi scanner will set you back a mere £995. It is compatible with the CPT 9000, IBM PC/XT/AT and compatibles.

Back-end peripherals

If 1960 was the year of the baby boom, 1987 was decidedly the year of the laser printer boom. A reflection perhaps of the complete demise of the daisywheel.

Despite the acceptance of Postscript as the industry standard page description language – Hewlett Packard's HPGL excluded – the vast proportion of new lasers do not offer Postscript support, but since the majority of serious WP users now employ a laser printer this is probably understandable.

In general we have witnessed an increase in speed from the typical 8 ppm to 10-12 ppm. Furthermore a greater range of engines – Hitachi, Konica, Kyocera and Ricoh – is now available. RAM has been increased often to as much as 3Mb. Some of the new engines (Hitachi) require separate consumables – toner, developer and fusing unit – as opposed to the straightforward cartridge replacement of the Canon engine. Input trays holding 100-250 sheets are now becoming standard.

The Xerox engines used exclusively in their own printers allow substantial monthly throughput compared with the recommended 3000 pages of the Apple Laserwriter. The Xerox 3700 model permits throughput of 60,000 pages per month, while top of the range 9700 supports 1.5 million. However at prices ranging from £27,000 to £240,000, they hardly fall with in the category of desktop publishing.

Increased resolution of 600 dpi and even 1200 dpi is challenging traditional typesetting devices. Despite this the Apple Laserwriter Plus is still pre-eminent.

Several concerns have emerged recently as it has become apparent that laser printers – given their high cost – are frequently used as low-run printing machines. The rated duty cycle (the frequency with which cartridges require replacement) can and should be improved upon and the emulation modes provided with the printer should be

Recent changes in the DTP scene

extended. In the DOS world the vast majority of non-DTP software packages do not offer Postscript support. It is seen as essential therefore that these devices offer HP Laserjet Plus, Diablo 630 and possibly a dot matrix printer emulation.

Below we have identified only those printers that offer Postscript support or that are worthy of mention for some exceptional feature.

QMS will be launching a colour Postscript printer in March 1988. Employing a Mitsubishi engine using thermal transfer technology the device will support a maximum of three colours at a resolution of 300 dpi. Printing speeds will not be record-breaking; approximately one page per minute when three colours are in use.

Data Technology's Crystal Print VIII is unique in that instead of using the usual small diode laser to create an image it uses liquid crystal shutters (LCS) to block out or transmit light. There is little noticeable difference from traditional laser output. However, it raises the question as to whether the current technology will, in the long term prove most effective. There is also evidence of some move to LEDs in the image-creation process.

NEC Silentwriter LC890 is a Postscript printer with HP emulation, switchable from the front panel. It is certainly not fast at 6 ppm, yet good for use with non-Postscript software. Serial, parallel and Appletalk ports are supported. The LC890 uses Postscript founts for HP emulation, thus some difference in character widths will be apparent. Supplied with 3Mb RAM and priced at £3950, the LC890 is an interesting proposition for the all-purpose laser printer user.

Texas Instruments Omnilaser 2115 uses the Ricoh 4150 engine and this Postscript device supports 3Mb RAM. It is geared for long print runs (by laser printer standards) and is supplied with two 250 page input trays but strangely no manual feed. The most significant feature is the 2115's speed rating of 15 ppm. The device offers HP Laserjet plus emulation. Both parallel and 25 pin serial ports are provided, the latter configurable at 16 different bit per second rates. A nine pin connecter that allows RS 422 or Appletalk is also built-in. Retail price £7195.

The AM Varityper VT600 was one of the first printers to break the 300 dpi barrier. Offering a resolution of 600 dpi and a speed rating of 10 ppm, the printer provides Postscript support. The VT600 retails at £15,750 and, although looking expensive, will replace traditional typesetting output in many circumstances.

10. DTP as a typesetting front-end

We pointed out earlier the value of the Postscript page description language in allowing desktop publishers to output to a Linotype phototypesetter via a Raster Image Processor (RIP). Other methods of harnessing the power of the typesetter – from the PC user's point of view – or harnessing the cost-effectiveness of the PC – from the publisher's point of view – are discussed below.

Compugraphic have a product strategy that reflects the desire to use PCs as low cost typesetting front-ends. CAPS (Compugraphic Automated Publishing System) is a high-end WYSIWYG workstation – beyond the cost constraints of the average desktop publisher – able to accept text and graphic files from PCs. Text files can be imported from most WP systems and vector graphics from MacDraw in addition to various CAD sources.

Compugraphic's PTS Publisher is MS-DOS based WYSIWYG publishing software that allows output to a range of laser printers in addition to the Compugraphics range of MCS phototypesetters including the 8000, 8300, 8400 and 9600. The software includes all the sophisticated features one would expect from a typesetter vendor. PTS Converter permits the conversion of DOS format into MCS format. The MCS system can then be linked into the Compugraphic network.

In facilitating this Compugraphic have been sensibly pragmatic in giving up a tranche of VDU sales to meet their trade customers' need to mix and match terminals with PC users.

Other players

Chelgraph offers the Ventura-Ace connection that allows Ventura files to be output to the Chelgraph IBX, a system that uses the bitstream library.

DEC's system PAGER – formerly DECset – runs on the VAX

Recent changes in the DTP scene

range of minis and can currently output to Linotype, Monotype and Autologic imagesetters.

An increasingly interesting area of development has been batch pagination on micro-based systems. The most impressive of these for general use on long documents – particularly conventional books – is Telos by Digital Publications Ltd.

This has no WYSIWYG facility so is not a true contender for DTP classification but is relevant because page make-up parameters are specified through a menu-driven program (called setparm) usable by any competent editor with a basic knowledge of typography.

Generic coding is used to identify elements of the document for typographical and make-up purposes and the program divides into pages at a spectacular rate, working on a chapter at a time. Ten seconds to paginate the average book chapter is normal on a PC.

With some experience setparm can be used to create page make-up rules which will accommodate most of the editor's preferred disciplines.

The system comes in two forms: a text editor, which is basically a word processor producing Telos-readable files, and the full system, which incorporates the word processor plus full pagination routines. Prices range from around £100 for the former to £5000 or so for the latter. Output drivers need to be typesetter-specific. There is no Postscript option but the system can drive the 300 dpi Cora Proofer.

Other significant recent developments include the increasing emulation on the part of high-end pagination systems of the WYSIWYG environment, and change in output from third to fourth-generation laser-based phototypesetters. This reflects the ability to integrate text and image in the page make-up process.

In addition we have witnessed an increase in the number of bureaux offering typeset output from PC originated CRC. Currently the UK boasts in excess of 30 such bureaux.

DTP – the future

Where are we heading and what developments can we expect in the near future? Firstly as we predicted earlier, more and more DTP software will fall by the wayside as PageMaker and Ventura retain and build up their market stronghold. The main threat will come from software developers who successfully combine the WP and DTP function. The major contender in this category is Lotus' Manuscript.

The Macintosh will not die as a result of the PS/2. Indeed it is currently going from strength to strength. A recent announcement that DEC has bought into Apple and now holds a 24% share will serve to enhance Apple's credibility significantly. The Macintosh II is living up to expectations and everything looks rosy for the future.

The IBM environment will go through a state – albeit temporarily – of confusion. As OS/2 products become available we may witness periods of incompatibility and problematic software integration as users struggle to overcome the limitations of the one-product compatibility box. The light at the end of the tunnel will shine when the majority of products are available under enhanced OS/2 with Presentation Manager. The Mac-alike IBM will have arrived.

Interesting developments are afoot on the Postscript front. Apple's co-founder, Steve Job, has set up a new company, Next, which is currently working on screen-based Postscript drivers. True WYSIWYG may be just around the corner, though how long it will take to navigate the corner is an unknown.

Laser printers will continue to offer higher resolution and increased facilities for colour. It is debatable whether the LCD (Liquid Crystal Display) approach adopted by some vendors will catch on, but it could well overcome problems associated with the properties of toner powder.

Grey scale TIFF will lead to more acceptable results in the scanning of half-tones, especially as scanning resolution increases.

Lastly, desktop publishing as an application is changing dramatically. To the publisher it will no doubt remain in the confines of a low-cost front end. The average business user, however, is perceiving the discipline more and more as an integral part of the office function. It has become merely a back end to service the primary office functions. Paper-based communication has benefitted tremendously from DTP but it has left the closed sanctum of specialists and discrete departments. It is a solution for all (even if the problems that it solved never really existed) and is perceived as such. If we were expecting a revolution we have had one – of sorts – but its major result has been in the quality of office documents, not in a plethora of new publishing.

1
'Desktop publishing' and 'publishing'

Desktop publishing is a generic marketing term for systems which can accept keyed input and maybe scan in graphics to a microcomputer, make up pages with varying degrees of flexibility and graphical facility and output the results on a laser printer or other high quality output device using industry standard typefounts.

These three functions of input, make-up and output are not, of course, unrelated and on many systems the distinctions between them are less than categorical, but for the purposes of this introductory chapter they are valid and we shall consider them separately before going on to debate the present and potential uses of desktop publishing.

Later chapters will consider individual systems in some detail but in this first section we will take the liberty of making sweeping generalisations which can later be refined.

As an aid to putting the whole subject into context in the printing and publishing industries, we will look at output first and will discuss it in terms of its quality, its speed, its sheet size and its colour limitations.

Output quality

This paragraph, like most of the rest of this book, has been composed

This paragraph, like most of the rest of this book, has been composed on a microprocessor and output on a laser printer which is part of the most widely used desktop publishing system... the Apple Macintosh running PageMaker.

This paragraph has been keyed on a typesetting front end system and, like most conventional books, output on a phototypesetter... in this case the widely-used Monotype Lasercomp.

**Illustration 1.
Enlargement of text output from the
LaserWriter and Monotype's Lasercomp.**

'Desktop publishing' and 'publishing'

on a microprocessor and output on a laser printer which is part of the most widely used desktop publishing system... the Apple Macintosh running PageMaker.

This paragraph has been keyed on a typesetting front end system and, like most conventional books, output on a phototypesetter . . . in this case the widely-used Monotype Lasercomp.

In illustration 1 we have printed both paragraphs again, this time greatly enlarged.

The difference in quality, discernable but less objectionable in the standard text size, is largely due to the output resolution of the machine. For the purposes of our comparison, we have deliberately chosen a typesetting machine which uses basically similar technology to the laser printer, i.e. the images are composed by a *raster image processor* - a RIP in computer jargon - the workings of which will be broadly covered later in the book.

The essential difference is that in the case of the laser printer, where the image is being built up by the RIP in a series of dots, the number of dots available to make up the image is 300 to the linear inch, i.e. 300x300 to the square inch, which equals 90,000 dots available to be used in each square inch of image. The phototypesetter, on the other hand, is building up images using a minimum of 1000 dots to the linear inch, i.e. one million dots available to be used within each square inch of image.

The new fourth generation (laser-based) phototypesetters which have been designed with halftone reproduction in mind are in fact capable of outputting at a resolution much in excess of 1000 dots or scan lines per inch and the comparison with these is therefore even more extreme.

For other technical reasons, including the screening process, the results on halftone reproduction are, as might be expected, disproportionately unsatisfactory, although both halftones and line drawings can be scanned into the system. In illustration 2 we show a halftone output on a laser printer alongside a conventionally screened and photographically reproduced picture.

But leaving aside the halftone problem, this output limitation on the laser printer should not be overstated, for there are several mitigating circumstances.

Firstly, except in a few peculiar circumstances, the conventionally-printed book does not employ the device of blowing-up text matter to unusually large sizes and thereby exposing the dot constituents of the

Illustration 2.
Halftones reproduced conventionally and by
the LaserWriter.

'Desktop publishing' and 'publishing'

typography; in normal text sizes and for some uncritical purposes the low-level resolution may be acceptable. Secondly, many publications are printed on paper which in any case absorbs some of the available definition of the text (this book is a mid-level example of that). Thirdly, development is going on apace to increase the output resolution of laser printers and we may confidently expect at least some degree of improvement within the next year or so.

What is acceptable to the publisher depends on his judgment as a marketeer of what will be acceptable to the reader. Experimentation is a help, of course, but can be expensive if you need to run the test through to the printing process.

To give some basis for comparison, we have typeset the glossary of this book by conventional means. On a finer quality paper the differences would, of course, be more marked but even on this book-quality stock the resolution is apparent.

One possible shift in fashion which may occur as laser printer typography becomes more universally accessible is that levels of acceptability previously the judgmental domain of the typographer or production expert may be overtly assessed by the reader or, in the case of periodicals, more likely the advertiser.

In the early 1970s much debate went on about the declining standards of typography available on the new, cheap phototypesetting systems. The reader knew little of this - Compugraphic's early founts looked little different to him from Monotype's high quality faces - but editors and production experts within publishing companies did make qualitative judgments and, rightly or wrongly, sometimes made decisions in favour of the higher quality typography and at one and the same time incurred expense on their own behalf and forced the manufacturers of bottom-of-the-market plant to upgrade their founts.

The 1980s version of this dilemma will be more publicly examined because the evidence is more clearly available to the general public and, more significantly, the ubiquitous man-in-the-street may well be using the bottom-end technology himself, in his home or his office.

It is difficult to predict the short-term consequences of this public appraisal of perceived quality but one strong possibility is the polarisation of typography into 'upmarket' and 'downmarket'... documents may more readily fall into distinct groupings requiring acknowledged levels of presentation. In some degree this is already underway with the creeping acceptance that desktop quality is suitable for newsletters, although it is certainly true that it is easier to replace a style that might previously have been word processed in any event.

Because of the certainty of a quick improvement in resolution it is likely to be unprofitable to dissipate too much energy in researching acceptability in the market place. Possibly more relevant in the immediate sense is the pure readability of documents.

The process of turning viewed typographic images into mentally assimilated information is in large measure facilitated by the rapid observation of the outline shapes of words and letters as groups. Given the obvious conclusion that low density of resolution must diffuse the shape of an image, it should follow that such text will, in any quantity, be more difficult to read.

As implied above, consideration of optical quality and its implications is one thing, marketability is another; and the two do not necessarily have a direct relationship. For example, academics have shown themselves to be very tolerant of research publications which sometimes have doubtful qualities of legibility when printed from often very scruffy word processor output or badly-presented typescript to be used as camera-ready copy.

Cynical publishers may claim this is because material which is not going to be read does not have to be very legible, but the market implications are not at all clear! Much literature is seriously not intended to be read at all, of course; it is for reference only and there is a strong argument against incurring the costs associated with high levels of legibility when only a few words or figures are to be scanned at any one time.

There is also the consideration that publishers, like most other businessmen, are additionally engaged in producing printed material which is not going to be sold to the reader in any event. Internal documentation, mail shots, regular publicity leaflets, and so on, are as important - or maybe more important - to the publisher as to most other commercial ventures.

And in these instances the quality of output is a consideration the publisher and all other businessmen must review on equal terms. A pattern will no doubt emerge.

Before we leave the question of output quality, we should point out that it is possible to interface the rather clever 'front end' of a desktop system - the micro and its page make-up software - with the 'back end' of a printing industry typesetting system...a laser-based phototypesetter.

'Desktop publishing' and 'publishing'

Linotype are already well along this route with the most popular desktop system linked up to their new high resolution laser setters.

In these circumstances the output is, of course, identical to the normal output from the photosetter since the programmed description of the fonts in the micro's or, more generally, in the intelligent printer's software must relate to the fonts resident on the photosetter.

One point which should be remembered, however, if this seems an attractive long term option, is that one of the enticements of the desktop publishing system is that the output device, although restricted in quality, uses plain paper, not expensive photographic film or bromide, and handles its own processing.

On the financial front, a development of plain paper laser printers to an acceptable resolution would have great advantages in material cost savings.

Output speed

Depending on the content of a page - and let us take A4 as the control standard since this is the normal unit used by the microprocessor industry - it might take 20 seconds to output the first copy of a page of text (say - one typeface, roman, italic and bold in two point sizes) on an inexpensive laserprinter driven by a small micro and 6 - 8 seconds to produce subsequent prints of the same page thereafter. Pages containing a variety of typefaces, and/or a high graphics content can take considerably longer.

There are fast-running laser printers - Xerox market one which could compete with a litho press on an impressions per hour basis - but these are also as expensive as printing machines and could not sensibly be included in a consideration of desktop publishing, whatever the criteria used.

The present technology at the desktop level therefore supports in terms of speed only a very short run as a printing machine or the production of camera-ready artwork for subsequent conversion to litho printing through the normal processes.

Output size

It seems unlikely to the initiated but it is nevertheless true that the general public believes books and magazines are printed a page at a time. The desktop publishing entrepreneurs, although they are probably better informed than the public about the 'old' technology of printing, are only just coming to terms with the binding limitations of single leaf output.

Most of the standard desktop systems so far support a maximum sheet size around the A4 mark. The maximum image size is somewhat less but this is probably relatively unimportant unless printed spreads are involved, since the software could control multi-page positioning.

The consequential disadvantage of this limitation is that nothing in excess of A5 can be saddle-stitched (or bound by any other technique which requires a folded sheet) and even sizes smaller than A5 must have a limited extent for mechanical binding due to the number of signatures presented or must involve a lot of hand-work.

Since our restrictions on speed anyway preclude serious consideration of the technique as a substantial printing system, the maximum sheet size is maybe not too critical, but it needs noting as a limitation needing to be removed or resolved if the next step in the development of desktop publishing as a printing method is to be taken.

As will be mentioned elsewhere, the problem has been taken on board by the manufacturers and is within sight of at least a partial solution with the recent arrival of A3-size laser printers. Albeit at prices slightly in excess of the typical desktop publishing spend.

Output and colour

The production of colour using xerographic techniques and the software necessary to instruct the raster image processor to split images (even for spot colour production) is a complicated study. We will look at the problem in outline in Chapter 9, but meanwhile we can simply note that colour is not yet available from the standard systems.

This is naturally a limitation if you wish to produce, say, a short run of publicity leaflets where colour would be an advantage, but in many instances either the present output quality would be unsuited to the type of work which needed colour or - if that were not a problem - artwork would be produced and the colour split handled by conventional camera or scanner techniques preparatory to litho printing.

No doubt the application of a lively imagination can create projects where short-run colour from such a system would be useful but they do not immediately spring to mind in the conventional publishing context.

Input

Word processing is commonplace these days. Most of us are used to the idea that characters, words, lines and chunks of text can be deleted or amended, blocks of material can be moved around or copied and searching and replacing of characters, words and strings can go on willy nilly until the author or operator is tired and emotional enough to stop changing his mind.

This is a technique which began seriously to impinge on our consciousness in the 1970s and by the start of the 80s was in full and productive commercial use.

What we are only now beginning to realise is that it is possible to take the art a stage further and see on our screens exactly what we will get when we print out the document...a page in the same typefaces, same size, with all the frills and fancies and none of the codes.

WYSIWYG - what you see is what you get - has come of age.

It is difficult to calculate what this means in terms of efficiency of input. Different desktop publishing text entry packages have different degrees of cleverness built in, of course, and some are easier to use than others. In some instances there may even be a trade-off of time at the input stage in exchange for ease and facility of make-up in page design.

Arguments continue over the advantages of different packages and in many instances the real issue is, to borrow the jargon, a simple case of WYUTIWIB...what you're used to is what is best. It is certainly true that one of the earliest and most difficult word processing packages, WordStar, is also shown to be one of the most productive when measured for speed of input, but this is largely irrelevant if you want to design the fancy pages possible with the new page make-up languages, because programs like WordStar cannot exploit the full range of facilities you need.

If a publisher is looking for speed of input of straightforward text and if the text is going to be run up and down in single columns once set, there is little need to see what it looks like in type and there is much to be said for a basic word processing program with a limited range of simple editing commands. If he wishes to design complex pages in complex typography it is arguable, although difficult to demonstrate, that inputting the text in WYSIWYG format is quicker and less susceptible to error.

It should be pointed out, to present a balanced argument, that many professional compositors claim that even with the more complicated pages it is still quicker to code in text on a fast keyboard and cut and paste it onto place on a grid...but that may be another example of WYUTIWIB. The keyboard itself is a special consideration. Generally speaking, micro keyboards, although they have improved significantly in recent years, are not designed to suffer the type of pounding at the sort of speed which purpose-built typesetting keyboards must take in their stride.

It was noteworthy that when Linotype developed the very successful APL front end system from the Apple II micro they completely re-built the keyboard, not only to expand access to the character set but also to speed up the response and extend longevity.

This is not necessarily an important factor unless continuous hard use is anticipated. Simply on grounds of human nature it seems likely that if the operator can see the shape and size of what he is creating rather than a series of coding strings fewer mistakes should result. It is also a logical extension of that argument that if the operator is also the originator of the text the ability to see the shape of what is created should induce a reduced incidence of changes of mind at later stages...but that may not be supportable on grounds of human nature!

Page make-up

Publishers and printers talk about page make-up systems. Desktop publishers refer to page layout packages, with (ideally) support for a page description (or descriptor) language.

There is more to the difference than the terminology.

Page layout software like Aldus' PageMaker has a mass of design facilities not available on most typesetting front ends and an ability to process text within the page environment which is only present in the most sophisticated industry systems. Output is determined by PostScript the *Page Description Language* (PDL) resident in the RIP of the printer. It is the combination of both programs that allows flexible input and high quality (relative to predominating PC standards) output.

It is a very, very clever system.

It also has gaps (rapidly being closed) in the area of graphic finesse which will make the typographic pedant's hair curl.

Because this is in some respects the heart of the desktop publishing system, it is given detailed consideration later in the book. By most standards it is a more-than-adequate page make-up device and has, indeed, been adopted by Linotype to front-end their fourth generation high resolution lasersetters.

'Desktop publishing' and 'publishing'

What it is not - and this is the only point which needs seriously emphasising at this stage - is an automatic page composition system.

You cannot ask a desktop publishing system in the PageMaker mould to take a text file from one source and a graphics file from another and pour it into page after page of book or magazine after the fashion of an Atex or Penta or Miles 33 front end.

It is a system well suited to designing pages individually or to systematically making up pages with a set design...but it is not 'automatic' in the sense of continuous processing of files into pages.

The penny has dropped, however, and increasingly we are witnessing the emergence of the 'automatic' composition system, frequently combined with a WYSIWYG preview facility, to satisfy current market demands. Examples of this new generation of 'document based' DTP software are supplied in chapters 3 and 5.

The uses summarised

There is information enough in this guide to enable the experienced printer or publisher to form his own views on desktop publishing as a tool but we have tried in this introductory potted description to present a few pros and cons which may lead him into one chapter or another or may suggest that all are worth reading.

In brief, the systems which are commercially available at present will enable the user to input and design pages of text and line graphics of some complexity to a reasonably high standard and to output laser printed sheets of a limited size in true industry-standard type founts at a low resolution and in one colour suitable for some types of text matter but generally unsuited for halftone reproduction.

The output devices are neither large nor fast enough to be used for long print runs and, because of the size limitation, are unsuited to documents of large extent.

Given that there are restricted uses for such systems, it is nevertheless important to watch their development closely because the limitations are being swiftly removed and it could well be that the publishing and printing industries are about to see a serious alternative presented to much of the present composition, output and printing technology. That challenge is coming from a new direction - the whizz-kids of the micro world - and there is a strong case for getting alongside them and helping them to take the next steps which will solve some of the industry's technical problems.

2
DTP: where it came from and what it is

It is widely accepted that the major forces responsible for instigating the desktop publishing revolution have, almost without exception, emanated from the micro computer industry. The professional print and publishing end of the spectrum has latterly become involved but still finds itself bringing up the rear. It is the PC that plays vanguard in this revolution.

It would be a fruitless exercise, moreover, to provide a potted history of the printing industry. The developments that lead from hot metal typesetters to the fourth generation phototypesetters of today cannot be said to have culminated in desktop publishing. There are similarities, in that the latter both employ laser technology to build up characters (raster images). However the net outcome is the convergence of technologies rather than some kind of historical linear progression.

There is nonetheless a feedback between the two technologies. PC-based desktop publishing takes its standards in both resolution of output and quality of typographical precision from the traditional print and publishing industry. If it is to gain credibility outside the traditional microcomputing arena, it is towards these professional standards that the DTP market is compelled to aspire. Conversely the print and publishing industry must surely apply itself to the ease of use and cost factors that lend strength to the desktop case.

Our aim below is to pinpoint the developments in microcomputing that enabled desktop publishing to become not only a technical possibility but an accepted - indeed, a demanded - reality.

Early micro involvement in typesetting

Typesetting and personal computers: to the pundits of both industries, each concerned with his own specific discipline, there was no apparent need for cross pollination; the needs, the tasks and the hardware performing those tasks were worlds away. In short, the twain would never meet.

Yet back in the late seventies the twain did meet, if only briefly. Linotype developed the APL series of front ends to run their typesetting software. The APL terminals, available with single or dual floppy drives are menu driven and hence simple (by the standards of typical typographic processes) to use. APLs provide their own communications software to allow data to be transferred directly, even to remote typesetters via modem and telephone lines. The APL terminal is a modified Apple ll, and the more recent portable APL50 is built around Apple's own portable, the llc.

The picture has changed somewhat. Today, it is possible to drive a Linotype 100 or 300 directly from an unmodified Macintosh; indeed the Linotron acts as another device on Apple's local area network. The only additional piece of equipment required is a raster image processor (RIP) which sits between the Appletalk Network and the typesetter. However, more of this later.

What we propose now is an examination of the technological developments that have led to this state of affairs, and the factors that initiated the so-called desktop publishing revolution. In addition we intend to outline the hardware and software options that make the whole process possible.

As a preliminary, it might assist the reader if we were to expand upon the definition given in the previous chapter, as to what desktop publishing is, whom it effects, the benefits, costs and considerations.

Typesetting and what it means

The term 'typeset' and 'typesetting' are subject to a wide range of interpretations. Ultimately all printed text is typeset, since typesetting by virtue of its name implies the setting/organising of letters (type) upon a page.

Hence, by producing documents on a manual typewriter one is

DTP: where it came from and what it is

effectively producing a typeset page at the most basic level. What the publisher must understand is that outside the industry the term is synonymous with the system of producing page layout prior to printing (whatever the method used). Hence desktop publishing is mainly a method of composing pages. In short, it is a means of producing screen-based, camera-ready copy, and/or camera-ready artwork, without recourse to the traditional cut-and-paste methods.

Three key elements

There are three main elements to desktop publishing, which can be broadly summarised as follows:

1. The personal computer or front end through which text and /or graphics is entered or into which text or graphics is transferred from other sources. This includes the importing of files from other micros, minis and mainframes and accepting images via scanners and digitisers.
2. A variety of output devices including laser printers with a minimum resolution of 300 dpi, using Xerographic techniques directly onto plain paper. The output device, typically a laser printer supporting a standard page description language, should allow the printing of combined text and graphics. It is desirable that any desktop publishing system be capable of sending the completed camera ready page/document directly to a professional phototypesetter, producing an output of 1200 dpi + onto light-sensitive paper.
3. Page layout or typesetting software allowing screen-based cut and paste from a variety of software sources and lending full support to the page description language resident in the output device.

Illustration 3 shows the constituent parts of the typical single user DTP system.

Having established a rudimentary but workable definition of desktop publishing, it is interesting to note the origins of such an innovative but eminently useful PC application.

Origins of DTP

It is nowdays generally accepted that the paperless office is a myth.

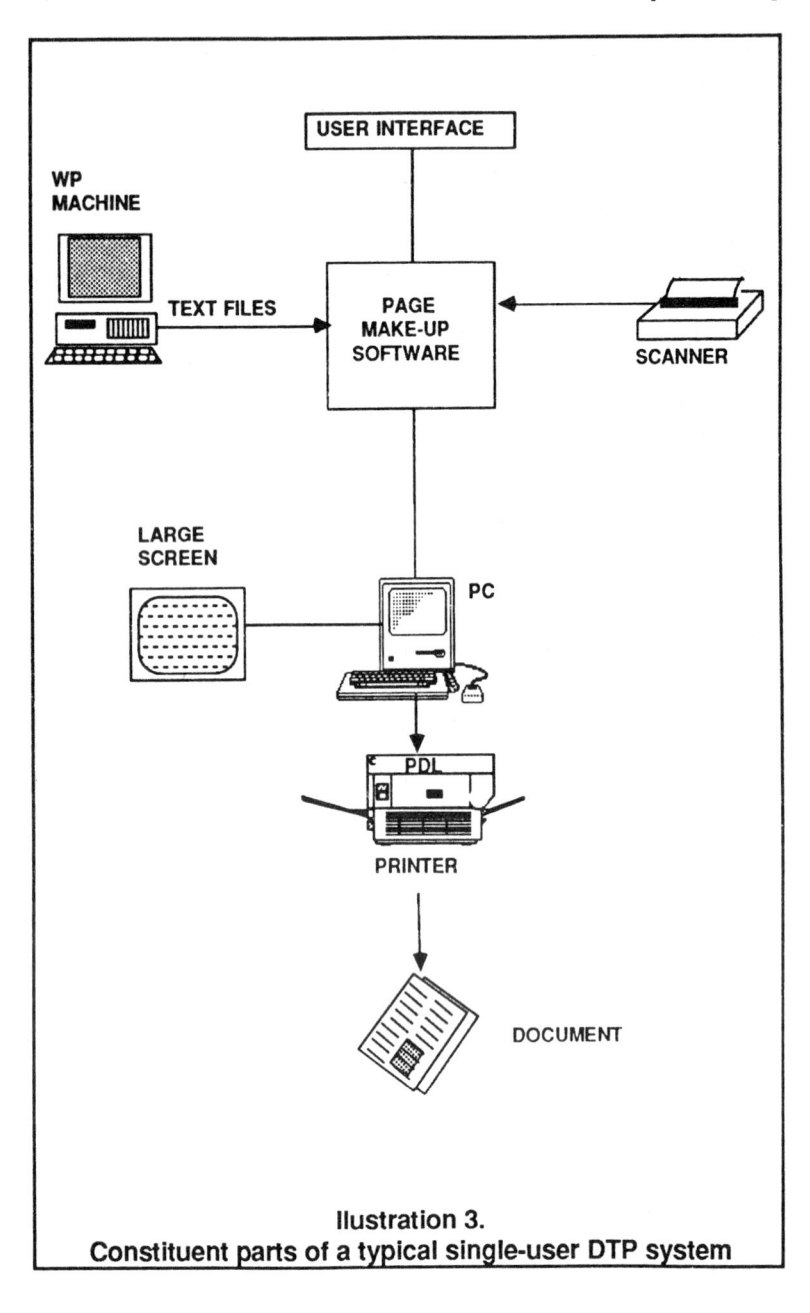

Ilustration 3.
Constituent parts of a typical single-user DTP system

DTP: where it came from and what it is

Indeed statistics abound informing us of the number of world trade centers we could build, or the number of times we could reach across the Atlantic and back, with the documents generated in one year. The reasons are many and human nature is slow to change. There is an inherent trust in the notion of hard copy, not to mention its portability; and while the fax may cut down on the movement of paper, it still continues to generate paper-based communications.

The advent of the microcomputer and the concept of wordprocessing served to enhance the written word.

If something becomes more effective, it will be used more frequently. Thus the wordprocessed mailshot, the personalised letter, came into being, proposals doubled in length, and the amount of paper in circulation increased.

As the power of the PC increased, and with it new dimensions of graphics software, so the production of charts and graphs gravitated down from their traditional place on the dedicated CAD/CAM workstation and the mini/mainframe environment. Programs such as Lotus 1-2-3 allowed the user to create effective business graphics in a matter of seconds. The power of the image as a means of communicating numerical information, statistics, trends, results and forecasts was realised and developed on the PC. This in turn led to the production of yet more paper.

As the number of wordprocessing and business graphics users increased, the demand for high quality output escalated. The options were restrictive. One could use a standard dot matrix printer which would allow graphics to be printed but offered very low resolution. The daisywheel printer evolved as the industry standard for text processing but by its very nature could not print graphics. The NLQ (near letter quality) dot matrix printer emerged, offering a 24-pin head as opposed to the standard 9-pin version of the traditional matrix printer. In simple terms, output resolution was increased, graphics could be printed, but each character was visibly made up of dots and hence not acceptable for anything other than drafting.

Ink jet and thermal printers met with limited success. The former were using new and unperfected technology (though they may have a part to play in the future), the latter required special paper, and output always appeared rather pale and 'watered down'.

To aggravate the situation there was no software that allowed for the integration of text and graphics. The latter would often be produced on a plotter and appended to text documents.

Developments

It was a technological advance in the form of the low cost laser printer that did most to forward the cause of desktop publishing. Using a mechanism not unlike that of a photocopier, the laser printer also included a raster image processor. This was key to the effective integration of text and graphics. The RIP treats both text and graphics as images to be built up line by line in memory and then re-created on the page. Depending on the available memory resident in the printer the ratio of graphics to text supported on any one page can vary.

The availability of the laser printer alone would not have been sufficient to allow such versatility of output as the DTP function required.

It was the implementation of the page description language (PDL), specifically Postscript, that was instrumental in the successful output of combined text and graphics, and the use of industry standard founts. We discuss the implications of PDLs in more detail below.

The acceptance of the WIMP environment (see chapter 3 for more detail) aided and abetted in the development towards DTP. In producing 'What You See Is What You Get ' screen layouts, it is simpler to move blocks of text or graphics with a pointing device such as a mouse, rather than using keyboard controls.

Furthermore, as a legacy from the CAD/CAM environment, packages emerged that allowed the user to draw on screen, a task that is frankly too cumbersome without the aid of a mouse.

Lastly, the art of page composition is not easy. The simple user interface provided by the WIMPS operating standard assisted the user in getting to grips with a complex procedure. Reducing most options to the level of icons or pull down menus served to create a very simple method of achieving a sophisticated end.

With affordable laser technology in place, an ultra-easy user interface and the ability to integrate text and graphics, it was just a matter of time before software writers took advantage of the available features. We have traced the growth cycle of Macintosh software - the epitome of the WIMPS/ WYSIWYG environment - to its current level of maturity in chapter 3. While Apple are universally acclaimed for having taken the lead, many others have followed, so that the current 'state of the art' in

DTP encompasses a wealth of other manufacturers, operating systems and approaches.

Traditional print influence

As we have mentioned above, the impetus behind the entire DTP revolution stemmed in the main from the PC arena. One cannot underestimate the part played by Xerox in the field of R & D but the fact remains that it was left to a microcomputer manufacturer to make that research a commercial reality.

The professional typesetting and publishing industry initially stood on the sidelines and waited for the whole thing to blow over. It didn't. Instead, it grew from strength to strength precisely because the DTP software developers looked to the traditional industry for their standards.

As PC-based page make-up software matured, it emulated the skills of the professional compositor. Not only did DTP adopt the professional jargon (often incorrectly), but increasingly now is adopting sophisticated standards such as finely-tuned kerning, industry standard founts, H&J, etc.

The restriction of 300 dpi resolution hindered the DTP process considerably. It was only when a few innovative typesetter manufacturers changed gear from a passive to an active role that the technologies converged.

Fear can be the greatest innovator. It was preferable, or so Linotype contended, to work with, rather than against, an industry that could, given the right technological innovations, elbow the established companies out of the business. In chapter 10 we examine other typesetting/PC combinations that serve to demonstrate how the technologies are converging and the lines of demarcation becoming daily more nebulous.

Indeed, so rapidly is the entire industry moving, that many DTP systems cannot now be accommodated on a desk, and the provision for linking to professional typesetting equipment almost detracts from the notion of the PC-based solution.

Once the initial excitement over the easiness of WIMPS had abated, many DTP users started demanding more precision, greater facility for long document runs, and sophisticated boilerplate, or style sheet, facilities. Moreover, they were not afraid of cashing in on the ease of use, in order to achieve greater flexibility.

In the field of DTP it is currently the more complex packages (many of which were developed and used long before the advent of the laser printer) that offer less ease of use and in general operate on the basis of embedded codes. Yet they are gaining momentum as the desktop publisher demands higher quality composition facilities. No doubt the WIMPs evangelists will catch up, but until they do it is interesting to witness a return to the old methods.

Possible advantages

In simplistic terms, the possible advantages of DTP are fourfold:

1. Cost benefits
2. Time savings
3. Control
4. Image/profile

Cost benefits

Cost savings are likely to apply to the company/organisation with an annual spend on external typesetting services in excess of one third of the system outlay (since capital expenditure is generally written off over a three year period) provided quality is acceptable and staff are available. Cost may also be saved in the area of forms production, graphics/artwork design for logos, presentation material and diagrams. As the system becomes familiar to the operators, more and more uses are discovered, devised and implemented.

Time savings

We are all familiar with the production cycle from galley to finished page. We are equally familiar with the time it can take. One attraction of a DTP system lies in the possible shortening of the proofing cycle.

The principle of time saving applies particularly to the newsletter. In a fast moving industry, product information is out of date almost as soon as its received (this book has been through at least four updates in the course of its writing). Copy must be created, input, laid-out and printed within a very short time span.

Control

The constant movement of galleys, paste-ups, proofs and completed

DTP: where it came from and what it is

documents between originator, typesetter and printer leaves room for human error and probably the most frequent cause for hold up in an already long-winded process is the mind-changing syndrome. The ability not only to edit but to allow for author alterations on one system maintains complete control over content and aesthetics.

Image/profile

The credibility of companies involved in selling, marketing, PR and any aspect of media or communications is frequently judged on the level of presentation. DTP implies the possibility of upgrading standards of internal documentation and - at the lower end of the scale - external promotion pieces.

In chapter 10 we touch upon the function of bureaux - typesetters who are able to offer a service in outputting PC-produced camera ready copy at typeset resolution. Many have already invested in a Macintosh, a RIP and a modem and as long as they have a Linotype 100 or 300 standing by the customer merely sends composed pages down the telephone line and receives back identical pages at 1200 or 2400 dpi. The innovative typesetter can find ways of co-existing with, and benefiting from, the arrival of DTP.

In the context of microcomputer hardware, with the notable exception of Apple it is now accepted that the only way to ensure a product's success is to follow the MS DOS standard. Not only do manufacturers have to adopt the DOS standard but now they have to be sure that the disks are standard, the BIOS is standard, the keyboard is standard - in fact that each machine is a clone of the other.

Typefounts are another matter. There is a need for the publisher to ensure that his system is using industry standard as opposed to 'bastardised' founts.

In the event that a non-typesetter specific face is used, the H and J will of course vary on output.

Desktop publishing must allow the user absolute control over selection of founts, fount attributes (italics, emboldened, underlined, etc) and fount sizes. Nor should there be any constraints as to the percentage of graphics to text or vice versa in any one page. The system should support at least one serif fount, usually Times, and one sans-serif fount, typically Helvetica. Most publications can get by with two typeface families.

A constant 'selling point' of many of the systems offering non-standard founts is the fact that the user has, say, 64 typefaces available to him. The novice desktop publisher throws up his hands in glee and rejects the eminently more suitable system because of its apparent lack of founts !

It is desirable, though not essential, that any desktop publishing system allows for the input of images through various means: scanners, video digitisers and optical character readers. Obviously, problems will arise in the event that images be scanned in one resolution and subsequently output through professional typesetting equipment at a considerably higher resolution. If, however, the scanned image can be transferred to software that supports a page description language, the problem will be overcome. In addition, editing at pixel level followed by image reduction would assist in overcoming resolution discrepancies. The standard for any scanning device should be that it produce files in TIFF format.

The development of desktop publishing has been largely influenced by the adoption of page description languages as a mechanism for controlling output. Without the use of a PDL, images would be transferred to the paper pixel by pixel and line by line, a slow process and highly consumptive of memory. The absence of a PDL creates output device dependency. Software with, for example, Postscript drivers, can output not only to the Apple LaserWriter but to any and all Postscript devices.

PDLs have been classified as the latest type of fourth generation language (4GL). They can be learned within a few days and enable users to embed their own Postscript commands in the document to achieve special effects or specific output commands to improve the efficiency of the DTP system.

The presence, however, of a PDL creates the need for significant processing power resident in the printer/typesetting device. Apple's LaserWriter offers more RAM than the Macintosh itself. PDLs allow output device independence since the output operation is essentially twofold:

1. Generation by the application program of PDL code for the required page, followed by
2. Translation of the code by the PDL interpreter resident in the output device to build up an image as defined by the instructions received from the front end.

DTP: where it came from and what it is

Postscript was the brain child of Evans and Sutherland, ex-employees of the Xerox corporation. The original idea of a page description language was conceived while they were employed in research at Palo Alto. Frustrated by the lack of commitment by the corporation to the ongoing commercial development of the project, they left Xerox to go it alone.

They were subsequently commissioned to carry out a harbour simulation project. The concept was to build a digital model of New York harbour to enable the simulator to project the view of the harbour as seen from the bridge of the ship. Finding no suitable means of outputting data of this type, they perfected the original concept of a page description language and came up with Postscript. Evans and Sutherland went on to form Adobe systems, the vendors of Postscript, and a company that has played a key role in the development of DTP.

There are a number reasons why Postscript has become the most widely used PDL. Firstly the language that is required for printing has to have straightforward syntax. Postscript is like Forth, a high level language, because the syntax is so simple to parse. This means that if the user needs to communicate with another processor all that is required is that the serial data is sent across the wire and it can be consumed by the processor on the other side in a straightforward way.

Another advantage is that new computer programs can be generated very easily. The straightforward, simple syntax has made this language a natural choice for a printing protocol because it is procedural-based as opposed to a static data structure.

At the last count Postscript was supported by 49 DOS based software products, with another 23 due for imminent release, 36 mini/mainframe packages, with an additional 19 just around the corner, and the majority of Macintosh software too numerable to mention.

Hewlett Packard's recent decision to implement Imagen's Document Description Language (DDL), has led to an upsurge in its popularity. Also in the running is Xerox's InterPress, which has recently been endorsed and accepted by ICL. Both parties are counting on this collaboration as a means of establishing Interpress as de facto industry standard - they've got considerable catching up to do! Despite this, Xerox's popular DOS based document lay-out package Ventura currently supports Postscript and will shortly provide DDL drivers. One wonders why Xerox have not implemented their own Interpress, if confidence in the language is so strong ?

Other PDLs currently under discussion include Prescribe and Express, both of which purport to allow programming by the illiterate user with the use of English-like commands. This does not, however, imply acceptance. In the field of database software DBase has remained market leader, over a considerable time period, despite marked unfriendliness. There is no reason to assume that late entrants in the PDL race will succeed merely because they purport to be easy.

Selecting equipment

All computer systems must be planned. In the field of DTP the most important starting point is to determine the end result, the kinds of publications to be produced. Desktop publishing can provide a wide spread of standards and facilities using the same basic 'engine': the personal or micro computer.

Begin by determining how the publication will look, its design and layout. Are you currently wordprocessing your documents ? Do you want to use photographs and line art? Do you want it to be output at a higher resolution than the 300 dpi of the standard laser printer? Do you want to print it in more than one colour? Each choice you make that involves higher quality generally means higher cost.

For many, the publishing tool at the center of the system, the personal computer, is already available within the organisation. Using a particular personal computer as a base, it is possible to build a publishing system by looking for compatible software that combines text and images in a manner appropriate to needs and selecting a printer of the requisite resolution. Should there be a need, if only on occasions, for higher quality output, it is worth establishing at this point that the facility for direct output to a typesetter exists.

The first decisions facing the DTP buyer are :

1. Whether the document requires layout using 'professional' typographical functions or whether standard text (as produced on traditional WP software) will suffice, in which case we leave the realms of DTP entirely.

2. What standard of output is required. How close does it need to be to professional 'print'. Will 300 dpi resolution (and hence a laser printer) suffice?

3. What type of publications are to be produced? A clear demarcation

DTP: where it came from and what it is

is emerging between page-based and document-based packages. The former allows total flexibility of layout on a page-by-page basis, though certain aspects such as margins, headers, etc will remain constant. The latter are designed with the long publication in mind, so that all verso pages will adhere to the same layout conventions as all other verso pages and likewise with recto and title.

The choices are many, but the personal computer you choose will effect your choice of peripherals. If it is planned to use an IBM PC or compatible personal computer, there is the largest overall selection of laser printers available, though not necessarily offering page description languages and by extension industry standard founts. The theoretical range of page make-up software on the IBM is now probably larger than on any other system, though it is hard to differentiate between 'vapourware' (that which is advertised but not actually available) and workable installed packages.

On the other hand, a Macintosh effectively reduces the choice of available printers to Postscript devices, since while it can drive many others without interfacing difficulties, it would undoubtedly be a waste of the Macintosh's resources to do so. The Macintosh supports a wider choice of graphics software and in general the page make-up systems available are more mature, tried and tested than its DOS based counterparts.

We have outlined above the basic hardware decisions necessary. Software charcteristics are more variable in terms of features and functionality. DTP software should include the following facilities:

Page layout

Columns, headlines, running headers and footers, WYSIWIG, ease of re-arrangement, simple user interface for moving, pointing, etc (i.e. mouse, graphics tablet).

Text composition functions

Choice of typeface, typeface style and point size, H&J (hyphenation exception dictionary and algorithm desirable), tabulation, proportional spacing, kerning, variable leading, control over widows and orphans, ability to wrap text around graphics/designs, overlay of text on graphics, acceptance of text files from other sources, and rudimentary text editing functions since in general page composition and WP are not combined.

Graphics

Ability to draw rules, boxes, circles, outlines and shaded areas. White text on black. Support for basic drawing functions and/or acceptance of graphics from other sources, (scanners, freehand and structured graphics software).

Macro facility/style sheets

Set-up and storage of re-usable format sheets, reflecting house and/or publication style, thus avoiding re-specification of typeface, point size, leading, column width etc. Simple editing of style sheets is desirable.

Page description languages

Given the importance of page description languages, any publishing system not supporting a PDL or supporting a non-industry standard PDL, must suffer in terms of output device independence and hence in terms of commercial appeal.

Standard operating characteristics

Given the WYSIWYG environment and the use of some pointing device (mouse/stylus) it makes sense to assume that a Macintosh-like environment be adhered to. Pull-down menus, windows, on-screen help, icons, click boxes, etc. We have drawn attention below to typesetting software that uses embedded codes, but this offers specific typesetting rather than general user appeal.

Output devices

Given an acceptable PDL, desktop laser printers and professional typesetting devices should be supported. Dot matrix printers are acceptable for draft runs at the galley stage, though not for proofing composed pages. Plotters for colour presentation material and preferably some peripheral sharing system, allowing many users access to one laser

DTP: where it came from and what it is

device... the item that constitutes the major cost factor in a DTP system.

The question asked by many professional publishers is how long will it be before the quality of output from a laser printer will be comparable to typesetters? The answer is that while standards of resolution are increasing almost constantly (400dpi printer is already available), the current technology cannot actually cope with 1200 dpi or more.

The physical properties of toner make it difficult to achieve very high resolution. Particles are quite simply too large to create the very clean, precise edges inherent in typesetter output. It is possible that thermal, ink-jet or LED array technologies will develop high resolution solutions or that modestly improved laser output will be adequate for unillustrated work.

PC hardware considerations

In order to run various software components of the total DTP system, several hardware considerations need to be borne in mind. The IBM PC or compatible in its standard configuration cannot support graphics or page composition software. A graphics adaptor and monitor must be added and memory must be increased to 640K or more. IBM PC hardware options are covered in more depth in chapter four.

The Macintosh Plus and SE by comparison are supplied complete with one megabyte of RAM and an internal high resolution graphics screen. In effect it is offered as a 'one buy solution' that requires the addition of no extra items, boards, operating systems or RAM, in order to be used as a DTP terminal.

When looking for a personal computer for desktop publishing one of the first questions to be asked is whether it will run the appropriate software. In some cases, software (such as PageMaker) is available in both the DOS and Macintosh environments, so factors such as cost, WYUTIWIB (what you are used to is what is best) or purely personal considerations such as aesthetic appeal, come into play.

A task as complex as page composition is extremely consumptive of memory. Furthermore the retention of images will necessitate significant disk storage. It is therefore vital that the computer has adequate processing power, screen display, memory and storage capabilities.

Displaying and processing the pages and images in high resolution require more computer memory than do normal applications. Depending on a personal computer's memory size, there may be a restriction in the size of document or quality of graphics which can be produced.

To produce high resolution screen images and print-outs, the computer must store the image by converting it into 'bits', tiny units of storage. A screen image and the data for the print-out are stored separately, requiring double the number of 'bits' of storage. The screen image, for example, results from the translation of the image into a grid of 'pixels' (picture elements). The more pixels, the better the resolution. For high resolution a computer must have enough memory to store all the data relating to the dots appearing on the screen and the dots that form the printout image.

Highly refined graphic images can have millions of pixels, many more than the average personal computer can hold in memory. The basic IBM PC addresses up to one megabyte of memory (1024K of RAM and ROM combined). Currently the Macintosh can be expanded to four megabytes.

In order to develop computer graphic programs, to produce images for a publication, the correct screen resolution of the computer's monitor is essential. The amount of detail that can be created on screen is representative of the amount of detail that can be produced on a printout. Screen resolution and printout resolution are not identical, however. The Macintosh displays at a screen resolution of 72 dpi, whilst the LaserWriter outputs at 300 dpi. Whilst this discrepancy persists, as indeed seems likely, the term WYSIWIG is only partly accurate.

In practice, outputting screen images will result in a sharper, clearer and less jagged illustration. In some degree, therefore, the intricacy of graphics is limited to the amount of detail that can be created on the screen.

The exception lies in the use of Postscript or any other programmable page description language. PDL commands can be send directly down to the printing device and translated into graphic images that are never displayed on screen. Obviously the benefit of WYSIWYG is lost but this method does serve to overcome screen resolution constraints.

Yet to work with and modify digitised images with ease, as well as to create images with graphics software, it is essential that you are able to see what is going on. The higher the resolution of your screen, the better can the work be viewed. Currently, the high resolution Macintosh screen produces images in a 512 x 342 pixel resolution. The IBM PC monochrome monitor can produce graphics of a 720 x 350 resolution but requires a special graphics adaptor card to do so. Given that the nine inch Macintosh screen is of a smaller size than that of the standard 12 inch IBM PC or compatible, the pixel to inch ratio is effectively reduced. The net result is that the Macintosh screen appears to offer a better resolution and hence provide a closer approximation to true WYSIWIG .

Personal computers mainly store information on diskettes and hard disks although other devices such as tape cassettes have been used in the past.

Volume of data is not the only consideration that dictates the amount of on-line storage required. As significant are the size and quantity of the software components involved in the production of a typical page. Xerox's Ventura Publisher, for example, is supplied on 11 floppy disks. An application of this type requires hard disk storage regardless of the length of documents produced. To operate the system successfully without a hard disk would be almost impossible. The bare minimum software components of a Macintosh DTP system include :

1. Operating system, including Postscript drivers
2. A wordprocessing package
3. A graphics package
4. Page layout software typically with Postscript drivers

It is possible that a spreadsheet or integrated program for the production of business graphics would be required together with a scanning/digitising drivers to allow the capture of half tones and other images. While the entire array of software is supplied on floppy disks, these would merely be retained for security purposes. The software could only be conveniently accessed if loaded onto a hard disk.

In the case of the IBM PC and compatibles the situation becomes even more complex since the average page layout software (Harvard Professional Publisher being a notable exception) requires an additional software application: the user interface, typically GEM or Microsoft Windows, that serves to create a Mac-like environment.

3
Macintosh the industry standard

Desktop Publishing, the term, is said to be the brain child of Aldus Corporation, Apple Computer, or both. Given that the two companies have worked closely together, let us assume the latter and allow the kudos to be shared. Suffice it to say, were it not for the Macintosh's eminent suitability for the task, the reality of DTP as we know it might not have happened, and the 'revolution' currently in progress might never have occurred.

Pre-Macintosh developments

Undoubtedly Apple took a considerable commercial risk in launching a series of computers that broke away so dramatically from traditional PC conventions. The Apple ll, despite its hard core following, was technically out of date, the Apple lll a fiasco and an embarrassment. Apple were desperately in need of a successful product if they were to retain credibility as one of the leading PC manufacturers.

The notion of 'What You See Is What You Get' is alien to the typical PC user. Under traditional CP/M and MSDOS operating systems the user would access files and directories through a series of learnt key strokes. The Macintosh through its innovative use of WIMPS (windows, icons, mouse, pull down menus) and WYSIWYG changed all that.

It didn't happen overnight. The Lisa, introduced by Apple in 1983, adopted and enhanced Smalltalk, the revolutionary development language developed by Xerox at Palo Alto Research Centre (PARC). SmallTalk was the first object-oreintated language that allowed the application developer to produce software utilising the concept of icons (i.e. meaningful pictorial representations of microcomputer nomenclature, e.g. files, folders, deletions, copying methods, etc).

The idea is simple: rather than having to type commands, or select an option from a menu, the screen shows a number of little pictures (icons). You point your cursor at the one in question, using a non-keyboard input device such as a mouse. Other features of this type of presentation include 'pop-up' or 'pull-down' menus, which appear only when requested. Often the screen is divided up into a number of windows. Some systems have the windows side by side, others have them partly overlapping, in analogy to papers lying around on a desk; each window represents a program or task in progress, or a document being processed. The mouse allows you to move around easily from one window to another.

See illustration 4 for a typical Macintosh menu

The Lisa had limited success due to three main factors. It was priced unrealistically for the performance levels offered. Apple's idea of a suite of software to cover general office and business applications was too inflexible, and the world of traditional micro users was wary of, and hence unprepared to accept, such radical changes.

Macintosh makes an entrance

A second generation machine was called for, one that not only appealed to the user's purse, but that offered increased flexibility, and was aimed at the 'individual' rather than the corporate user. So the Macintosh was conceived in its original form - an innovative, small, one box solution (closed architecture, no add-on boards, no options) offering a rather humble 128K of RAM and 400K disk drives.

Initially the Macintosh fared no better than its predecessor. There is a myth in the computer industry (indeed it is prevalent in most technical industries) that power is synonymous with complication. By extension, any computer that permitted users to be up and running in a matter of

Macintosh the industry standard 33

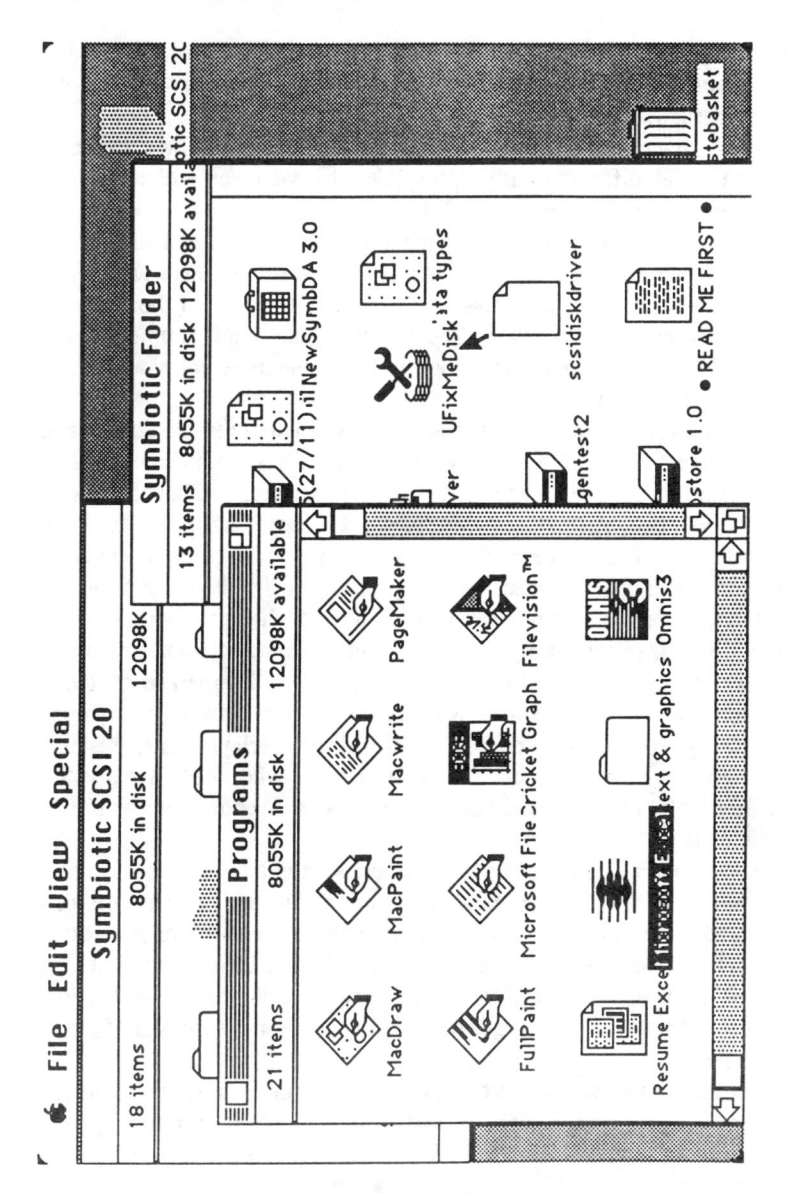

**Illustration 4.
Typical Macintosh Menu**

minutes rather than hours, was viewed with suspicion and relegated to the status of toy/designer workstation. Trendy and friendly but not particularly serious.

As hardware and software become more powerful, they can also become more difficult to use. To explain what we mean with a concrete example, let us consider the telephone.

Everyone knows how to use the telephone to make a call, or to answer a call, because the procedures are almost self-evident. There is no switch to turn it on, other than the action of picking up the receiver, which you need to do anyway. The process of dialling is simple because the numbers on the dial correspond to the numbers which you have in front of you or in your mind when you make a call.

Nowadays, however, telephones are becoming more sophisticated, and that is where the trouble starts. Modern automatic systems have all sorts of useful facilities; you can dial the last number again without keying in all the digits; you can get the system to keep ringing an engaged extension until it is free; you can tell the system that you are moving temporarily to another extension, and your calls will follow you there.

There is only one thing wrong with having all these facilities: it is very difficult to remember how to use them. Some instruments have a few extra keys, with rather obscure letters and codes marked on them, but for the more sophisticated systems the facilities have to be obtained by keying in a numeric code. For the full-time telephonists, this is a very good arrangement; but for the executive, who needs a particular facility only once a week or so, the codes become impossible to remember.

The same is true for personal computers. It is all very well to use a PC with Lotus 1-2-3 or some accounting package if you use that package every day. The trouble starts if there are three or four other packages to be used, say, once or twice a month. Unless the system is as self-evident in its use, like a telephone, it will not be used. More office automation systems fail because of their complexity than for any other reason.

On closer inspection there appeared to be great advantages in the enhanced icon based 'Finder' adopted as the Macintosh operating system. Not only did it allow true WYSIWYG screen representations, but every software package, third party and Apple's own, operated in precisely the same way. The user was therefore spared the hassle of re-learning basic operations every time he used a new piece of software.

RAM upgrades soon became available, as did a new model, the 512K or 'Fat Mac'. At this point had Apple positioned the product more realistically, as a powerful, business PC , and a viable alternative to the IBM, acceptance would no doubt have arrived sooner.

It was the introduction of the Mac Plus with 1 megabyte RAM and available hard disk options, coupled with the advent of desktop publishing, that caused the computer world not only to sit up and take notice but to dedicate considerable time, money and research in emulating what so recently they had been writing off as unviable. The Macintosh SE and Macintosh ll, new additions to the Apple range, will, whilst allowing limited compatibility with the DOS environment, continue to uphold their well-established standards. Ease of use epitomised by the WIMPs approach remains central to Apple's approach.

Desktop publishing is born

The WYSIWYG enviroment adopted and advocated by Apple was the perfect vehicle for desktop publishing. Simplicity of operation, coupled with low cost and effective results, offered wide appeal for the creation of CRC and CRA. The benefits were tremendous, not only in terms of time and cost savings, but, perhaps most critically, in terms of control. It suddenly became realistic to create, design, amend (again and again if required) and output entirely on a low-cost desktop system.

However, the advent of true WYSIWYG and a screen adequate to support complex combinations of text and graphics was not enough without an output device able to improve upon the screen resolution. Certainly the production of a low cost laser engine, around which Apple could build its powerful LaserWriter printer, was yet another factor contributing to the product's overall suitability as the ideal DTP tool.

In adopting certain desktop publishing conventions, as outlined in chapter 2, the Macintosh total DTP system became de facto leader almost by default since little else was available. Industry standards emerged and it is against these standards that every other desktop publishing system is measured.

Macintosh - the hardware

Built around the Motorola 68000 32 bit chip, the Macintosh SE, Apple's current top of the range model, is supplied with a built-in 9" high resolution screen displaying at 72 dpi, two 800k floppy drives (or one 800K floppy plus a 20MB hard disk) and one megabyte RAM as standard. The current version of the operating system can support up to 4KB RAM, and allows user definable RAM cache of up to 768K.

The following interfaces are supplied: serial, for modems, printers, plotters etc; SCSI (Small Computer Systems Interface), a recently adopted industry standard that provides a fast data interchange rate and is ideally suited for the attachment of hard disks. An AppleTalk (Apple's low cost peripheral sharing network) port is also provided. A slot at the back provides the facility for plug in cards, to be supplied by third party vendors. It is anticipated that a MS DOS card will shortly be available allowing the SE (if used inconjunction with the Apple 5.25" disk drive) to run DOS applications.

With availability of the SCSI interface, the addition of a hard disk makes the Macintosh a very fast and powerful PC. Various hard disk options are available - Apple's own 20 Megabyte HD20 SC which sits neatly underneath the Mac, thereby retaining the compact 9" x 9" footprint, or a wide variety supplied by other manufacturers : Symbiotic, Quisk, MacBottom and Hyperdrive to mention but a few. The Hyperdrive was the first internal hard disk available for the Macintosh. Initially the installation procedures involved were daunting, though this is now said to have been improved.

There is a certain appeal in such a logical development of the one box solution and other manufacturers were quick to jump on the internal drive bandwagon. There is now a wealth of such products offering both SCSI capability for the MacPlus and SE and standard interface for 512K users. Our contention is that the Mac was designed as a sealed unit and should remain so. Furthermore, the convenience of carrying around your life on a lightweight hard disk has definite advantages - you merely plug into an available Macintosh and immediately have 20 megabytes of data on stream.

The Macintosh as a DTP tool

Several hardware considerations should be borne in mind by the prospective desktop publisher. Whilst the pros and cons of floppy vs hard disk based systems is covered in greater depth in chapter 9, the following guidelines are worthy of note :

1. The serious DTP system should most certainly be based around the Macintosh Plus or the new Macintosh SE. The importance of the RAM, supplied as one megabyte upgradeable to four, cannot be

overstressed, particularly in the area of image processing. Use of the SCSI port as supplied with both models speeds up disk accessing quite noticeably compared with previous models.

2. Consider carefully the purchase of your hard disk. There is a certain wisdom in buying the constituent parts of a system from one manufacturer. Not only does this policy ensure onward compatibility in terms of hardware and software upgrades, but assists in the smooth running of maintenance contracts in the event of system failure. (Which thankfully seems to happen less frequently on the Macintosh than on the standard open architecture PC). In addition, dare we mention, the aesthetic aspects of such a strategy? The computer is going to be part of the desk furniture for a long time, so it might as well be pleasing to the eye. Beauty and functionality can mix.

The majority of third party Macintosh hard disks available in the UK are supplied by companies holding distribution rights, rather than representatives of the manufacturer per se. Hence, though they may appear more cost effective initially, be warned. Technical support and spares availability may be less than perfect. Symbiotic, a British company, are a notable exception and their products offer the UK user a viable alternative to Apple's own.

3. Make use of the available utilities to speed up the Mac's operation. 'Switcher' and 'Mini finder' enable you to move from one application programme to another without having to return to the desk top (WIMP equivalent of disk directory) to reload programs.

4. Do think twice about using an Apple Imagewriter as a low-cost proofing device. The Macintosh screen based founts were designed with a 72dpi screen and dot-matrix output in mind. The founts are adequate approximations of their industry standard counterparts. Hence Apple's GENEVA is the screen based equivalent of Helvetica, NEW YORK corresponds to Times. Any fount referred to by a city name (MONACO, VENICE, LONDON, etc) is an Imagewriter fount. A page designed, made up and sent down to an Imagewriter will not therefore be an identical representation of the same page produced on the LaserWriter. The Imagewriter has a role, but this should be restricted to the non-justified printing and proofing of 'galleys' prior to make up, and not the finished article.

The term WYSIWYG, though a relative newcomer to the PC environment, originates in the print industry where make-up terminals like the Xenotron and systems such as Xyvision are already in use. Text can be manipulated with great flexibility and in some cases half tones and line drawings can be shown correctly placed on the page.

That the Macintosh operating system was geared to data manipulation and flexibility makes it admirably suited to the DTP task at a fraction of the cost of its professional counterparts. Moreover, that the Mac is supplied as a complete unit with the correct hardware and software configuration to allow this to happen is yet another plus point. This advantage will become clearer when we go on to discuss the IBM PC and look at the range of add-ons needed to bring the system up to a workable specification.

Most significant, however, is the fact that "The Apple Macintosh is currently the only DTP system where data interchange between applications is fundamental to the way the computer works" *(Systems International, Febuary 1987)*. In effect, the cut and paste facility is available as standard, regardless of which application package is in use.

The Macintosh system provides the user with a 'clipboard' - a temporary storage area in which data is held pending pasting into another file/page/document. The 'scrapbook' is a permanent storage area, designed to hold re-useable text and images, obtained from any source, for subsequent pasting into the required document.

It was no accident that US software developers Aldus originally selected the Macintosh as the vehicle for their PageMaker package. The rest is history.

Future developments

Apple's recent announcements include, in addition to the Macintosh SE mentioned above, the Macintosh II. Hence the Macintosh family now covers the MacPlus, Mac SE and Macintosh II. The latter is a powerful workstation based on the Motorola 68020 chip and providing open architecture for the installation of add-on cards. RAM can be increased up to 8 megabytes, and hard disk storage to 80 megabytes. Colour screens are supported, as well as larger displays. Unix will be implemented on the Macintosh II later this year.

Macintosh software

Before examining in depth the make-up systems currently available, let us first consider the software elements and the roles they play in total page production. The constituent parts can be broken down under the following headings:

- Wordprocessing software
- Structured graphics
- Freehand graphics
- Business graphics
- Scanning software (see chapter 9)
- Page make-up
- Communications

Wordprocessing

Wordprocessing continues to play a major role in the inputting of text. Nor need the text originate on the Macintosh: communications and the ability to pull in files from other sources for subsequent layout is discussed briefly below. WP alone is satisfactory for the production of letters, textual reports, or indeed any document that requires neither columns, integrated text, nor sophisticated typographical facilities. If 300dpi output resolution can be obtained in an industry standard fount, we can refer to the wordprocessing of documents as DTP.

MacWrite

MacWrite, Apple's own proprietary WP software, is more than adequate for standard text production. Though lacking the bells and whistles of sophisticated WP systems, the assumption here is that major text manipulation will be performed in the page make-up package.

Predictably, MacWrite offers all the advantages of WYSIWYG operation. Founts, styles and sizes can be changed throughout the document at will, merely by pointing at and clicking on the portion of text to be changed or by a rapid scroll throughout the entire file. Style changes for individual words, headers, etc, can be performed using a toggle principle, i.e. two keystrokes turn the style on or off. Nothing superfluous or meaningless appears on screen apart from text in the specified style.

A significant number of functions can be accessed without using the mouse - a boon for the touch typist who is naturally less than delighted at the prospect of periodically diving for the mouse when keyboard controls would prove faster. Apple have helpfully supplied keyboard equivalents for many of the mouse controls such as cut and paste, align, justify, find and style changes. Moreover, the controls used are simple to remember because they are so totally logical. Thus 'B' represents bold, 'U' underline, 'O' outline, 'S' shadow and yes, you guessed it, 'I' not suprisingly stands for italic.

Since text editing is somewhat cumbersome in a typical page make-up system, it is advisable to make all alterations, wherever possible, at the WP stage.

See illustration 5 for an example of a typical MacWrite screen

Microsoft Word

Word offers a greater level of sophistication than MacWrite in terms of traditional WP facilities. It has been found adequate by some users for the production of books and technical manuals and this achieved without dumping the whole lot into a page layout package.

According to Microsoft, however, WHNSAY ! which roughly translated means 'We Haven't Seen Anything Yet'. Word version 3.0, due for imminent release, offers more functionality than any other WP package available on the Macintosh to date. So much bearing does Word version 3.00 have on the enhanced wordprocessing versus desktop publishing debate, that we have examined its properties more closely in chapter 9.

Such a product must surely assist Apple in improving its position in the marketplace, if only in making Macintosh-based WP respectable.

Structured graphics

The creation of organisation and flow charts, technical diagrams, forms, etc can be subsumed under the heading structured graphics (as opposed to freehand).

The almost uncontested leader among graphics packages of this type is Apple's MacDraw. Able to support the 300dpi of the LaserWriter, Macdraw offers some interesting features. In addition to what you would expect - lines of varying thickness, boxes, circles, arcs, polygons, a choice of hatches or fill patterns including various shades of grey -

MacDraw allows for acceptable precision. On-screen rulers allow specific object sizing and a grid covering the entire work area allows objects to be easily lined up, using the 'snap to grid' facility that recurs

Macintosh the industry standard

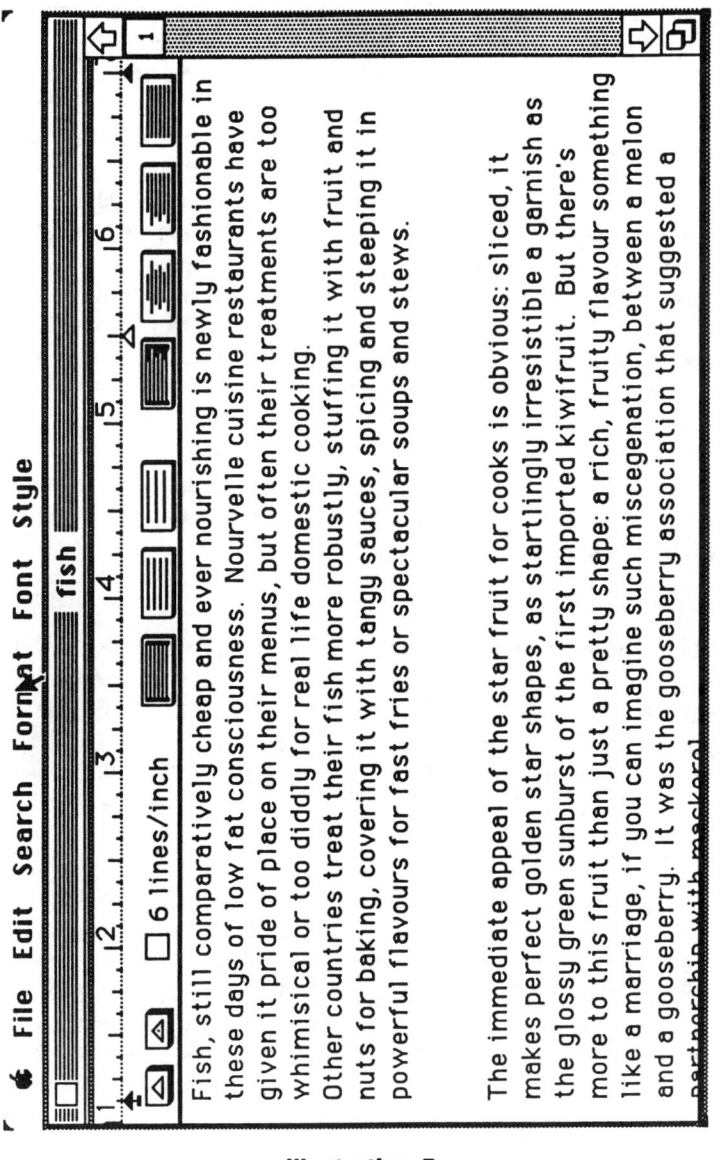

> Fish, still comparatively cheap and ever nourishing is newly fashionable in these days of low fat consciousness. Nouvelle cuisine restaurants have given it pride of place on their menus, but often their treatments are too whimsical or too diddly for real life domestic cooking.
> Other countries treat their fish more robustly, stuffing it with fruit and nuts for baking, covering it with tangy sauces, spicing and steeping it in powerful flavours for fast fries or spectacular soups and stews.
>
> The immediate appeal of the star fruit for cooks is obvious: sliced, it makes perfect golden star shapes, as startlingly irresistible a garnish as the glossy green sunburst of the first imported kiwifruit. But there's more to this fruit than just a pretty shape: a rich, fruity flavour something like a marriage, if you can imagine such miscegenation, between a melon and a gooseberry. It was the gooseberry association that suggested a partnership with mackerel.

**Illustration 5.
Typical MacWrite screen**

throughout any examination of Macintosh software. Co-ordinates can be shown on screen to verify that circles and squares are true.

Objects once created can be duplicated and aligned against various criteria. A complex image made up of many objects can be 'grouped' so that all constituent parts act as a whole. Grouping allows the easy manipulation of images, through 'dragging' (i.e. grabbing the graphic with the mouse and hauling it around the screen) cut and paste or duplication.

MacDraw allows you to work at actual size or at display-entire-page size. Text can be input directly; up to 48 point is supported, as are the LaserWriter founts. Text and objects can be created and placed on top of or behind other objects, hence creating a collage effect with as many layers as required. Objects can be sent to the back, or bought to the front, depending on the desired result.

Rotation in any direction is supported, other than through diagonals. Lastly, though the LaserWriter limits output to A4 sized chunks, very large documents can be created under MacDraw. A suprisingly powerful package for under £100. See illustration 6 for an illustration of a typical MacDraw document.

Freehand graphics

Freehand graphics allow the production of line drawings that are not dependent on specific shapes. Typical applications include the freehand design of logos, cartoons and illustrations in general. So popular has computer aided 'art' become that exhibitions are now being held dedicated to precisely this discipline. The most impressive results can best be achieved with the use of a graphics tablet and stylus, tools to which the user can most readily relate, in preference to the mouse.

MacPaint is the original freehand drawing package upon which all others have been based. Available tools, represented in true WIMP form as icons, include pencil for fine line drawing, paintbrush, aerosol can for the graffiti effect or merely to assist in shading, a paint pot to fill predefined shapes with shades or patterns, the usual squares, lines and circles and for obvious reasons an eraser. Perhaps MacPaint's most useful facility is the 'fat bits' option which allows a portion of the screen to be blown up to pixel level for precise editing. This is an important facility in the editing and general tidying-up of previously scanned images.

Unfortunately, and here's the rub, MacPaint was designed to support the Imagewriter printer and will only output at 72dpi. Other software

**Illustration 6.
Typical MacDraw document**

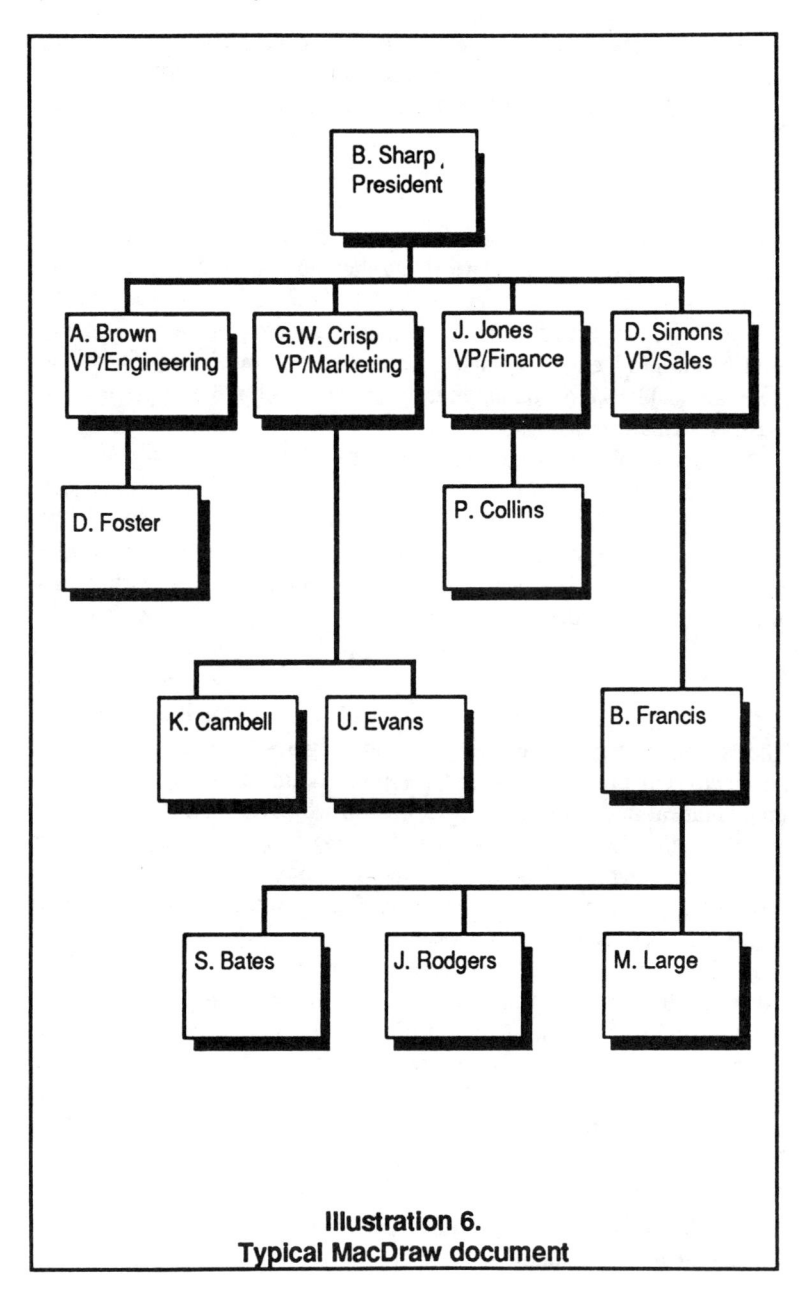

houses have been quick to jump on the bandwagon and produce MacPaint clones with full LaserWriter support. The desktop publisher with a need for freehand design would therefore be well advised to opt for FullPaint or SuperPaint.

Business graphics

It is widely accepted that graphs convey trends, results, indeed any commercial messages, more effectively than do columns of figures. The manual creation of graphs, however, is tedious and time consuming - especially if the results keep fluctuating. Business graphics are widely used in the production of financial and statistical reports, presentation materials, published accounts; indeed any publication that has a need to illustrate numerical data.

Business graphic packages cover a spectrum of the most widely used chart and graph styles : scatter, line, bar, column, pie, xy, etc. Traditionally business graphics were offered as a function of the spreadsheet or integrated software package, the trend having been set by Lotus 123 in 1984. The beauty of this approach is the ease with which graphs can be re-plotted once the data changes.

Lotus Jazz

Lotus Jazz was the first serious integrated software for the Macintosh. The spreadsheet principle allows text and figures to be placed in cells arranged in a grid of rows and columns. Formulae entered performs mathematical and statistical calulations on whatever data relates to that specific cell. In order to produce a graph using Jazz one merely selects an area of data using the mouse, opens a graphics file, selects the graph type and gives the plot command, all performed using pull-down menus. The graph appears almost immediately.

At this stage considerable editing options are available, legends and titles can be arranged using the standard LaserWriter fount families. Shading and fill patterns can be specified and of course the graph can be cut or copied into the scrapbook or saved for subsequent use in a page layout program. Any changes to the original data will be reflected in the graph until such time as it is cut out.

Microsoft Excel

Microsoft's Excel operates in much the same way but offers enhanced spreadsheeting capabilities. As our concern lies in the production of

Macintosh the industry standard

graphic images we will not expand on this. If the idea of using an entire spreadsheet system merely to produce some graphs sounds rather daunting, then opt for a package which performs the latter without the cost of the former.

Professional Business Graphics' Cricket Graph serves such a purpose.

Relative software costs are as follows: Lotus Jazz offering WP, spreadsheet, database, graphics and communications - £295; Microsoft Excel, combined spreadsheet, database and business graphics - £395. Cricket Graph, business graphics only - £170. See illustration 7 for sample graph produced under Jazz.

Communications

Communications software exists to enable text generated on another computer to be imported into the Macintosh for subsequent manipulation and formatting. There is no need therefore to relegate existing WP machines to the scrap heap, since text created on the majority of popular systems can readily be transfered in ASCII format onto the Macintosh. Why upset the Applecart by asking WP operators to learn new systems when in reality there is no need.

This chapter was input on an IBM PC using WordStar and transferred onto the Macintosh using a serial cable and 'MacLink ' software. Some formatting was required at the Mac end and the entire operation took about 10 minutes.

Page make-up

For the sake of clarity we have outlined the functions of each package before providing a brief overview of relative strengths and weaknesses, as judged against the 'ideal' proposed in chapter 2. We have added some additional criteria, based in the main on personal experience.

Given the wealth of available DTP software it is impossible to cover every package. The criteria for inclusion was twofold - did the software come close to the ideal and did we feel it had sufficient following and credibility to be around in the foreseeable future. As software continues to be developed, some products come to the fore and as market leaders enjoy a successful life cycle. Others make an appearance and then for a variety of reasons disappear.

What we have done is to mention the former and something of the

**Illustration 7.
Graph produced under Jazz**

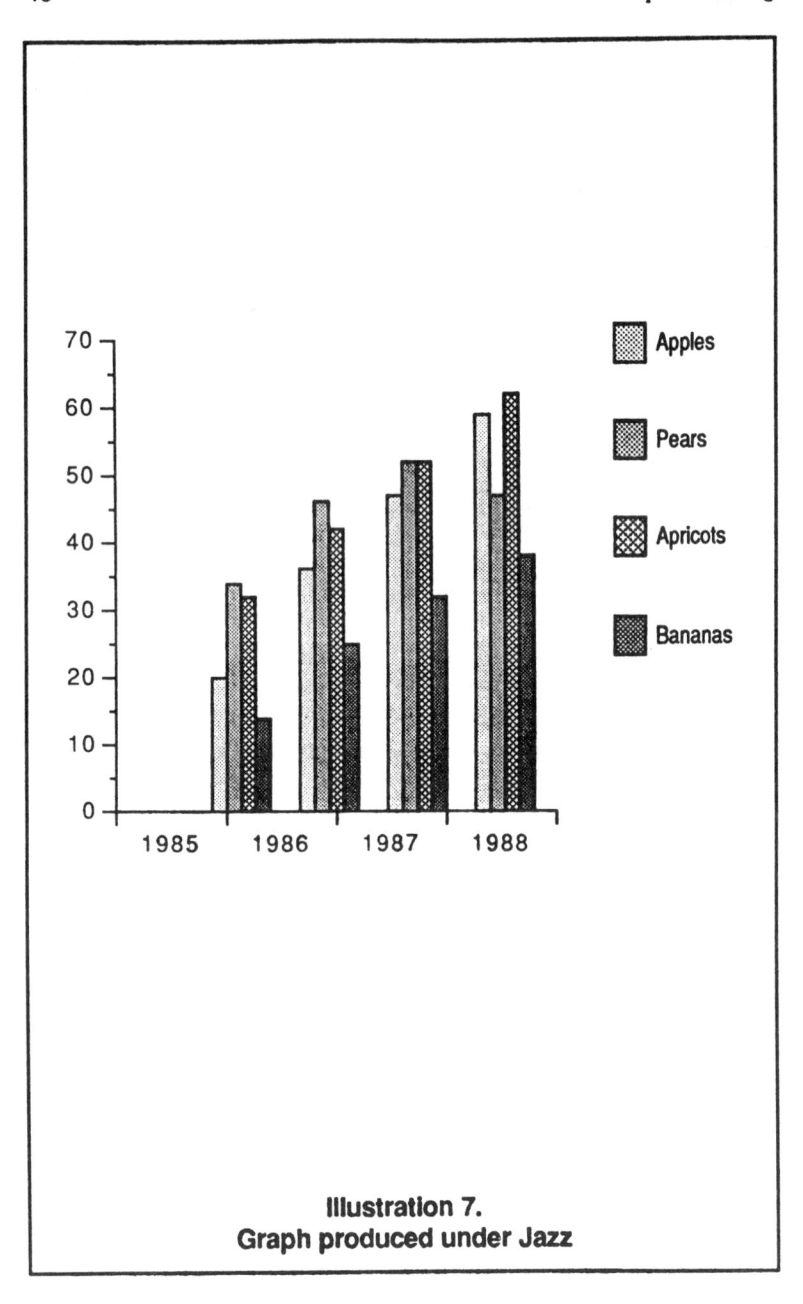

packages that offer particularly innovative features.

Aldus PageMaker - (page based)

PageMaker must surely be at the time of writing the most widely-used PC based page composition package available (over 30,000 copies sold in the first year). So significant has been its impact that it can be said to have defined, if not created, the DTP market as we know it. It has set standards and become regarded as the benchmark that other software developers must follow if they are to win a slice of the market.

At the time of PageMaker's initial release there was very little around in the way of strong competition; Ready Set Go version 1 was available, MacPublisher in a rudimentary form and very little else. Hence, despite a glaring lack of typographical functions and little concern for aesthetics, PageMaker's simplicity, speed and effectiveness, its ability to manipulate text and graphics from other software sources, and its Postscript support made it a clear winner.

It must be understood that pre-PageMaker there were no DTP standards and no significant products by way of comparison. Futhermore there was no clear definition, not only of whom the primary users would be, but what levels of professionalism they would demand. It is only very recently that awareness has increased and the divide between professional publishers, typesetters and graphic designers on the one hand, and PC users on the other, has closed considerably. The latter are now demanding typographic sophistication previously unknown (and certainly not understood) by the traditional microcomputer user and dealer alike.

At the time of writing, PageMaker release 2 for the Macintosh was not officially available, but it appears to address and overcome many of the functions that were seen to be lacking.

Text manipulation. Interactive page composition program, which provides a screen-based electronic cut and paste facility for the production of camera ready artwork/copy. Text taken from WP (MacWrite, Microsoft Word) is flowed (snaked) into pre-defined columns. Text can be edited at any stage, through one of the five viewing sizes, i.e. entire page, two facing pages, 200%, actual size and 70% . It is not advisable, however, to use PageMaker for text entry per se. Slow screen redisplay realistically limits the user to minor edits. Any changes made will 'ripple' through the entire document. Hence if text is rearranged to allow space for a graphic to be inserted, the resulting extra text will automatically flow into subsequent columns.

Whereas earlier releases of PageMaker allowed typographic changes, such as changes to fount, fount type and size, to be made only column by column, release two overcomes this cumbersome process and allows users to make changes across the entire page through a 'select all' facility. Individual objects, be they blocks of text, graphics or headings can be moved freely and repositioned within the document.

Page formatting. All column guides, margins, gutters,etc can be specified in inches, millimetres or picas and points. Ruler guides are available to allow precise placing of headlines, graphics and half tones. Text automatically re-wraps upon the changing of column widths.

Typographic features. Automatic pair kerning and manual kerning in positive and negative increments. The former is pre-defined according to the manufacturer of the fount used.

Hyphenation and justification are more in keeping with professional typographic standards. PageMaker offers three levels of word spacing for justified text, in addition to flexible hyphenation. A 90,000 word dictionary is supplied to cope with auto hyphenation. Supplied by Houghton Mifflin, the dictionary stipulates the acceptable point at which a word can be hyphenated, hence avoiding potentially unprofessional results in the event that words such as titular or prickle be hyphenated inappropriately! Users can add up to 1000 words to the dictionary and will in addition be prompted to hyphenate manually any words not included, should excessive white space result from not so doing.

The dictionary cannot be modified, since it is supplied in compressed form. It can, however, be turned off. In order to fit words on a line PageMaker runs through the following procedures. Firstly, it tries optimum word spacing, calling on the dictionary to hyphenate the last word in a line if necessary. In the event that this fails, minimum word spacing is tried, with recourse to maximum spacing and, if you have permitted, letterspacing. The last resort, if all fails, is to hyphenate manually. The entire exercise is of course transparent to the user, apart from the last step, when a manual hyphenation prompt will appear. In effect, an inter-word spacing range is pre-determined, and if PageMaker can't sort out a line within those parameters, the operator is forced to take over.

Leading. Whilst PageMaker will always default to the leading considered appropriate to the point size in use, it can be adjusted manually in half point increments.

Graphics/scanned image support. In addition to accepting documents created under traditional Macintosh graphics software (MacDraw, FullPaint, Cricket Graph, Jazz, etc), files can also be developed using the Postscript language, for subsequent insertion in the document. The concept of programming in Postscript and other PDLs will be explored in more depth later. All graphics images can be scaled to fit allocated space. Additionally the facility exists to crop a graphic taken from whatever source.

PageMaker provides you with a 'tool box', which contains a number of icons specific to certain functions. Included are basic graphics tools for the creation of lines, boxes and specified fill patterns or shades of grey. Rudimentary graphics can therefore be created directly on screen.

PageMaker supports all files produced on what in PC terminology are referred to as 'high' resolution scanners (typically 300dpi) that use the 'tag image file format '(TIFF). Examples include Microtek, DEST and Datacopy scanners. See chapter 9 for further explanation.

Document production. Unlike earlier releases, PageMaker version 2.0 can create documents of up to 128 pages in length. The previous constraint of 32 pages had been a purported cause of concern amongst users. However, bearing in mind that PageMaker is *page based* as oppposed to *document based* and is thus not geared to typical long extent productions such as manuals, books, etc, the page constraint has never been, we maintain, a real obstacle.

Master Pages. PageMaker does not support any style sheet or macro facility. You can, however, set up 'master pages' which retain a predefined format throughout the document. Margins and columns can be pre-determined, as can headers, footers, boxes, shaded areas, rules, etc. Verso and recto pages can hold distinct formats.

Page description language. PageMaker offers Postscript support, enabling use not only with the Apple LaserWriter but other high resolution Postscript compatible typesetting devices. Graphics files written in Postscript can be placed in PageMaker, and cropped or scaled accordingly. Postscript files developed in this way can be viewed only when placed on the page.

Ease of use. Once you have learnt the normal Macintosh WIMP conventions, any program that adheres to them is relatively easy to grasp. We managed to find our way around it and make up a page without once referring to the manual. Admittedly it wasn't the most pleasing page ever produced, nor is it recommended that first-time Mac users do likewise.

The 'file' menu is positioned where one expects to find it and includes the normal options of print, save, etc. It also offers a PageMaker specific option 'place'. Upon selecting 'place' a disk directory is displayed, a double click on the required file allows it to picked up for positioning in PageMaker. Icons inform the user of the type of file he is placing. The 'snap to guides' facility discussed above comes into effect and enables the text or image to be placed precisely along the column marker. Text flows into the columns, stopping only when it finds a box, line or graphic already in place. Column widths can be altered, even when text has been placed.Subsequent page formatting will not effect preset text and graphics.

It is very difficult to go seriously wrong using PageMaker. The same file can be placed, deleted and replaced ad infinitum, since you are using not the original but merely a copy. Changes, amendments and alterations can be made simply and easily.

PageMaker is developed and supplied by the Aldus Corporation and costs under £500.

Manhatten Graphics Ready Set Go3 - (page based)

Thankfully, Ready Set Go3 bears very little resemblence to either RSG1 or 2. The latest release is recognised as a serious rival to PageMaker and fulfils much the same purpose. Recent endorsement of the product by Letraset, who have adopted it in preference to Boston Software's MacPublisher ll, can only serve to create greater credibility and acceptance in the marketplace. What makes RSG3 unique is its ability to double as a wordprocessor, an option not normaly found hand in hand with the page make-up facility.

Text manipulation/ page formatting. RSG3 offers standard wordprocessing functions, and allows text entry as the page is being made up. WP facilities include search and replace, glossary options and a 60,000 word spelling checker.Ready Set Go3 pages are composed of text frames (or blocks), graphics frames and ruled lines. Text is keyed directly into the former which can be linked to allow text flow from one to another, even across page breaks. Text changes throughout the document, be they additions or deletions, result in an automatic reflow of text through the linked frames. Like PageMaker, RSG3 offers five preview and edit modes: double size, for fine editing, actual size, half page, full page and facing pages.

Text runaround, or the flowing of text around a graphic, occurs automatically if text and graphics frames are manipulated so that they overlap. The concept of building up a series of connected or overlapping text and graphics boxes allows considerable flexibility in layout. Dropped caps, for example, can be achieved by placing the large character in a text frame and positioning this adjacent to the initial paragraph. Custom rulers specified in inches, centimeters or picas and points can define page size and layout. In addition, design grids allowing column numbers and formats can be modified to precise requirements. The use of grids enables use of the 'snap to guide' function mentioned above for accurate positioning of text and graphics.

Point size can be user-controlled, i.e. you can override the defaults supplied with the Macintosh system. Ready Set Go can support anything from 6 point to 255. We have yet to find a use for the latter !

File import. RSG3 offers file import facilities so it is not mandatory to use the program for text entry. MacWrite, Microsoft Word and standard ASCII files can be directly read in. No file export facilities are available.

Kerning. Fount based pair kerning and manual kerning in one point increments are supported.

H&J. Hyphenation is controlled through means of a linguistic-based algorithm and can be turned on or off for a predefined section of text. If the algorithm is switched on, hyphenation and justification occur at the same rate as standard word wrap. H & J will be correctly and rapidly readjusted through all linked text frames in the event of textual alterations and edits. There is no facility for maxium, minimum or preferred word spacing.

Leading. RSG3 makes use of standard leading-to-point-size assumptions over which the user has no over-riding control.

Graphics/scanned image support. MacDraw and MacPaint images can be imported directly into RSG3, where they can be scaled or cropped. By extension any scanned output file supporting the TIFF convention can be imported into Macpaint and thereafter into RSG as a bit-mapped graphic.

Document Production (length). Document size is constrained only by the amount of disk storage available.

Master pages/style sheets. Ready Set Go3 like PageMaker is page-based.

Whilst we are beginning to witness the emergence of page-based make-up packages with facilities for long extent documents, the former do not usually offer a true style sheet option. Like PageMaker, RSG3 allows the creation of master pages, so that formatting - headers, footers and even the positioning of text and graphics frames - can be set up for odd and even pages and carried through the document. In reality, the typical page-based document, a newsletter, magazine or even a fairly basic report, will not adhere to a standard format regarding the positioning of line drawing and text on every page. Hence whilst the master page option has limited usefulness, the notion of linked text frames has far more significance. Changes made to fount, point size and style are reflected throughout the entire area of linked text.

Page description language. Adobe's Postscript is supported, as is the facility for embedding Postscript code directly into the document, in order to achieve a variety of 'special effects'. Sophisticated pages can be produced without recourse to Postscript. This merely serves to reinforce the view that any page make-up package offering PDL support can be enhanced and is less likely to be 'outgrown'. It follows that RSG can drive the LaserWriter and any other device with a Postscript raster image processor (RIP).

Ease of Use. Ready Set Go is a WYSIWYG package that conforms to the standard Macintosh operating procedures. The use of text and graphics frames, whilst less simple to grasp initially than the PageMaker system of flexible columns, does have its advantages. The speed with which text can be reformatted with simultaneous hyphenation and justification makes for very fast operation.

Ready Set Go version three, offers some interesting facilities: runaround of text, the ability to have several documents open at one time and cut and paste between them is also useful. Manhattan Graphics have obviously followed PageMaker's lead in incorporating more sophisticated typographical functions. At the end of the day, however, they still have improvements to make in this area. This is obviously a case of closely examining requirements, since some users may prefer a fast package at the expense of aesthetics and professional quality.

Ready Set Go is available from Letraset Page and Print, and costs £295.

Knowledge Engineering's Just Text - (document based)

Remembering our enthusiasm about the ease of use of the Macintosh, its friendly environment and the fact that it offers a continuity of operation regardless of the software in use, we've finally come up with the exception that proves the rule !

Just Text, unlike the Macintosh software reviewed above, does not operate in a WYSIWYG environment nor does it adhere to the WIMP conventions. Of all Macintosh software, Just Text is possibly the most difficult package to learn and use. It warrants special mention for the simple reason that, being based on conventional typesetting software, the package offers typographical precision unsurpassed by any DTP software examined above. The user who is prepared to dedicate a degree of learning time, can be assured of greater control over the printed page.

In the abscence of WYSIWYG, Just Text uses embedded codes, a concept not alien to the typesetting industry. To the traditional Macintosh user the notion of not being able to see what you are going to get is a daunting prospect but a screen preview facility is available for users of version 1.1, although only one viewing size is permitted. That said, for those with a requirement for long, professionally set documents, particularly if there is continuity of point size and type face (such as in a book), Just Text appears to be ideal. Written in assembler, the program is extremely fast, noticeably so when printing.

Text manipulation. Like RSG3, Just Text offers wordprocessing facilities, but there the similarity ends. The standard of facilities is more akin to professional WP as we know it. At the level of text entry, pull down menus and a recognisable Macintosh enviroment is available to the user. It's when you start typesetting that the fun begins ! However, many functions can be simplified by the use of a macro facility that assigns commonly-used routines to specific keys. Fount, type and style can be controlled by embedded codes, as can fount width. Both expanded and compressed characters can be produced.

File Import. 'Text tools' enables MacWrite and Word files to be converted into Just Text format but they may still require editing since the translation is normally not 100% perfect. Unformatted ASCII files can also be imported (or rather, the format will be lost if it exists).

Page Formatting. Any number of columns of varying widths can be specified, as can horizontal and vertical tabs. Verso and recto offset is provided. Text is flowed automatically into the predefined columns, moving on to the next column when the page end is encountered. Graphics are avoided in this continual flow. If they fill up the entire width of the column, Just Text will merely leapfrog the image and continue. In the event that white space remains around the graphic (i.e. it has been placed as an outline not surrounded by a box or any rules) Just Text will perform a neat runaround.

Pages can be defined as broadsheet, tabloid, A4 and smaller. The Postscript output for each size will be correct, despite the fact that a printer such as the LaserWriter will have to output the finished page in sections. Obviously Just Text is geared to driving any and all output devices with a Postscript raster image processor.

Kerning. Comprehensive kerning options are offered. Customised global pair kerning can be specified, to override standard defaults. Manual kerning on a one-off basis is also possible. Just Text allows very precise negative and positive kerning. Commands can be entered in terms of fractions of a point.

H&J. Automatic and discretionary manual hyphenation are supported. A small exception dictionary may be built up. Columns can be justified, centered, left or right aligned. Given that the correct embedded codes are entered at the begining of the document or at the precise place when a format change is required, H&J will tend to look after itself, the flow of text pausing only when Just Text is defeated in trying to obtain a 'fit' and calls for operator intervention.

Leading. Very specific control is offered over line leading.

Graphics/scanned image support. A utility refered to as 'text tools' controls the import of graphics files from MacPaint. Scanned images from Thunderscan (see chapter 9) can also be accepted, for conversion into Postscript files. Sadly, there is at present no facility for importing MacDraw images. Basic graphics tools are available via embedded codes for the creation of boxes and rules in various widths and patterns.

Master pages/style sheets. In the event that you are using a specific house style, Just Text is adequate. All instructions in the form of embedded codes (i.e. commands contained within {} brackets) can be entered at the beginning and remain so until resest.

Page description language. Not only does Just Text support Adobe's Postscript; it makes considerable use of it. It is used in two distinct ways. Firstly, Just Text translates the embedded codes and generates a Postscript listing to be sent down to the printer. This element is transparent to the user. Of most significance is the fact that Postscript commands and routines can be embedded in the text to produce a wealth of special but useful effects. Text can be created on diagonal axes, can be curved, can encircle an object. These effects require complex algorithms and knowledge of programming the Postscript language. However the serious desktop publisher may find that he wants to get to grips with this, if professional quality output is to be achieved.

Ease of use. It is probably superfluous to expand in any more depth on Just Text's user unfriendliness. As always in dicussing the pros and cons of any software package, it boils down to what you require in terms of quality, flexibilty and typographical sophistication, what type of publications are to be produced, and what skills are available in-house. Those who have mastered Just Text find it no more difficult to use than WordStar. It is only in the light of traditional Macintosh products that this package appears so complex.

Just Text is currently used by several newspapers, the most notable being the New York Times, the Wall Street Journal, and the Boston Globe. It is a typesetting software package with a specific orientation toward the professional user and heralds we believe a demand for higher quality output and greater flexibility over typographical functions. That it is outside the mainstream WYSIWYG environment and that Postscript offers no user-friendly interface are not prohibitive, but leave room for improvement if a package of this power is to command mass appeal.

Just Text is distributed by MacEurope and costs £195.

Other page make-up software

Worthy of mention, though not serious contenders:

Orange Micro's Ragtime . An 'integrated' package offering rudimentary WP, spreadsheet, graphics and page layout. Works on the frame or box basis , rather than using columns. No kerning, hyphenation or control over inter-word spacing. Postscript support. Not intended for the serious desktop publisher, but useful, given the built-in spreadsheet, in the production of financial reports.

Boston Software's MacPublisher. Until recently Letraset's only DTP package, marketed under the guise of Letrapage. Has recently been elbowed out (temporarily we are told) in favour of Ready Set Go3. Letraset has bought rights for both packages, though MacPublisher had not, apparently, developed as they had hoped. However, enhancements continue to be made which will gear MacPublisher/Letrapage towards the graphic arts industry rather than DTP. Its facilities remain impressive: page-based, WYSIWYG software operating on the 'frame' principle. Auto-hyphenation using extensive word dictionary and algorithm. Pair plus manual kerning, the latter in one point increments. Vertical and horizontal justification. Creates automatic table of contents. The theoretical limits of Letrapage are claimed to be 1024 pages, containing 1024 text files and the same number of graphics files. We haven't actualy tried this so cannot comment !

4
The IBM PC

The IBM personal computer, which made the concept of personal computing respectable in business circles, now has the capability of lending credibility to, and hence promoting, desktop publishing.

We define a microcomputer, or rather a micro-based computer, as one in which the central processing unit is a single chip microprocessor. Today, this covers a wide variety of machines, single-user and multi-user, eight bit, 16 bit and 32 bit. In effect, the development from eight to 32 bit means quite simply that the latter is able to process information and access data faster than its predecessor. Hence the 16 bit micro offered more speed than the eight bit and logically the 32 bit facilitated improved response over the 16 bit.

The original generation of micros used eight bit processors such as the Intel 8080 and were limited in their capabilities. Even so, many organisations used them very successfully for solving business problems: stock control, accounting, word processing and information management.

The increasing adoption of micro technology lead to a dramatic reduction in the cost of hardware. Moreover, the potential market for software became so large that it was worthwhile expending effort to produce sophisticated packages that would sell cheaply in large numbers.

Another factor in the early days of micros was the existence of an industry standard operating system, in the shape of CP/M (Control

Program for Microcomputers), which was available on all computers using the Intel 8080 or Zilog Z80 microprocessor. It was CP/M, in the first place, available on so many different machines, that promoted the growth of generic software such as wordprocessors, database management systems and spreadsheets. Apart from certain low cost machines aimed primarily at the home user, business computers have changed fundamentally since this heyday of CP/M.

Meanwhile, Apple went its own way. Apple utilised a different operating system - their own - and based their machines on the Motorola 6502. That the Apple ll has sold more than any other personal computer cannot be ignored. It did more to raise public awareness and develop a microcomputer market than any other product. Our ubiquitous man in the street will have heard of Apple. He is unlikely to know of CP/M. Undoubtedly IBM would have met with success in their PC venture under almost any circumstances; however the fact that a hard core of committed micro users existed due to the success of the Apple 11 aided and abetted the process.

Recent developments

Four developments have changed the face of microcomputing over the past few years: 16 bit processors, networking, multi-user systems and, finally, the entry of IBM into the personal computer market.

Networks dramatically extended the power of the micro. In the office automation arena, they allowed many users to share files, share data and exchange messages. More generally the network allowed the equivalent of mainframe computer power to be built up from smaller units. Multi-user micros are now available in environments where a mini computer would traditionally have been used. Again, the lower cost of the micro is making a whole area of computing available to a new class of user.

The IBM personal computer has had a dramatic effect, particularly in making the concept of microcomputing respectable. It has set an industry standard in the 16 bit user area; it has led to new developments in networking.

A key advantage of the IBM PC in the early days was that its main operating system, DOS (also called MS DOS or PC DOS; we will discuss the implications of terminology later) was in its first version very similar to CP/M. It was not difficult for software houses to convert their existing CP/M software, so there was a readymade source of

The IBM PC

software packages - the wordprocessor WordStar, used to type a small section of this book, is a prime example. Later, of course, these packages were much improved and new ones written to take advantage of the extra features of the PC, so that now it has an enormous range of software, far in excess of that available under CP/M.

Importance of the IBM PC

To anyone who has had exposure to computers and office automation, the name IBM - International Business Machines - needs little introduction. IBM is important as the dominant influence in computing, and increasingly in other areas of technology. It is also the most profitable company in the world and has achieved that position by a coherent blend of technological excellence and more importantly an unrivalled skill in marketing.

Of course, IBM was not the only company to attempt to dominate the lucrative PC market place. At the outset, the IBM PC was one of a number of machines that were very similar in their specification, with difference in detail and in standards. Other machines used the same 5.25 inch diskettes, but formatted in a totally different way, so that they could not exchange data or programs. The importance of the IBM PC was that by dominating the market it set a standard.

Today, if a new desktop machine appears, it is almost obligatory for it to be IBM compatible (the most notable exception being the Macintosh). The 'incompatibles' of the early days have either disappeared from the market altogether, or have been relegated to the backwaters of the industry. The IBM PC thus became the accepted standard, which competitors had to imitate if their machines were to be able to run the latest software. Only five years after entering the PC market, the IBM standard is dominant .

A recent independent survey carried out in the US, reflecting results for the last three months of 1986, showed Apple winning a larger market share than IBM. The combination, however, of the IBM PC, the Ollivetti, Compaq and Hewlett Packard compatibles collectively accounted for the vast majority. Though the IBM PC DOS standard may dominate, it is diffused over a plethora of other vendors' products

Another reason for the success of the IBM PC and compatibles has been the multiple expansion slots which have been used for plugging in a wide variety of extra devices, either IBM or third party products. This expandability has meant that the PC has become much more than a personal computer. With the facility to support networks, external communications and act as a terminal to mini and mainframe installations the PC now has the potential to become the multifunction workstation, that office automation so desperately needs.

IBM PC and DTP

The PC has the advantage of being a more open, or expandable, hardware system, which can easily accept different graphic boards for the addition of colour and high resolution displays, as well as memory expansion boards. It is this essence of expandability, coupled with the significant quantity of installed machines, that leads the DTP pundits to predict that the IBM and compatibles will pick up the lion's share of the market.

Until recently PC applications could only use the Apple LaserWriter in the so-called Diablo 630 emulation mode for text and severely limited graphics output. The net result was restriction to the use of Courier as a typeface, or recourse to other printers offering a wide selection of bastardised founts. With the addition of recently announced Postscript drivers, a considerable number of MS DOS applications will be able to exploit the graphics capability of the LaserWriter and other high-end laser printers. Of greater significance is the introduction of a PC AppleTalk card, which effectively allows the DOS machine unrestricted access to the LaserWriter and hence quality output that is not limited by the presence or absence of specifically written printer drivers. Apple's philosophy has apparently been 'if they're going to beat us, let it be with our equipment'.

The availability of Postscript compatibility will permit output through such devices as the highspeed LZR laser printer from Data Products and the Linotype 100 and 300 typesetting systems.

There is, and will always be, a facet of human nature that is resistant to change. The MS DOS user is unlikely to perform a U turn in his computing strategy and opt for a totally different environment. Yet another case of WYUTIWIB (What You're Used To Is What Is Best). Before the availability of DTP software on the IBM PC, many companies adopted the Macintosh system since by default there was no other route to take. The results of those who did so are encouraging. Now the communications between the two system are easy and effective and - with the advent of the Macintosh SE - you will be offered all the benefits of traditional Macintosh ease of use, coupled with an MS DOS option (achieved through the addition of an MS DOS co-processor card, and an additional 5.25" disk drive).

The 'typesetting' process was held up considerably without the ability of the IBM PC to preview printed output, since the user had to rely on a trial and error method. This was exacerbated when multiple columns of text and graphics were being produced. Ironically, it is due to the addition of a Macintosh-like user interface, such as Windows or Gem, covered in depth in chapter five, that the IBM can succeed in the DTP arena. Human nature works in mysterious ways. The very real conviction of WYUTIWIB is turned on its head by the adoption of precisely that environment it was intended to avoid.

5
Desktop software under MS-DOS

The foundation of all hardware is the operating system, the set of programs which manages the resources of the system : the disk drives, screen display, output ports and input devices such as keyboard and mouse. The application software, sitting on top of the operating system, is released from these tasks to process text, compute figures or make-up pages. To understand what desktop publishing can do on the IBM PC, it is important to understand MS-DOS, the PC operating system, with all its facilities. Note that MS-DOS is often referred to in its abbreviated form of DOS (i.e. Disk Operating System).

What is an operating system?

Software these days is becoming more and more complex: it may help to see it in terms of an onion, with the different layers of onion skin representing the different layers of software, which all need to interract together if the user is to benefit from his investment.

The outermost layer of the onion is the application program - word processing, page composition or whatever piece of software is required to accomplish the task in hand.

The next layer down is the user interface, the way the computer interacts with you as you sit at your keyboard or mouse. In some cases this is part of the application program, in other cases it comes with the operating system. There is a new generation of general purpose user-interfaces being produced - programs which enable the IBM PC to emulate as closely as possible the Macintosh WIMP environment. Examples include Microsoft's Windows and Digital Research's GEM, to be examined in more depth below. These user interfaces permit a variety of different software to look as similar as possible, thus avoiding the need to keep learning new ways of doing the same thing.

Finally we come to the operating system itself - the software which looks after all the detailed handling of the various devices that make up the computer, interpreting the keys you press, deciding what character to display on the screen, handling errors and interrupts.

Much of the operating system will be concerned with managing the disk and the files stored on it, keeping track of where each file starts and ends, allowing you to copy files, rename them, add to them, delete them, etc. Another part deals with programs, finding each program when you want to use it, loading the application into memory, taking over when the program has finished, and stepping in if the program needs to use an input or output device.

DOS vs the WIMP environment

We have already explored above the need for user-friendly systems, as a means of eliciting acceptance of, and by extension maximum productivity from, the system in use. Compared with some of the more powerful operating systems available, most specifically those designed for a multi-user environment such as UNIX, PC DOS may be considered easy to use. Compared with the Macintosh 'Finder', however, MS-DOS scores fairly low in the user-friendly stakes.

The key to the difference between the MS-DOS and Macintosh environments lies in the keyed-in command versus the WIMP approach. Some examples of how the same procedures would be performed by adopting such diverse approaches are outlined below.

Accessing files

Much of MS-DOS is concerned with maintaining details of files on the various disk drives. Indeed the very name 'Disk Operating System' implies that this is a key part of DOS's function. Normally a PC has two disk drives, referred to as 'A' and 'B' on a twin-floppy machine, 'A'

Desktop software under MS-DOS 65

and 'C' on a machine with one floppy and one hard disk. When referring to a file in DOS, the filename can be preceded with A: (or whichever drive you are accessing) to indicate which drive it is on. At any time one of the drives is the current default drive, where the system will look for a file if you do not prefix the filename with a drive letter.

The Macintosh allows each individual disk, rather than the drive, to be named. Hence whilst a rudimentary drive naming convention applies (internal drive, external drive and hard disk) it is not a key factor in using the system. An icon of the current disk appears on screen complete with its name, which can be up to 27 charcters long, and hence meaningful to the user. A disk could be named, for example, *"Pub's guide to DTP/ chap 5"*. In order to find a file, the mouse is merely dragged onto the disk in question and clicked twice. The disk opens and reveals all its contents, in Icon form, or as a listing according to type, size or date of creation.

Files contain all sorts of data. For instance, one file could be a document prepared using a word processing program, another might be the word processing program itself. One file might be a list of employees with their telephone extension numbers, another might be a week's accounting transactions, waiting to be posted to a ledger. Some files may be divided into 'records'; for instance, one record per employee or per transaction, but DOS knows nothing about this - a file is basically just a string of bytes.

The Macintosh, in contrast, uses a specific icon denoting the type of file held. By adopting simple logic, it becomes apparent that an icon showing lines of text is a MacWrite file, columns of text, a PageMaker file, etc. Program files are represented with unique icons. Selecting the 'view by type' option will provide a listing of all files, and the application used in their creation.

Filenames under DOS end in an optional three-character 'extension', delimited by a full stop. Extensions are used to indicate the type of file (for instance .BAS for a BASIC source file, .EXE for an executable program). Some extensions have special meanings to DOS or to particular application programs, but it is a good idea to generate your own standards such as perhaps .LET for a letter, .TMP for a temporary file which can be erased afterwards, and so on.

Subdirectories

DOS verion 2.0 which coincided with the launch of the IBM's hard disk machine the PC XT, permitted the creation of subdirectories (i.e. file directories within directories). These in turn could include other subdirectories, so that the number of files allowed on a disk was limited only by the physical space for data storage. The real benefit of subdirectories comes when using a hard disk. A hard disk can easily contain very large numbers of files, so that it becomes impossible to remember what they are all used for and difficult to find meaningful names for them all. Using subdirectories, files can be grouped in a logical way, perhaps by relating them to the same subject matter.

The use of directories is crucial for desktop publishing, which tends to involve large numbers of documents generated and keyed in by different people, especially when the machines are linked by a network. In the DTP environment, not only the use of sub-directories, but also standards for how to use them, can become extremely important.

The Macintosh equivalent to a subdirectory system was also made available with the release of Apple's hard disk. The rationale in terms of ease of location when hundreds of files can be held on a hard disk is the same in both cases. Macintosh named their enhancement the 'Hierachical Filing System' commonly referred to as HFS. However, in keeping with the WIMP tradition and the desire for continuity, Apple retained the notion of icons as representations of every-day items (disks, trash cans, a wrist watch denoting 'wait') and presented the subdirectory in terms of a folder.

Hence one conceives of the disk as a filing cabinet, containing folders, which in turn contain other folders. Subdirectory naming conventions are more flexible under the Macintosh system, since folder names can extend to 31 characters, whereas the IBM subdirectory provides a mere 8. It is perhaps easier to identify a folder entitled 'Fashion editorial, 3/4/87 KC' than 'fed347kc'.

Paths and pathnames

Under DOS you can move around from one directory to another. If you refer to a file by its name, DOS will look for it in the current directory, but additionally you can specify a full 'pathname', including a directory as well as the filename, and it will look for it in the directory specified. The special character '\' is used when specifying pathnames. For instance if you are currently in directory 'Book', the filename 'Chap1.Doc' would relate to a file in this directory. Its full pathname would be

Desktop software under MS-DOS 67

'\Book\Chap1.Doc'. The pathname '\' on its own means the original or 'root' directory of the disk in question.

The Macintosh allows subdirectories to be accessed merely by clicking' on a folder to reveal its contents. No interraction with the keyboard is called for, which could shed light on the DOS limit of an 8 character naming convention, since repeatedly keying in names of up to 31 characters could verge on the tedious.

Housekeeping commands

In general both the DOS and Macintosh environments allow for the same facilities in terms of general system 'housekeeping'. Both allow files and disks to be copied, files to be renamed and deleted. Under DOS everything is excecuted as a result of keyed-in commands, whilst a WIMP system will depend instead on pointing clicking and dragging. Renaming obviously requires keyboard intervention, but only after the appropriate file has been selected with the mouse.

Whilst DOS is quite powerful it can also prove inflexible and dangerous, even to the initiated user. For instance, in DOS you can delete a file very easily with a single command. If you enter the wrong filename by mistake, it is just too bad. Again, you may have a file that you keep a spare copy of, on a separate disk. If instead of 'Copy a:Myfile b:' you type in 'Copy b:Myfile a:' (easy to do, particularly if you are tired at the end of a long session of typing) then you may end up losing all your work. More disastrous, if you have a hard disk and for some reason you type in 'Format c:', you can irretrievably wipe out ten megabytes of information at a stroke. Remember as well that DOS is essentially a single-user operating system, and therefore has no means of protecting one user's file from another. This may seem perfectly OK for a single-user computer, but in practice one PC may have multiple users, though not of course at the same time. If you have data kept on the hard disk, it may be unwise to rely on other users not erasing it by mistake.

The Macintosh's friendly approach makes it difficult to lose data through operator error. During any deletion process you are prompted and informed of what you are doing. In the event that you try and throw away a program file, a dialogue box appears asking 'Are you sure?'. The supreme fail-safe, however, lies in the notion of the Wastebasket (actually an icon of a dustbin, but something got lost in translation from the American 'Trash can'!). Any file for deletion is unceremoniously dumped in the wastebasket, but it is only when you command the system to 'empty wastebasket' that the file is actually lost. Plenty of room for error avoidance.

Limitations of DOS for DTP

There is currently a move away from computing for computing's sake. The rapidly developing conviction among professionals is that they wish to perform their jobs as expertly, efficiently and profitably as possible, without becoming bogged down in the complexities of computer operation. The adoption of PCs to perform certain tasks is a means to an end.

The comparisons above serve to demonstrate the simplicity of the WIMP approach over conventional disk operating systems as epitomised by DOS. That is not to say that a pre-requisite to desktop publishing is studiously to avoid any DOS-based PC, nor should we infer that page make-up software cannot operate satisfactorily in a DOS environment. On the contrary, it can and does.

However, the reasons for condoning the Macintosh approach for the uninitiated are twofold:

1. The 'expert ', whatever his trade or profession, wishes to concentrate his energies on that specific area of expertise. Any PC-based solution must therefore perform as a tool enhancing rather than hindering the task in hand. At current price levels , PCs will be going onto many more desks than at present, and the typical user will no longer be a full-time typist or computer operator. A manager who uses the screen only occasionally will need to be helped and guided by a visual and friendly approach otherwise he may give up using the system. For this reason, ease of use and by extension a short learning curve is key.

2. The nature of PC-based page make-up software demands, with a few notable exceptions, a WYSIWYG standard, that can best be achieved in a WIMP or Macintosh like operating environment. DOS in its raw form does not support the facilities implicit in the concept of Windows, Icons, Mice and Pull down menus. Where it does fit in, however, is in supporting Macintosh-like user interfaces, as mentioned above, which provide the user with the ideal operating environment for DTP.

Imitating the Macintosh on the PC

Not surprisingly, the impression that the Macintosh has made on the market has given rise to a number of imitations. The closest imitation,

Desktop software under MS-DOS 69

in the IBM PC environment, has been Digital Research's GEM suite of software. Unfortunately Apple were not flattered by the imitation, which was so close that Apple threatened legal action, and GEM had to be withdrawn for cosmetic surgery to make its icons less Apple-like.

GEM is not the only product of its class. The main rival to GEM is Microsoft Windows, to be examined below. Other windowing products so far announced have included VisiOn from Visicorp, Taxi from Epson, and Topview from IBM itself. There is not room for so many contenders in the market and several of them already seem to have disappeared.

What is GEM?

GEM is several different facilities: a standard method of presenting information to the user, a standard method of dealing with the screen and keyboard, and a series of programs, of which the GEM desktop is the first one you are likely to use.

When you start GEM up, a 'desktop' appears on the screen, with two windows open. Normally one of these represents the system as a whole, with several icons already displayed, one for each disk drive you have in your machine. The desktop program allows you to do everything you could normally do by using MS-DOS commands, but in many cases you manipulate the icons on the screen rather than having to type commands. Generally, in respect of operating procedures GEM apes the Macintosh way of working.

As well as the GEM desktop program, there is a variety of GEM application software, offering for example graphically oriented 'Write' and 'Draw' programs similar to Apple's MacWrite and MacDraw. These programs are specially designed to work with the GEM desktop and use the same conventions for the mouse and the opening and moving of windows.

For some computers, such as the Macintosh, the WIMP type of presentation was introduced right from the start, so that virtually all Macintosh software follows the same conventions. With DOS-based PCs the situation is different, since the majority of software was written to run under MS-DOS without reference to GEM, and so does not use the GEM approach. Once you exit the GEM environment, that's it: you're stuck with DOS.

GEM Paint. Like MacPaint, GEM Paint is a freehand graphics package, essentially a tool for the illustrator. In other words, GEM Paint gives you the equivalent of a pencil, a ruler and compass, a variety of paints and paintbrushes, an airbrush, an eraser, and a paint tap which you can turn on to flood an entire area with colour. There is even a microcoscope, the equivalent to MacPaint's 'Fat Bits' which you can use to focus in on a particular area to work in fine detail. In their efforts to avoid Apple's threatened lawsuit, Digital Research have made considerable changes to the nomenclature of features and design of icons without losing the benefits of the original Macintosh system.

GEM Draw. As the name suggests, GEM's answer to Apple's structured graphics package MacDraw. GEM Draw offers much the same flexibility, features and functions one would expect to find in the latter.

A favourite tool of the graphic designer today is the Letraset sheet of standard symbols (now available in Macintosh format - but more of Letraset later), to be put onto the page in the appropriate place. The electronic equivalent is the GEM Draw Business Library, which has a whole variety of special borders, organisation templates, electronic circuit symbols, and so on. The Macintosh offers a plethora of graphics design libraries including such topics as architecture and landscape gardening, in addition to more general special effects, standard diagrams and forms. These packages though inexpensive, (normally under £50) must be purchased separately. GEM provides a rudimentary library with the total system, from which selections can be copied as required into your GEM Draw diagram, to give the whole thing a professional and consistent appearance.

GEM Paint and GEM Draw will obviously be compared with the MacPaint and MacDraw. In fact the programs are very similar, apart from restrictions imposed by different screen resolutions; on the other hand, the GEM versions are able to work in colour.

GEM Graph. The idea that 'a picture is worth a thousand words' has been applied in business, particularly to the generation of so-called 'business graphics', to bring numbers to life. GEM Graph like the Macintosh package 'Cricket Graph' can be used either as a standalone product, which you can feed with the figures you want graphically displayed, or as a vehicle for the output of data from another program.

GEM WordChart. The 'illustrated lecture' was a favourite entertainment in Victorian times, when the magic lantern or the epidiascope were the available technology. Today the overhead projector foil and the 35 millimetre slide are the favoured medium for business presentations. Visual aids can add a great deal to the impact of a talk, but in the past it has been expensive and difficult to produce really professional-looking material.

GEM WordChart is specially designed for this sort of use. It contains a series of templates into which you fit the words you want to include in your slides, so that the text is automatically centred or arranged in columns as you wish. You have a choice of founts and styles, and output in colour is possible if you have the means of reproducing it. Additionally you can surround the text with plain or decorative borders, produced either in GEM WordChart itself, or perhaps in GEM Draw.

Special typefaces. Much of the impact of good graphic design comes from the careful selection of founts and typefaces. The GEM Fonts and Drivers Pack comes with a library of different sizes and types of text characters, as well as patterns and sample pictures for use with GEM Paint. Of greatest significance, given our overriding concern with desktop publishing, is the fact that Gem provides Postscript drivers. The usual output device, if industry standard founts are to be obtained and full page graphics supported, would be the Apple LaserWriter or a Postscript phototypesetter.

Microsoft Windows

Despite being officially announced over three years ago, it was mainly with the success of desktop publishing on the Macintosh and the realisation that a similar environment was called for on the IBM PC, that Windows received recognition in the marketplace. Certainly, the decision on the part of Aldus to adopt Windows as the vehicle for their PC DOS version of PageMaker aided and abetted this process. By putting pressure on Microsoft to enhance the product (for example, by building in Postscript drivers), Aldus contributed to its new-found acceptance .

Windows uses considerable storage and processing overhead. Unlike GEM, which runs on all IBM PCs and compatibles, the minimum workable hardware configuration required by Windows is an AT class machine, i.e. one based on the 80286 chip. Anything less will slow down operation of the application software quite considerably. A perennial problem facing any IBM PC based DTP system lies in the RAM constraint of 640K imposed by DOS. To overcome this, Windows supports the standard memory expansion solutions now available such as the Lotus/Intel Above board and AST Rampage board with RAM increases of up to two megabytes.

Windows, acting as an extension to DOS, provides the user with a Macintosh-like interface. Like GEM, however, the environment is limited to those applications that support the user interface.

Application software. Microsoft Windows, like GEM, is supplied with its own suite of application software: Windows Write, Paint and Draw. Basically, these follow the standard conventions of their Macintosh counterparts and as such do not warrant in-depth examination.

Microsoft are intent on expanding the suite of available software and are looking to other software houses to develop applications written for Windows. A few major coups include the implementation of Windows-based PageMaker. Other products in the pipeline include a PC publishing package from Micropro, the makers of WordStar; and from Micrografix, the company responsible for the development of Windows Draw, a business graphics package-Windows Graph.

Linking data. In order to enhance the 'electronic cut and paste' associated with the WIMP environment, Microsoft will shortly be releasing their own Dynamic Data Exchange (DDE) protocol for windows. This will allow the linking of data from any applications that are written to run in windows and support DDE.

As yet no application has implemented this protocol and we cannot comment as to it usefulness in the DTP environment. We have always found the cut and paste feature not only simple and workable but extremely logical, since it effectively emulates an activity that is recognisable to the user. What DDE will provide is dynamic data links. What this means in simple terms is that any related data, albeit in different files, will be simultaneously updated.

Dynamic data links, whilst extremely useful in some cases, should be treated with caution. Let us take an example. We link a pie chart produced in Window Graph to a Write text file to create a financial report. When a new set of figures is released, the pie chart is manually amended to reflect changes. At this point the chart in the financial report is automatically updated. Depending on what was intended, this could be a tremendous aid or a total faux pas. Caution is needed.

Microsoft has also developed a text transfer protocol called Rich Text Format (RTF). Like IBM's Document Control Architecture (DCA), RTF accepts text files from other packages without losing formatting, fount and typestyle attributes. Given that many PC application packages have already adopted the DCA protocol, are Microsoft confusing the issue by promoting another?

MIRRORSOFT

THE SOFTWARE THAT MAKES HARD BUSINESS SENSE

▶ *for desktop publishers*

FLEET STREET EDITOR for PCs and compatibles is ideal for everyday desktop publishing tasks such as press releases, simple advertisements, flyers, and newsletters. It includes a variety of typefaces in different sizes and styles, a disk of ready-to-use artwork, and printer drivers for dot matrix, HP LaserJet and PostScript printers. Text and graphics can also be imported from other PC software.
Recommended retail price £109.95 inc VAT and 90 days' hot-line support.

◀ *for timekeepers*

TIMESLIPS and its big brother, Timeslips Plus, are designed for anyone who charges or monitors time as a business cost. The integral TSTIMER program can be run as a memory-resident stopwatch, so that even the shortest phone call doesn't get left out of the invoice. TSREPORT, the other part of the program, can produce a wide variety of reports and invoices containing as much or as little information as you want. Lotus 1-2-3™ and dBase™ compatible.
TIMESLIPS recommended retail price £69.99 including hot-line support.
TIMESLIPS PLUS recommended retail price £149.99 including hot-line support.

▶ *and for everyone*

FILE RESCUE PLUS is an essential purchase for every PC user. As well as rescuing damaged or corrupt files, as its name implies, the program will also recover data from physically damaged DOS and non DOS disks wherever possible. A variety of other useful functions in FRP include: file optimisation, the facility to locate specific information within a file without knowing the filename, pinpointing bad or empty sectors on a disk, and repairing disk errors. Context sensitive help screens in plain English are available throughout the program. **Recommended retail price £24.99**

MIRRORSOFT LTD, Athene House, 66-73 Shoe Lane, London EC4P 4AB Tel: 01-377 4645 Telex: 93121200112 Fax: 01-353 0565

MIRRORSOFT

Please send me further details on:
- ☐ Fleet Street Editor PC
- ☐ Timeslips/Timeslips Plus
- ☐ File Rescue Plus

Name _____

Company _____

Address _____

_____

_____

Postcode _____ Tel _____

CSAR

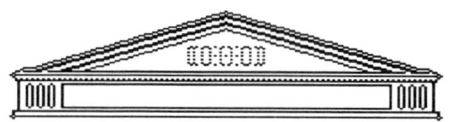

A complete DTP service
.....under one roof!

Software and Hardware Sales
DTP Consultancy
DTP Bureau Service & OCR Scanning

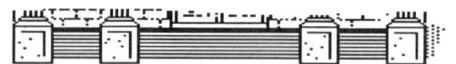

Welcome to the world of DTP. In the early days everyone will be your friend. Buy your first system, encounter the inevitable problems and see who your friends are! Only people who *use* the equipment regularly can provide the experience to bale you out when the chips are down. Slick demonstrators stumble over practical examples - Studio Box don't. We have our roots in publicity services and understand the meaning of urgent jobs.

Who do **you** want to deal with; people strong on theory or strong on practice. **Call Adrian Goodman on Reading (0734) 482575**

▢ Studio Box
Far End, Priest Hill, Caversham, Reading RG4 7RY

▶ ONE STOP
FOR DESKTOP PUBLISHERS

Whether you're already a user or are planning to start up and enjoy the cost-cutting and time-saving benefits of DTP, we can help you get the best from your chosen system.

LINOTRONIC 300 OUTPUT BUREAU
- ▶ Text and graphics at up to 2,540 dots per inch.
- ▶ Output from Macintosh or IBM compatibles of all software generating Postscript.
- ▶ 24 hour turnround - usually faster.
- ▶ Modem link & electronic mailbox facilities.
- ▶ Also conventional Linotronic 300 typesetting, design, artwork and printing.

HARDWARE, SOFTWARE, TRAINING
- ▶ Authorised Apple resellers, and agents for other major DTP producers.
- ▶ Full training at competitive rates.

ADVANCED GRAPHIC
COMMUNICATIONS
34 Hereford Road, London W2 5AJ. Telephone 01-221 6036. Fax 01-727 0986

Desktop software under MS-DOS 73

Windowing. One advantage Windows offers over the Macintosh/GEM system is a multi-tasking environment. This allows several applications to be open on screen at one time, permitting the user to jump from one to another. The term multi-tasking can be misleading, since only one application can actually be used at any moment; the others are, as it were, in stand-by mode. They are loaded and ready, but doing nothing. The only activity that can proceed in background mode is printing, but the addition of a print spooler to the Macintosh Finder can provide this too.

DOS user interface vs the Macintosh.

The primary difference between the DOS and Macintosh user interfaces has its foundation in the hardware constraints imposed by the Macintosh or, to look at it another way, the hardware flexibility of DOS-based PCs. Despite its clarity and high resolution, the Macintosh screen is monochrome. The IBM PC and compatibles, by nature of their 'open architecture' design, can support a range of display options. As outlined in the previous chapter, the ideal PC-based DTP system would include an enhanced graphics adaptor and a high resolution colour screen.

Both GEM and Microsoft Windows make full use of the available colour facilities. Whilst this offers certain advantages in the aesthetics of graphics creation, its use in simplifying colour output is limited by the effective quality and use of such output. Chapter nine reveals in more depth the current state of the art in colour printing.

Gem and Windows both reside between DOS and the application software. The user is thus denied one consistent environment in which to work. The dedicated DTP user can, however, avoid too much contact with DOS, in which case as vehicles for WISIWYG software these Macintosh-like interfaces are perfectly acceptable. One thing is clear: the Gems and Windows of the computer industry have allowed the PC to mature into a viable desktop publishing tool.

Desktop software under DOS

Page composition software is nothing new to the IBM PC. Prefis' Book Machine, and PagePlanner have been around for several years. They were basicaly text-only packages, offering relatively precise typographical features, combined with columnar layouts - a rare facility at the time.

One impediment to their success lay in the lack of any high resolution yet low cost output device; another in the prohibitive cost (£2000 +), and a third in the fundamental fact that desktop publishing had not emerged as a concept. Prefis have now enhanced their existing software to an acceptable DTP standard, which we will examine below.

It is only since the latter part of 1986 that DOS-based page make-up packages able to conform to true DTP criteria have emerged. Even then many were still at the 'Vapourware' stage - we'd all heard about them, magazines had reviewed them (often incorrectly, probably due to not having access to them), but you couldn't actually purchase them. Where were they ? The entire DTP market ground to a temporary halt whilst prospective desktop publishers waited. Whether to go for the tried, tested and proven Macintosh system or wait for the much-vaunted DOS-based solutions ? They remembered the old adage 'No-one ever got fired for buying IBM'.

It was worth the wait. The quality and choice of page make-up software for the IBM PC that became available almost overnight was impressive. The majority of current IBM PC compatible DTP software was announced at the Seybold Conference held in San Francisco in September 1986. Hence the sudden surge of products. The US software market is generally about three months ahead of the UK. It was therefore not suprising when the same pattern was repeated in the UK in January '87. A European re-run of the San Francisco conference launched a wealth of products and generated a level of interest and demand that could not be immediately satisfied. Three products in particular have emerged as clear market leaders in the US: Aldus PageMaker, Xerox's Ventura Publisher and Harvard Professional Publisher. UK trends to date appear to be following closely US developments so we have concentrated our energies on close examination of the three packages mentioned above. Attention will also be given to products that for reasons of their origins or specialised appeal warrant inclusion.

Aldus PageMaker - (page-based)

The sucess of PageMaker on the Macintosh, due in part to Apple's enthusiastic endorsement of the product, has been astounding. However, whilst Apple's promotion undoubtedly boosted PageMaker sales, the reverse is also true, since it is reckoned that one in three of installed Macintoshes (excluding pre-PageMaker/LaserWriter product availability) were primarily purchased to allow use of PageMaker. Our experience

Desktop software under MS-DOS

tends to support this. PageMaker has the world's largest installed base, is available in eight languages, and is said to hold 90% of market share in the US. It was an obvious move, therefore, to offer the world's leading DTP package on the world's leading PC!

From early on Aldus planned to use Microsoft Windows as the interface vehicle with which to crack the PC market. However modifications were obviously required, since despite Windows *apparent* similarity to the Macintosh, the former is very different in architecture and more complex for the programmer to work with. In order to make optimum use of the strong features of the two environments, Aldus completely rewrote the package (using 'C') to run under both systems.

PageMaker Version 1.0 for the IBM offers the same functions and features as the Macintosh Version 2.0 outlined in chapter three. Once loaded on the PC it is almost impossible for the user to tell the difference between the two. It is therefore superfluous to itemise again the characteritics of the package. The key difference lies in the lack of uniformity of IBM PC software. You cannot simply cut and paste text and graphics from one software package to another; therefore we need to examine the type of data that can be accepted by PageMaker.

File Import. Text and graphics can be imported by using the now familiar 'place' command. IBM's DCA (Document Content Architecture) is fully supported hence type characteristics and formatting will not be lost in transfer. The following programs are supported :

Word Processors:
- Windows Write
- Microsoft Word
- WordStar 3.3
- Multimate
- XYWrite
- ASCII text files
- DCA format files

Graphics:
- Windows Paint and Draw
- PC Paint
- PC Paintbrush
- AutoCAD
- Lotus 1-2-3 and Symphony
- TIFF files

Microsoft Windows is not supplied with PageMaker. A copy must therefore be purchased prior to using the software.

Xerox Ventura Publisher - (document-based)

Ironically, it is due to Xerox that desktop publishing ever emerged at all: firstly with the development of SmallTalk that formed the basis of the Lisa and Macintosh WIMP environment, and secondly with initial work in the field of page description languages that lead ultimately to Adobe's Postscript and to Xerox's own Impress.

Despite offering the Documenter (discussed in chapter eight) as a complete desktop publishing system, Xerox, realising the potential of the IBM installed base, chose to market a software product aimed exclusively at the IBM PC market. The resulting program, Ventura Publisher, developed by Ventura Software, is tending to detract from Documenter; is not boosting Xerox laserprinter sales (the preferred printer continues to be the Apple LaserWriter) and is hence costing the company valuable hardware revenue. At the end of the day, 'if you can't beat 'em, join 'em' obviously continues to hold sway.

User Interface. Ventura is supplied with a 'run time' version of Digital Research's GEM. This means that Gem does not have to be purchased separately. It is not, however, a full-blow version, but merely the GEM desktop which serves to provide the required WIMP/WYSIWYG environment Keyboard shortcuts are provided through the use of control keys. Ventura Software opted for GEM in preference to Windows (the developers came from a Digital Research background). The GEM environment does allow support for lower specification machines than does Windows, and could therefore be advantageous for the existing PC user.

Text manipulation. Like PageMaker, Ventura offers limited text editing and is geared for page make-up using previously created text files. Once again the advantage in this approach lies in the opportunity for users to continue using preferred, existing WP software. Text files, depending on their origin, can be imported with character attributes intact, or transferred in straight ASCII format. Supported wordprocessors (i.e. those offering the former transfer facilities) include:

                Microsoft Word
                WordPerfect
                Windows Write
                GEM Write
                Multimate
                WordStar

Letters, words and blocks of text can be specified in, or changed to : bold, italic, small caps, strikethrough, all caps, all lower case, subscript, superscript and underline.

Using the 'text' mode, editing can be performed at any stage. Four viewing levels are supported, 100% (actual size), 50%, 200% and facing pages. 'Real time' reformatting occurs as text is edited, hence a deletion in one line will cause all remaining text to be automatically hyphenated and formatted. If a graphic is encountered during the flow, the text will merely runaround the obstructing image.

Page Formatting. Ventura operates in four program modes : Frames, Paragraph Tag, Text and Graphics. The formatting of pages works on the basis of creating distinct frames intended to accept graphics or text. The paragraph tag facility allows definition of a specific paragraph's format, by assigning fount size, type , indentation, leading and text alignment.

Up to eight various width columns can be set up per page or frame. Verso and recto pages can be formatted independently. Headers, footers and automatic page numbering are supported. The latter can be specified in Arabic, Roman, or numbers spelled out.

Five page sizes can be defined including A4, B5, and American quarto. *Typographical Features.* Automatic H&J, if specified occurs extempore as text is flowed into frames or edited, based on algorithm and dictionary. Leading control in fractional point sizes is supported. Dropped caps, vertical and horizontal tabs are also featured.

Graphics/scanned image support. In common with the all WYSIWYG make-up systems, limited graphics tools are supplied to add aesthetic finish to the document. Lines, boxes and circles of various thickness can be drawn directly onto the page. Graphics generated by the following software can be placed directly into frames using the Graphics mode :

>AutoCAD
>GemDraw
>Gem Graph
>Gem Paint
>PC Paintbrush
>Lotus 1-2-3 and Symphony
>CAD DXF (Data eXchange Format) files
>TIFF files from Microtek and Dest scanners.

Graphics once imported can be repositioned or scaled to size.
Document production (length). Ventura is orientated towards production

of long documents such as books, manuals, etc. Chapter size is dictated by RAM constraints. Up to 64 chapters can be linked together in one document. Page count provides numbering from 1-9999. Automatic table of contents and index generation serve to support Ventura's onus on the long publication.

Master pages/style sheets. Control over document format is accommodated by the use of style sheets. User created 'Tags' define the format of all text or one paragraph. Each tag is named and can subsequently be stored for re-use. The collection of tags used in one document is saved as a style sheet. Features regulated under the tag system include the typographical functions outlined above, character attributes, standard page formatting specifications, such as margins, columns, page breaks and control over widows and orphans. In addition, indents, paragraph spacing and text alignment can all be specified.

Tag names can be embedded directly into a wordprocessed document or assigned directly to paragraphs in Ventura. Once 'Tag' mode is selected a directory of existing tags appears on screen, text is selected and the appropriate specification attached. Tag characteristics can be amended at any stage, whereby all text assigned to that specific style will reflect the changes. This facility provides a simple method of making overall changes to (say) point size throughout the document.

For the benefit of the amateur desktop publisher, Ventura is supplied with a library of pre-defined style sheets. As we discussed above, the most difficult aspect of page make-up for the first time user is getting to grips not with the software but with standard layout conventions. The addition of sample style sheets for such publications as newsletters, books and product lists provides the uninitiated with guidelines for the creation of professional publications.

Page description Languages. Ventura supports the Postscript page description language and will be incoporating DDL drivers later this year. The package also offers a variety of Bitstream downloadable founts for use with the Hewlett Packard Laserjet printers. Typefaces over and above the standard Times and Helvetica include Avant Garde, Bookman, Optima and Palatino. Width tables stored in memory must be specified for each fount used. By implication, the more founts used in one document, the less memory will be available. The Postscript fount width table can be loaded to allow use of the Hewlett Packard as a proofing device for Postscript typesetting devices. This will ensure that each character/word/line claims the same amount of space as it should

Desktop software under MS-DOS

under industry standard typeface conventions.

Obviously the simplest way of ensuring true output would be to drive a Postscript laser printer from day one.

Ease of use. Ventura is supplied on eleven disks, which is initially a little daunting. A significant amount of the three megabytes of program is dedicated to printer drivers, of which there are many, downloadable founts and fount witdth tables. Under most circumstances, you would not need to load the whole lot. Given that Ventura Publisher operates in the Windows environment, it is by implication relatively simple to learn and use. Getting to grips with the basic operational modes (Text, Graphics, Frames and Paragraph Tag) is perhaps the least demanding area of the program to be absorbed. The printing options, typographical functions and creation of style sheets may prove less obvious to the first-time publisher. The documentation supplied is good, and a comprehensive tutorial section is provided.

Ventura adheres to the concept of dynamically-linked files. Changes in the original will thus be reflected in the publication. As discussed above, this facility is considered by some (mainly vendors of software that support such a feature) to be an advantage, in keeping all published material constantly up to date. We continue to hold reservations about the security of such a process.

In DTP market parlance Ventura is considered to be *the* package able to pose a real challenge to PageMaker's current supremacy. The two are orientated towards slightly diverse target users, the former being admirably suited to the production of long publications, the latter clearly geared to flexible design of individual pages. If the pundits are right and the potential for desktop publishing is as significant as we beleive it to be (by the end of the decade it is reckoned that three billion pages of information will be published by businesses worldwide) there is surely room for at least two leading software solutions. Competition can only benefit the publisher who will surely use the enhancements resulting from software vendor 'one-up-manship' to advantage.

Bestinfo's Harvard Professional Publisher (page-based with document facilities)

Marketed by Software Publishing Corporation, Bestinfo's HPP is primarily in the PageMaker vein, with the addition of a style sheet facility. Whilst less dedicated in application than either Ventura or

PageMaker, HPP offers general-purpose desktop publishing, yet provides sophisticated typographical features and Postscript drivers. An unusual aspect of HPP is that it uses neither Windows nor GEM as a user interface. The program runs directly on DOS, and as such can operate on a standard hard disk PC. As always for DTP applications, a 286 or superior machine is recommended. In not adopting an existing WIMPS environment upon which to base HPP, Bestinfo have enabled the program to consume less RAM and disk space but in so doing have in effect re-invented the wheel, since HPP operates in a WYSIWYG mode.

HPP's advantage in competing against an evergrowing plethora of IBM packages is twofold. Harvard Presentation Graphics from the same source has a sound reputation and a well established base among IBM PC users. Morover, Professional Publisher derives from Bestinfo's Superpage ll, of which it is basically a rewrite; though much less sophisticated, aimed at a larger audience and hence offered at lower cost. SuperPage ll, also available on the IBM PC, handles the entire pre-press production process, including text entry, page composition and output through a selection of over 25 typesetting devices. At approximately £7000 SuperPage ll cannot realistically be subsumed within the category desktop publishing.

Text manipulation. Facility for restricted on-screen text editing, which automatically updates all other text. HPP offers limited wordprocessing capabilities and is in the main dependent on text import from other sources. Any WP packages able to ouput in ASCII or DCA file format, plus any spreadsheet print file, can be accepted. Pages can be reviewed using HPP's zoom facility at the following levels: 200%, actual size, one page, or facing pages.

In addition to the standard typeface styles type can be expanded, condensed or reversed (white on black). Dropped caps can be specified.

Page formatting. Multiple columns, automatic page numbering, headers and footers, alignment of lists and tables and continuation messages are all supported. Any number of master page formats can be used within one document. Text can be flowed page by page or throughout the entire document. Widow and orphan control is permitted.

Typographical features. Automatic pair kerning and tracking (i.e. the automatic reduction of spacing between characters and words in a given line) are supported.

Text is automatically hyphenated and justified (if specified) as it is

flowed into the document. Hyphenation is controlled by means of an algorithm supported by a dictionary. Manual hyphenation is also supported. HPP attempts to obtain word fit through wordspacing and letter spacing facilities. User definable leading is available.
Graphics/scanned input. HPP accepts graphics files generated under the following software:
> Harvard Presentation Graphics
> Lotus 1-2-3
> PC Paintbrush
> Windows Paint
> PC Paint Plus
> TIFF files from high resolution scanners.

Once accepted grapic images can be scaled or cropped. Standard rudimentary graphics tools are supplied for the creation of rules and boxes. The latter can be filled with varying grey scale tints to produce special effects and mark areas for susequent pasting of half tones, in the event that scanned input is deemed unacceptable. Text performs automatic runaround when an irregular image is encountered.

Master pages/style sheets. Long documents can be pre-formatted using the style sheet option. Global changes can be effected throughout the document merely by amending the attached style sheet. Piping, or the flowing of text onto many pages, assists in this process. Shorter or single page documents can be most efficiently altered using on-screen editing.

Page description languages. Harvard Professional Publisher supports all Postscript devices. Bit mapped output is not supported but as mentioned above we are not overly concerned with dot matrix output other than for checking text at the pre make-up stage. Given that Hewlett Packard LaserJet drivers are also supplied, it seems likely that DDL will be supported in the near future.

Ease of use. Not as simple to set up, nor as logical to work with as PageMaker. The decision to conform to the preferred WYSIWYG operating environment obviously implies a certain ease of use. We found text editing frustrating, insofar as a dynamic link with the original text file means you are restricted to editing portions of text within a frame, and not as laid out on the page. Hence it is only when an edit is completed that you return to the true WYSIWYG representation. We also had difficulty locating the piece of text to be edited, having to scroll through the frame to find the precise letter or word to be changed. This may not irritate the first time user, but those accustomed to page, as opposed to window editing, may find this a definite drawback. If we are to assume a continuity of What You See Is What You Get, it is desirable to see it as you are getting it.

Other IBM packages worth note

It would be impossible and boring in the extreme to cover all available. IBM PC based page make-up and composition software in depth. We have extracted the salient features of a cross section of the 'others' in an attempt to define the current state of the market. Other contenders include:

Studio Software's Front Page /Front Page Plus. Page-based layout system, using frame concept. Boxes drawn on screen and text flowed in. Most common typographic features supported. Mainly WYSIWYG, though some operations require user to insert composition parameters into raw text file. Slow recomposition into WYSIWYG form. Less easy to use than most DTP software despite good documentation. 12 Boards (style sheets) supplied (helpful to the novice desktop publisher) with the standard version. Front Page Plus offers a macro facility which allows the set up of bespoke style sheets and more sophisticated features. Both offer Postscript support. Software add-ons in the form of typesetter drivers (Linotype, Compugraphic) can be purchased as can a typographer's utility program, to allow for the setting up of width tables. Despite page-based layout, the macro facility under Front Page Plus makes it ideal for the long-run publication.

Mirrorsoft's Fleet Street Editor, Fleet Street Publisher. Mirrorsoft, originally part of the Mirror Newspaper Group, first developed Fleet Street Editor to run on the BBC Micro for the educational market. Implemented on the IBM PC and Amstrad CPC and PCW range, a WYSIWYG package operating on linked text box principles, offers adequate typographical features given the very low price (under £200). Text can be keyed in directly, any ASCII wordprocessed file accepted. Standard graphics facilities in terms of cropping and scaling, imports graphic screens (using a Snap Shot feature) *not* graphics files per se. Supplied with library of graphic images. An ideal starting point for the less ambitious desktop publisher. Limited number of columns (four), both bastard and standard allowed. Postscript drivers available.

Fleet Street Publisher will offer more sophisticated typographical features and page formatting controls.

The men and the boys

The software packages outlined above point clearly to the emergence of certain standards. All support some form of user interface and operate in a WYSIWYG environment. We have omitted those that :
1. Do not offer Postscript or some other industry acceptable page description language and by extension cannot output the made-up page directly to a typesetter .
2. Are no more than glorified wordprocessing systems with a lack of typographical functions considered essential for page make-up.
3. Are still at the 'Vaporware' or beta testing stage.

Lastly, some of the most powerful software packages around are those that do not conform to the WIMP conventions and that cannot be said to offer a true WYSIWYG facility although they are significant in the development of low cost systems that offer viable typesetting front end capabilities. Software of this nature is more common under DOS and in many cases has been available long before the DTP revolution was conceived. Because of the importance of these products and the implications not only to the professional publisher but also to the direction of DTP generally, we have dedicated a section to exploring the pros and cons of this more complex, but ultimately rewarding approach.

6
Enhanced wordprocessing and DTP

As manufacturers and software developers, desperate to jump on the DTP bandwagon, rush out their product offerings, the tendency is to take the shortest route to the desired end. It is expedient, or so they think, to beef up a wordprocessing package, add a facility for column support, and provide some links with graphics software. The 'piece de resistance' arrives, of course, when they develop a page preview facility and immediately lay claim to the WYSIWYG environment. Success is guaranteed. Or is it?

The demarcation between true DTP page composition systems and enhanced wordprocessors is significant and should be understood. We examine below enhanced wordprocessing and its limitations to the desktop publisher. We also examine the potential convergence of the two technologies and the resulting implications.

Concept of wordprocessing

In essence WP is the manipulation and arrangement of words. Unlike using a typewriter the words do not go directly onto paper. They appear on a screen which becomes the medium for alterations and edits. Only when the entire document is correct is it committed to paper. In this way a great deal of effort is saved and the operator is free to work at the full typing speed, since any errors can be put right later.

The total saving in time can be quite dramatic and the final printed output can be free from the ubiquitous Tippex and manual edits that once had to be endured.

Through the use of wordprocessing, moreover, standard documents can be stored for subsequent editing and re-use, cutting down on operator time at every re-draft.

The original generation of wordprocessors used special-purpose hardware, dedicated solely to wordprocessing. However, the various components of the system - screen, keyboard, disks, and so on - are the same in principle as those of the personal computer.

Today there is no reason to use such a specialised machine in preference to the much more flexible PC. Since the early days of the microcomputer, wordprocessing packages have been available. These were once regarded as poor relations of the dedicated wordprocessor with its specialy configured keys that left little room for operator error or forgotten key strokes. By comparison, WordStar, as originally implemented on CP/M machines, was far from user-friendly.

Today's wordprocessing packages are extremely powerful and generally emulate dedicated wordprocessing systems very closely. Indeed, they improve upon the latter because of the facility of linking to other PC software: databases, spreadsheets, names and addresses lists and more recently to desktop publishing. Wordprocessing today does not merely speed up the physical process of typing; it makes the whole task of document creation more rapid, efficient and effective.

For this reason, organisations would normally be far better advised to select equipment such as the PC, which offers the ability to process words and data, keep records or appointments, enable electronic communication; in short provide general personal computing. We should hence regard wordprocessing not as a piece of hardware, but as a software option capable of running on every home and business computer.

All the widely-accepted wordprocessing packages today are expected to offer certain basic functions. In identifying them, we have taken the features included in the current version of WordStar, (the all-time de facto leader in PC wordprocessing software) which may be considered as a yardstick for comparison purposes.

Editing options

Many of the functions of a wordprocessor relate not to the initial input

Enhanced wordprocessing and DTP

of text, which is relatively straightforward, but to editing and formatting text which already exists. Generally speaking, you have a choice of insert mode and overtype mode, which act on a 'toggle' basis (i.e. each mode can be switched on or off). In overtype mode, what is typed overwrites what was there before. In insert mode, the new text pushes the existing text to the right to make room. At this stage, WordStar requires the user to reformat the paragraph. In most contemporary packages, re-formatting is performed automatically.

Cursor movement

Cursor control allows movement around the text by line, character, screen or page. Scrolling through the text can be made more rapid by specifying beginning or end of document. More recent WP software generally supports a 'Goto' function, allowing the user to select the required page.

Search and replace

Specific words or character strings can be located in the document using the 'Search' command. Once found, global or individual replacement can be specified. This is obviously of great value in cases such as standard letters or contracts where one merely wants to change a name or a date throughout the document.

Text movement

Under WordStar, text can be moved in blocks that require 'marking' through the use of control characters. Hence the reasonably logical command *control KB*, signifies the beginning of a block, and the less meaningful *control KK* marks the end. One can thereafter specify whether the block is to be copied or moved, and mark the new position accordingly.The command for the latter, in keeping with the policy of meaningless characters, is *control KV*.

Text attributes

Depending on the printer in use, the attributes of the text can be defined (for instance, underline, bold, etc.). Given a non-WYSIWYG environment, certain techniques are used to signify that certain text will be output in a specific style. Hence the relevant portion of text may be displayed in reverse video mode.

Dot commands

WordStar allows the page length to be defined at the beginning of the document, through the use of 'dot commands', not unlike the type of instructions that would be embedded in a standard non WYSIWYG page composition program. Dot commands, so called because each instruction is preceded by a dot, are effectively a message to the output device that the text is for reference only and must not be printed. Page breaks can be inserted at any point throughout the document, but must be done so manually. There is no automatic control over widows and orphans.

Other dot commands control top and bottom margins, headers, footers, page numbering, etc. Not particularly friendly, but highly effective (if the user can rember them all !).

Other features

Text can be justified, centred, or aligned left or right. Line spacing can be specified in increments of 1-9. Unlimited tabs can be placed throughout the document. Paragraph indents can be specified.

WordStar also offers a very rudimentary columnar facility, which often defeats the average user (the authors included !).

WordStar offers much-needed on-screen help at various levels. The competent user is therefore presented with a blank screen, whereas the novice must contend with over a third of the available display being taken up with menus and options. Oh the joy of the pull-down menu!

This very brief overview does not cover WordStar's full range of features. Despite disparaging asides, WordStar is a very powerful piece of software, as is borne out by the fact that it is still in use almost ten years after it was first developed. The example is given to reveal the functionality of the typical wordprocessing package, in order that the new generation of 'enhanced WP' programs can be put in context.

Enhanced wordprocessing

There is a fairly clear line of demarcation between those WP packages that offered enhancements as a result of the need to compete with the dedicated wordprocessing systems such as Wang, IBM's DisplayWriter and Digital's DecMate, and those that have done so in an attempt to penetrate the DTP market. In some cases there has been a logical development from one to another, but what is pertinent for the purpose of this discussion is to examine the latter and their suitability as vehicles for DTP.

If we take a motorised lawn mower, add a chassis, four wheels, some seats and a modified steering device we have a car.... of sorts. It will be underpowered, unreliable and in all probability none too safe. It would not meet Department of Transport standards and would thus be relegated to pottering around the garden. Cars are designed to meet certain performance standards from the moment they are envisaged. There is therefore a continuity in aim as regards the finished product.

We contend that the same can be said of page composition systems. Their roots may lie in the concept of text manipulation, but the orientation towards the final goal must be inherent in the design from day one. It is thus the generic page composition packages that will continue to dominate until such time as WP software vendors effectively re-write, rather than modify, their offerings.

Several new products are emerging that are 'borderline' insofar as they represent substantial rewrites of their predecessors, or are developed with the WP/DTP market in mind. The latter can be said to result from two strategies. The first is to satisfy the corporate user with an office automation policy already in place. The assumption, which conflicts with that adhered to by DEC and Apple, is that this category of user will not want to go all the way in the electronic publishing sphere, but will be content with high quality output of integrated text and graphics. Secondly, there are those packages that attempt to provide the 'total solution' and in so doing run the risk of becoming Jacks of all trades and masters of none.

It may be helpful to provide examples of software packages that conform to our classification of enhanced wordprocessing. In addition we will examine others that fall between two stools in an attempt to understand how appropriately they fit into the total DTP scenario.

Wordcraft Elite

Wordcraft Elite is offered as an enhancement to Wordcraft Version 3, a flexible wordprocessing package aimed at the office user. Wordcraft software is supplied with the Canon desktop publishing system, running on the Canon A200 EX, IBM compatible PC AT. Not suprisingly, a Canon laser printer, the LBP-8 A2, completes the bundle.

The first time we saw a demonstration of the Canon system we were amazed that there was no facility for displaying text and graphics on one page. Forms design involved creating the graphic layout on one screen, inputting text on another (basing text positioning upon the page coordinates of the graphics frames) and seeing the finished result only upon producing hard copy. To give due credit to Canon, it was the first IBM solution available, and included a most impressive 300 dpi scanner (see chapter 9), which was under-utilised due to lack of RAM.

Wordcraft Elite offers improvements over the original system. It combines the functions of Wordcraft 3 wordprocessing which include a 100,000 word spelling checker (user editable), sophisticated calculation facility, MailMerge, re-useable phrase storage option, better than average search and replace, verso and recto headers and footers, automatic pagination, widow and orphan control and hyphenation prompts. All in all a versatile WP package.

Wordcraft Elite provides its own ImageMaster program to make up pages of text and graphics. Text is recalled in the form of word processed files and is displayed on the screen as a text map, i.e. you are presented with little blocks *representing* the outlines of the text. You can select 'edit mode' which shows a portion of the page and allows the normal WP features to take over. At this level, thankfully, text is text and not a text map as in the total page preview feature.

Graphics can be placed at the text map stage. Hence at no time can the user preview an entire page combining text and graphics. Not a lot has changed since our initial demonstration. Wordcraft is a WYSIWYG package at WP level, but not at page make-up level. What a shame it's not the other way round !

The implication is, therefore, that all typeface conditions, including style and size, must be established and saved at WP level. Subsequent amendments, which may only be made apparent at output stage, necessitate a return to the WP environment.

Justification and proportional word spacing is supported; leading and kerning are not, nor is any page description language. Wordcraft have a long way to go before they can lay claim to a viable DTP product.

Samna IV

Samna offer a range of wordprocessing packages that cover needs to

Enhanced wordprocessing and DTP

various levels of sophistication. The higher level versions were offering columnar support, basic line diagrams, and a text map page preview facility long before the much vaunted DTP revolution came into being.

It comes as no suprise therefore to witness Samna attempting to break into the DTP market. With a well-established corporate user base they are intending to capitalise on existing Samna devotees who require a publishing facility. The question is have they done enough ?

Samna is not a WYSIWYG package It operates in the DOS environment without recourse to a Gem or Windows-like user interface. Text styles such as bold, underline, double underline and sub and superscript cannot be shown on screen as they will appear on the printed page. The use of colour monitors displays fount styles in different colours, which is a helpful indicator, but far from perfect.

The main criticism of Samna IV from the DTP perspective lies in the fact that points are not used as measurements. The emphasis appears to be on users of dot matrix or daisywheel printers. Pitch may be set between five and 20. Point size cannot be defined, unless one is prepared to go to the trouble of performing the appropriate conversions. Hence, the Daisywheel standard of varying line spacing is 1/48 inch, compared with the traditional printing standard of points measured in 1/72 inch. Currently neither the Apple LaserWriter nor any PDL is supported.

A Samna page can support up to ten columns, limited dictionary hyphenation is provided, or discretionary hyphenation may be used. Justification must be specified, since Samna will default to left alignment. There is a rather nebulous 'proportional space check' which does the best it can, but with no facility for inter-word or inter-character spacing control documents will tend to show a rivering of white space.

A 'zoom' facility allows the entire page to be previewed, as Wordcraft, in Greek format, which at least allows the user clearly to see an overall map of text blocks, and by extension the severity of any rivering.

Samna can accept business graphics. Charts and graphs created under Samna's Decision Graphics can be placed directly into the document. As in earlier releases, facility exists for producing simple graphics - rules and boxes - on-screen.

Samna Word IV is a very powerful piece of wordprocessing software. It includes many options over and above those normally found on a standard WP package. Most impressive is the Word Base Manager (available with Samna IV plus) which allows words and phrases to be located and retreived on a multi-file basis. It then prints a report listing line and page number, file name and directory name. Index generation and a Math mode are useful additions.

Undoubtedly the DOS-based desktop publisher can benefit from using Samna. However, its place in the production of a finished document must remain fairly and squarely in the field of text entry. Samna offers very little in the way of high quality output support, limited typographical features and graphics integration. It may suffice for the production of in-house reports but cannot realistically be slotted into the classification of page layout software. Samna files can be output in both ASCII and DCA format; it therefore makes an ideal bedfellow for packages such as Xerox's Ventura.

Microsoft Word Version 3.0 (Macintosh based)

Even early versions of Microsoft Word on the Macintosh permitted the user to make use of Postscript and the RIP for high quality output in true industry standard founts. Indeed we know of several innovative users who have produced long publications, manuals and reference books included, using Microsoft Word alone.

Microsoft Word version 1.05 proved adequate for document production. Version 3, with a wealth of enhancements may well prove to be one of the few WP packages that sucessfully 'crosses the line'.

Word allows sixteen 'windows' or files to be opened simultaneously, useful if you are doing considerable cutting and pasting from one document to another. The menu system has been improved, allowing novice users a set of primary menus, as with the standard Macintosh environment. A 'toggle' facility reveals the more comprehensive menu options, hence providing different learning levels. Menus are to a certain extent user-definable and can be customised to reveal only those options that are likely to be used.

New text attributes not in the old version include double underscore, dotted underscore, strikeout, all caps, small caps and hidden. The latter permits the insertion of Postscript commands for direction to the printer. All standard Adobe supplied founts are supported, be they resident in the Postscript device or down-loadable.

Word version 3.0 allows up to six columns per page. MacPaint graphics can be placed on the page and borders, boxes and rules can be produced. Those ready and able to get to grips with Postscript can produce almost unlimited graphic effects, those who are unprepared to go to such lengths can make use of a rudimentary macro language that permits production of simple graphics for incorporation in the page.

An extremely useful new tool is the enhanced preview facility that displays two pages side by side. Dotted lines indicating margins can be moved and stretched, causing the text to reformat automatically to accommodate the area change. Page preview allows repositioning of headers, footers and page numbers, thus even a style sheet type approach has been implemented. Individual pages can still be modified. On the subject of style sheets, Word offers a very simple facility referred to as 'outlines'. It is a capable tool for re-organising long documents and the package is supplied complete with nine modifiable document outlines - a useful aid for the novice user.

Word makes no claims to anything other than wordprocessing status, though it does claim to be one of the most comprehensive available. The level of sophistication offered for the professional setting of type is therefore restricted.

Word is due for imminent release in the UK. It is not hard to predict that it will be well received. As it stands it offers considerably more than many so-called composition packages, not least in its support of Postscript, a true WYSIWYG environment, and little added extras such as the command language and the facility for outlines. If we are to consider any enhanced word processing packages as encroaching on the document composition domain, this must surely be a contender.

The majority of true composition packages examined in earlier chapters are aimed at two types of publications. Firstly, long documents of a general nature, where most pages will conform in the main to the same layout and typeface attributes. Secondly, those publications such as newsletters where it is assumed that each page will be unique in some respect. We have made it clear that the division is not rigid.

In the PC industry where average application package costs are low, the user can afford to purchase specialist software for specialist applications. That this software differs in many respects from the norm is not to imply that it does not meet our criteria for 'publishing' as opposed to wordprocessing software. We examine below MacAuthor and Lotus Manuscript. Both were written with specific areas of publishing in mind. The features offered are therefore relevant to the target user group.

MacAuthor- (Macintosh based)

MacAuthor, as the name implies was designed with the writer in mind.

It is currently being used as a wordprocessing package that also generates camera-ready copy. Like the great majority of Macintosh software, MacAuthor supports Postscript.

A British product, MacAuthor was developed by an author as a direct result of his frustration at not being able to find software suitable for writing needs. It holds special appeal to the script writer, insofar as the set-up options are ideal for typical script layouts. See illustration 8 for sample MacAuthor output.

Mac Author works on the basis of frames and 'Paragraph Styles'. Frames can be created within frames, within frames ad infinitum, and are designated for either text or graphics. The paragraph style option allows the creation of a basic boilerplate specifying fount, point size, style, indent, etc. It is then named and automatically added to the appropriate pull-down menu.

Let us assume that the example in illustration 8 is actually being created. Text would be entered freely and at speed, probably in the default Macintosh fount, Geneva. When a scene was completed, the author would then define which areas, or blocks, required a specific style. In this case three styles have been predefined, as suitable definitions for the character's name, the actual dialogue, and instructions pertaining to actions, stage positions etc.

The reason that MacAuthor is successful where others fail is that it is not column-based. Hence if we were to attempt to achieve the same end with, say, PageMaker, we would have to use tabs, which would slow down input considerably and would not allow wordwrap of the discreet areas. Conversely, the use of columns would necessitate the creation of text in three distinct chunks, since text flows down columns not across them. There is, moreover, no guarantee that once the separate files (i.e. for character, dialogue and instructions) had been placed, that the columns read across correctly. The probability is that Bill would be reading Fred's lines, whilst performing Sarah's actions.

MacAuthor is one of the few packages that succesfully combines wordprocessing with page layout facilities. It is specialised and does not purport to be a general purpose tool, but because it was envisaged and developed from scratch, it performs the desired function well.

Lotus Corporation's Manuscript - (DOS Based)

Another package conceived and developed for the more specialised user, Manuscript, like MacAuthor, also combines text entry with page layout.

THE TEMPEST

SCENE I. *On a ship at sea ; a tempestuous noise of thunder and lightning heard.*

Enter a SHIPMASTER *and a* BOATSWAIN.

MASTER. Boatswain !

BOATS. Here, master ; what cheer?

MASTER. Good! Speak to th' mariners ; fall to't yarely, or we run ourselves aground ; bestir, bestir. [*Exit.*

Enter MARINERS.

BOATS. Heigh, my hearts ! cheerly, cheerly, my hearts ! yare, yare ! Take in the topsail. Tend to the maasters whistle. Blow till thou burst thy wind, if room enough.

Enter ALFONSO, SEBASTION, ANTONIO, FERDINAND, GONZALO, *and* OTHERS

ALON. Good boatswain, have care. Where's the master ? Play the men.

BOATS. I pray now, keep below.

ANT. Where is the master boson ?

BOATS. Do you not here him? You mar our labour; keep your cabins; you do assist the storm.

GON. Nay, good, be patient.

BOATS. When the sea is. Hence! What cares these roarers for the name of king? To cabin ! Silence! Trouble us not.

GON. Good, yet remember whom thou hast aboard.

BOATS. None that I love more than myself. You are counsellor; if you can command these elements to silence, and work the peace of the present, we will not hand a rope more. Use your authority; if you cannot , give thanks you have liv'd so long and make yourself ready in your cabin for the mischance of the hour, if it so hap. - Cheerily, good hearts! - Out of our way, I say. [*Exit*

GON. I have great comfort from this fellow. Methinks he hath no drowning mark upon him; his complection is perfect gallows. Stand fast, good Fate, to his hanging; make the rope of his destiny our cable, for our own doth little advantage. If he be not born to be hang'd our case is miserable. [*Exeunt*

Re-enter BOATSWAIN.

BOATS. Down with the topmast. Yare, lower, lower! Bring her to try wi' th' maincourse. [*A cry within*] A plague upon theis howling! They are louder than the weather or our office.

Re-enter SEBASTION, ANTONIO, *and* GONZALO

Illustration 8.
Typical output from MacAuthor.

The product's onus is very much on the 'technical' user who may wish to produce reports or manuals. Given that a maximum document size of approximately 800 pages is supported (this will depend primarily on the mix of text and graphics), it is well suited to the latter.

Manuscript overcomes the page versus document question by providing two modes of use, structured, which allows a style sheet facility to be evoked; unstructured, which allows pages to be built up bit by bit. The package allows import of ASCII and DCA files, as well as from Lotus 1-2-3 and Symphony. Tables can be integrated into the page, as can business graphics.

Manuscript offers some interesting facilities such as spelling checker, word count, automatic generation of table of contents, table of tables and table of figures. A document revision comparison checks word by word throughout the file and highlights any amendments.

Sophisticated equations include diacritical marks, binary operations, eight varieties of brackets and matrix and vertical stacking. Manuscript will no doubt appeal to the hard core spreadsheet user looking for high quality reports... without losing any of the finer technical detail. The significance of which is lost on mere mortals (such as the authors).

Manuscript offers as much typographical sophistication as some of the dedicated page layout systems mentioned above. Micro-justification, hyphenation and widow and orphan control, global document formats allowing for title, verso and recto pages. Scanned image support (TIFF files) and, perhaps of most significance, Postscript support. A WYSIWYG preview feature allows the made up page to be displayed, thankfully in readable as opposed to 'text map' form.

Manuscript may, unwittingly perhaps, have paved the way for a generation of 'task specific' composition systems. As long as standards are maintained the importance of PDLs and by extension the output of true founts are realised, this development can only serve to further the cause.

The market diversifies

Having defined early on our criteria for an acceptable desktop publishing system, it should be clear that enhanced wordprocessing does not currently make the grade. Yet the traditional PC user, while developing more typographical know-how and more sophisticated demands, has always been cost-conscious. Witness the annual death rate of PC dealers who, through the demand for cut-throat discounting, have gone out of business.

Given the appeal of economy (real or perceived) different levels of 'publishing' systems are emerging.

Certain business sectors freely admit that they do not require industry standard founts, have no intention of outputting to a typesetter, and wouldn't understand H&J if it jumped up and bit them in the face. These constitute, in the main, businesses that have until recently been dependent on typewriters or rudimentary WP.

The main criteria in opting for high quality output are to raise company profile, ensure greater readability of publications and in short keep abreast of the competition. Prime examples would be building contractors, solicitors and surveyors. These companies 'publish' a considerable volume of printed material, often of a poor quality, with the token splodges of Tippex, poorly aligned text, and no supporting diagrams or plans other than costly hand produced drafts.

The typical user in this bracket wouldn't and shouldn't be concerned with typographic niceties. What he should be concerned with is ease of use, and in general it is the enhanced WP software which presents limitations on text and graphics integration, true WIMPs environments and WYSIWYG representations. Moreover, a system that requires embedded control codes to inform the printer of changes in fount attributes (such as would be case if using a standard wordprocessing package with the Hewlett Packard Laserjet) could not lay claim to simplicity. The commercial publisher is unlikely to find such systems adequate.

The process for the professional publisher needs to be somewhat more sophisticated.

In chapter ten, we investigate in some depth the options for harnessing PC-based DTP systems as front ends to traditional typesetting systems.

Worthy of mention at this stage are the growing number of partial WYSIWYG packages which offer a modus operandi not unlike that already used by the professional typesetter.

Our decision to cover the Macintosh-based software 'Just Text' in some depth stems from the apparent appeal of command driven, or non-WYSIWYG software, particularly to the professional user. The reasons for this are twofold: the results obtained from a traditional command-based package are, generally speaking, typographically more precise.

Furthermore, the traditional typesetter is familiar with systems of this ilk and hence not daunted by the prospect of learning what are to him meaningful commands. That these commands are probably no more difficult to grasp than those required for the operation of WordStar leads one to surmise that such software does have a place in the DTP arena, especially as nowadays most allow for a preview feature. The desktop publisher is not therefore going in blind, but has recourse to a limited WYSIWY (are eventually going to) G facility.

As the growing demand for increased typographical precision and control gains momentum, packages such as Prefis' Book Machine, initially developed well over four years ago, are at last finding a niche in the market, and a well deserved following. Implemented originally for the Apricot PC, Book Machine has been modified for the IBM PC and compatibles. It is not easy to use, since the abundance of keyboard commands (no mouse facility) requires that each of the IBM's 10 function keys be allocated with four different commands. Furthermore the fact that it is still supplied with an Apricot manual (albeit with an IBM-oriented keyboard amendment) does little to assist the user.

Book Machine doubles as a wordprocessor of significant capability. It can accept ASCII files from other sources but only via a special conversion utility that necessitates exiting the program. Nor does Book Machine accept graphics directly into the document as yet... developments are underway to allow scanned image support.

The package is designed for the production of long documents and reformats the entire publication in one pass. This can be slow but obviously depends on document length and hardware configuration. The Prefis equivalent of style sheets allows page definition of one to three columns, fount specification (type families provided are : Times, Univers, Helvetica and Plantin) and point size. The latter provides a spectrum of 5pt to 50pt in half point increments. Book Machine is a quasi-WYSIWYG package, hence fount types are recognisable, if not entirely accurate on screen.

Book Machine offers considerable potential for the user who may require more than the traditional 'cut and paste type' packages can provide. The most significant feature lies in the printing, which is cumbersome and unfriendly. What is important, however, is the fact that output files are converted into DVI (device independent) format, precisely as T_EX files are. This allows considerable flexibility as to choice of output device, including a range of professional typesetters.

Enhanced wordprocessing and DTP

We will be covering T$_E$X systems in more depth in chapter ten. Our basis for including some reference to Book Machine is to strengthen the case for a clear demarcation between enhanced WP and DTP. To all intents and purposes Book Machine operates in a manner more akin to a wordprocessor. Commands are entered via the keyboard and must be remembered. Menus are not of the pull-down type and thus the program is less logical in approach. What it will do is produce camera-ready artwork that can be accepted by a professional typesetting device and that is aesthetically pleasing and typographically precise.

It must be said that in general this type of software has a text-based document orientation and is therefore suitable for publications such as books. As the aesthetic standards of the WIMP camp improve, we may see a move away from this unfriendly but precise software, but for the present it has a part to play. Indeed as the user becomes more sophisticated in his output requirements the demand for the Just Text/Book Machine genus of software is on the increase. They will probably never rate in the top ten but they could offer a few suprises to the hard-core WIMP exponents. At the end of the day it is, for a section of the DTP fraternity, the quality of the document, not the means of achieving it, that is key. As long as control over the creation of CRC remains in the hands of the user, as long as savings are made on the use of external typesetting services, and as long as documents can be produced without the never-ending (and time consuming) to-ing and fro-ing from originator to paste up artist, to typesetter to printer... an extra day's learning is of no great significance.

7
Desktop publishing under networks and UNIX

Such is the power and flexibility of the personal computer that it is tempting for the desktop publisher to think it is the only computer he would require. In fact a single-user micro is not the answer to every computer need. There is often a place for bigger and more powerful computers, although in many cases the personal computer still fits into the picture as a terminal or a workstation.

Multi-user systems

The main reason for choosing a bigger machine is that a multi-user system is required. A network of personal computers can sometimes be an alternative to a multi-user computer but if there is a need to share data and processing power - for instance, when a number of authors are producing one document or a large database has to be shared among many users - then a multi-user system could well be the most effective solution.

It is possible to use the IBM-type machine for multi-user working, under operating systems such as XENIX, UNIX or PICK, but there will be a need for bigger disks, bigger memory, and a more powerful processor than the personal computer can provide in its basic form.

These multi-user machines come in many sizes and can be classified under a number of headings. Most of these machines fall into one of three categories:

1. Mainframe computers, particularly the IBM machines and the plug-compatibles
2. Minicomputers, particularly the DEC VAX range
3. A variety of minis and supermicros running UNIX and PICK.

The machines that can be subsumed under the multi-user desktop publishing banner are primarily the latter: supermicros running UNIX.

Local area networks

A local area network (LAN) is a group of workstations (PCs) controlled by a central file server, generally a more powerful model of the same type, and connected in one of two ways. Either they can be linked in a star formation, each PC communicating independently with the controller, or each constituent machine on the network can be daisy-chained in a ring formation. A LAN is more than the sum total of a collection of PCs linked by cables. It necessitates the use of sophisticated software and the addition of controller boards to each participating PC in order to manage the constant demands made on the central hard disk or file server. The type of network system adopted will in turn dictate the composition and arrangement of the PCs.

The software that enables a group of PCs to work together from a central file-serving device also ensures levels of file security. This serves to prevent users from unwittingly editing, for example, the same document simultaneously. Networks can reduce overall equipment costs quite considerably by permitting several users to share storage devices and printers. AppleTalk, Apple's rudimentary but efficient peripheral sharing LAN, achieves precisely this cost saving, and is discussed in more depth in chapter nine.

LANs for the IBM PC and compatibles are at a more sophisticated level of development and would prove ideal vehicles for the desktop publisher. Despite the fact the the page make-up software outlined in chapter 5 is not specifically multi-user the benefit of the LAN approach lies in providing individual users access to the same document in order to perform their discreet function in the publishing process. Examples of

Desktop publishing under networks and UNIX 103

popular LANs include Torus, which makes use of a WIMP-like user interface, Novell Netware and IBM's Token Ring.

Examples of networked personal computers in a publishing environment are Eddie Shah's new systems at both the *Stockport Messenger* and *Warrington Guardian* groups. The installed hardware consists of Macintoshs linked by AppleTalk running under the AppleShare file server software, which allows files to be passed from one user to another.

Talbot Dialtext Editorial Software performs all text inputting and composition functions and allows reformatting to a predefined standard at the editorial stage. Quite simply, format codes are applied and typeset copy is generated. Collectively the *Messenger* and the *Warrington Guardian* group are operating with 86 Macintosh workstations, spread over 14 sites. Shah is said to have saved over £1m by selecting this rather than the Hastech system used for production on *Today*.

Single vs the multi-user environment

The difference between desktop publishing on a supermicro running UNIX and the DTP systems mentioned so far is in essence the difference between 'single' user and 'multi-user' systems. There are certain cases when a multi-user or networked system will be more effective. One such case is the area of office automation, where the desktop publishing system is an integral part of the office system. The terminals or workstations could be used as a wordprocessing stations or telex terminals or data entry terminals.

The multi-user set-up would have different software running on the system, not all of which would interface with the desktop publishing. One very large example is the system in the US Department of Defence which has thousands of terminals linked to a number of supermicros running UNIX. They are used to handle all the routine office automation requirements as well as publishing many of the thousands of documents concerned with commands and equipment specifications used by the department.

Implementing a multi-user system

There are a number of reasons for providing a multi-user environment. These include:

1. To share computer power
2. To share the benefits of expensive peripherals such as scanners, digitisers and laser printers
3. To share data and text files
4. To allow users overall communication with others on the system.

Sharing processing power

Before the advent of inexpensive processing power in the form of personal computing there was a need to reduce the cost of a system by maximising the sharing of processing power. Mainframes and minis able to support multiple users were thus the most commonly adopted computer solution.

However, as the price of processing power decreased, so the need to distribute it between users became less acute. In many cases it became more cost-effective to provide single-user PCs to those requiring access to computing facilities.

The multi-user computers still have their place for certain types of application involving centralised processing. In many situations there is a need to have a powerful machine at the centre, essentially as a 'file server' with a large disk holding common files.

Sharing peripherals

In the desktop publishing environment sharing peripherals can be important. This does not apply, of course, to matrix printers, which are now so inexpensive that it is cheaper to give a printer to each user. However, the state of affairs has not yet arrived whereby laser printers and digitisers can be provided locally for everyone. They are expensive items and are likely to remain so for some time to come.

Sharing files and data

The sharing of data and text files is a more fundamental need and one more difficult to fulfil. Nonetheless, whenever several users need to access the same data it can be dangerous for them to have their own copy, as the different copies may get out of step. Files therefore need to be shared.

This is essential in operations where more than one user will need to access the same document/file, albeit at different times and for diverse purposes. To put it in perspective, user 'a' enters copy, user 'b' edits and alters copy, user 'c' makes up a page having accessed a graphics file

Desktop publishing under networks and UNIX 105

produced by user 'd'. User 'e' proofs and checks final page before output. At any stage in the process the document is accessible from the central file server and while file security protocols must exist, such that one file cannot be updated simultaneously, this method of working saves a lot of leg work !

The main problem with sharing data arises when several people do try to update the same data at the same time. This can easily lead to the data becoming corrupted. It is therefore essential to provide some means of 'locking', so that if a particular record is being amended it is locked and cannot be accessed by anyone else, other than for viewing, until the update is completed. The UNIX operating system allows this to be carried out.

For the purposes of this exercise the UNIX operating structure allows files to be assigned as 'Read Only' (*ro*), or 'Read/Write' (*rw*). Assignments can be amended only by the system housekeeper, or in the case of private files, by the originator. The status of a file may differ from user to user, a device which is maintained through the use of passwords. This system ensures absolute security of data while permitting many users access to documents under controlled conditions. The status of a file can also be determined by its use at any time.

Let us assume that file 'DTP ' is assigned as *rw*. We have six users, of whom two are allowed access to files on a read-only basis. Any user may access the file (indeed all users may have the file open at the same time). However, UNIX works on a 'first come first served' basis; hence whichever of the four users permitted to write to files accesses 'DTP' first, may amend it. To all other users on the system the status of DTP effectively changes to *ro*. This must by neccessity occur regardless of the status of the user.

Conversely, should the file be claimed first by a user holding an *ro* assignation, it is still available in *rw* status to the next permitted *rw* user. In a desktop publishing environment this level of document security is ideal and ensures that each user with a part to play in page composition be accorded the level of file access commensurate with his task.

Electronic mail

The final reason for providing a multi-user environment is to enable office workers and desktop publishers to communicate between each other. The key activity here is electronic messaging, or electronic mail.

When a number of people from different departments are producing a desktop published document it is useful and effective if they can send parts of the document by electronic mail to each other. The editor also has an easier time since texts from different sources can be obtained from a central source and combined.

Refinements to Unix-based DTP

Despite a wealth of graphics software available under UNIX, there is as yet little available in terms of DTP packages. The hardware, however, is ideal, and the traditional graphics orientation has led to the development of UNIX-based graphics workstations, offering a resolution suitable for the desktop publishing environment.

Troff (Typesetting RunOff)

One of the first super-micro-based publishing systems is Troff, a program within the UNIX operating system. It is available as a formatting utility, forming part of AT &T's powerful document preparation tools, collectively referred to as the 'Documenters Workbench'.

The standard UNIX Screen Editor VI is a development of Ed, which originated in the pre-VDU teletype days and as such offered non-interacative editing and no screen respresentation of the text. Vi offered improvments over this. The document formatters, by extension, evolved from the same hardware constraints and are thus far from WYSIWYG.

Troff constituting the major formatter was designed to produce high quality output on a typesetter. Multiple founts and point sizes are supported, in addition to facilities such as paragraph styles, headings, footnotes, etc. Troff can also output directly to laser printers. Given that Troff cannot support a WYSIWYG style, text is first prepared with embedded formatting commands under Vi.

Several powerful pre-processors extend the capabilities of Troff - Eqn, Tbl, Pic and Grap - by providing layout facilities for equations, tables, graphics and graphs respectively.

Troff is not used often now because, despite exceptional power and flexibility, it is very difficult to use.

SoftQuad (Unixsys UK)

Softquad claims to provide 'Troff without tears'. An enhanced derivation of AT & T's Documenter workbench, it combines the power of Troff with considerably more ease of use. Its appeal to existing UNIX users lies in the fact that it can accept any standard Troff files.

SoftQuad's salient features include:

1. A preview facility of any formatted page and document
2. Simple reformatting of entire documents by making changes to one formatting file
3. Macro formatting tools to allow programmers to develop specific in-house format requirements.

The original AT&T hyphenation algorithm is used, supported by an exception dictionary. Kerning is dealt with through the use of software supplied to generate kerning tables for founts found on the target output device.

SoftQuad can accept and reformat files produced under non-UNIX software, including output from wordprocessors, spreadsheets and databases.

Supplied with Softquad are tools for the generation of charts, diagrams and graphs. Tables can be laid out as required and the creation of boxes and rules is supported.

Softquad supports the Postscript PDL and can thus drive the Apple LaserWriter, the Linotype 100 and 300 phototypesetters and any other Postscript device. Transcript and imPRESS, other supported PDLs (or 'intermediate languages' in UNIX parlance), increase the range of output devices that can be driven.

SoftQuad publishing software is available on standard UNIX-based machines running the following variants of UNIX : Version 7, Berkeley 4.2, System V and Xenix. These include IBM PC XT and AT, Olivetti PCs, Pyramid, Sun, Apollo, AT&T 3b range and the DEC Vax and PDP 11 machines, to mention but a few. Given that SoftQuad can cost anything between £700 and £20,000, depending on the machine and UNIX implementation, it is obviously only the low end super-micros and PCs that should concern us in the context of DTP.

UNIX as an operating system is difficult to get to grips with. It would therefore be unwise for the novice desktop publisher to leap on the SoftQuad bandwagon, unless UNIX expertise was readily available. The attraction of this composition system must realistically be said to apply to existing UNIX users. As yet there is no true WYSIWYG facility, other than the preview feature, nor is a WIMP-like user interface in place. We understand that moves are being made in that direction, but to date SoftQuad, though simple in comparison to Troff in its virgin state, cannot be classified as easy.

Interleaf WorkStation

Possibly the most serious contender in UNIX-based publishing systems is the Interleaf Corporation. Their product, Interleaf Workstation Publishing Software (WPS), is implemented on the IBM 6150 UNIX machine in addition to DEC, SUN and Apollo configurations. Interleaf WPS offers the UNIX user a WIMPS and WYSIWYG environment and is thus far less daunting than packages along the lines of SoftQuad. To date it has been used mainly for technical and/or corporate publications. The reason for the former stems from the traditional role of UNIX in the field of CAD/CAM. Whereas DTP on the stand-alone micro has its roots in the text editing/WP environment, UNIX-based DTP tends to have evolved from existing graphics systems, and the onus to a certain extent lies in this direction.

Interleaf is a document-based composition system. The processing power of the current generation of super-micros make them admirable vehicles for such packages. The speed with which overall document formatting occurs could not be equalled on a comparable PC-based composition system.

Interleaf have supplied a user-friendly interface that serves to provide a type of WIMPs environment and perhaps more significantly to shield the user from the complexities of UNIX. In many respects Interleaf WPS operates in much the same way as the single-user software outlined above. Hence the mouse supplements keyboard entry, pull down menus are supported and a 'cut and paste' facility allows text and graphics to be moved from one document to another.

Obviously the same limitations are present as on a DOS-based system, i.e. once the user-interface is exited one is confronted with the operating system in its raw (and not so friendly) form. The facility to cut and paste will not, therefore, apply overall to any and all software on the system. We have already established that in this facility the Macintosh is unique.

Interleaf offers some facilities normally associated with WP software, such as :

1. Search and replace
2. Automatic spelling check
3. Goto facility to avoid laborious scrolling

Text can be accepted in a variety of formats and from various WP

Desktop publishing under networks and UNIX

environments, including DCA, Wang, Xerox 860 and our old friend WordStar. Interleaf includes a communications program that allows data transfer from PCs operating under DOS. Nroff (a less sophisticated relation of Troff) files are also supported.

As with the majority of page make-up systems explored above, Interleaf WPS is not specifically designed for text input, though editing at all levels is permitted.

A stylesheet or boilerplate facility allows the pre-formatting of documents in terms of columns, justification, etc. The pre-formatting of typeface components, however, requires the use of a 'property sheet'.

Real-time automatic pagination and formatting occurs as text is fed into the document or when edits and alterations are made. Widow and orphan controls can be specified. Hyphenation is based on an algorithm plus an 86,000 word dictionary, which is user expandable. Line spacing can be controlled and specified in the property sheet.

Interleaf supports the 'frame' concept for the creation of graphics and their subsequent incorporation into the document. Three graphics types are available :

1. *Business graphics*. Over 40 types of charts and graphs can be generated from data input directly by the user. The communication's option also allows graphic files to be accepted from PC-based packages such as Lotus 1-2-3, Visicalc and Multiplan. Data held in tabular form anywhere in the document can be transferred into chart format.

2. *Free form diagrams* . Interleaf provides graphics primitives for the creation of rules, curved lines, boxes, circles and ellipses. Objects once generated can be sized, both directionally and numerically. The latter makes use of 'sets ratio' to ensure precision. Alignment, grouping, duplication, rotation and movement of objects is also supported. Interleaf's free form graphics editor is based closely on the 'draw' family of software in providing the same basic functions as MacDraw and Gem Draw. A 'graphics cabinet' acts as a library for images to be pasted into any document. A selection of basic shapes such as stars, borders, arrows, etc. are provided with the software. Customised shapes can also be retained for subsequent use.

3. *CAD files*. Drawings created under CAD systems can be accepted into Interleaf documents in the following formats: output (print) files in Calcomp 960, Calcomp 925 and HPGL. The latter may be edited using Interleaf graphics tools.

When first announced Interleaf WPS provided no support for any industry standard page description language. A 'language' known as PMP organises the downloading of founts as required for each page. However, IBM have recently announced plans to adopt Postscript as the preferred environment for their electronic publishing products. Interleaf for the IBM RT (6150) will now be supplied complete with Postscript drivers.

DEC's implementation of Interleaf also offers Postscript support. IBM's descision will allow Interleaf to output quality as professional as that available on the low-end Macintosh and IBM PC.

Interleaf uses a supermicro with a hard disk system and processing speeds and storage capacities beyond those of most personal computers. The Interleaf software runs on the Sun workstation (Sun Micro System) with 2 Mb of memory and a 42 Mb hard disk system. This is the hardware that is often associated with CAD/CAM workstations and gives some indication of the quality that can potentially be provided with these UNIX-based systems.

There are a number of other benefits, one of which comes into play when large documents have to be processed. Interleaf running on a UNIX-based system can repaginate long documents in seconds whereas a personal computer might take minutes. The system can also be interfaced to Monotype, Compugraphic, Autologic, and Information International typesetting machines.

Increasingly it is the high-end software developers and hardware manufacturers who are subsuming desktop publishing into office automation.

8
Other players in the market

The majority of installed desktop publishing systems use a standard PC such as the Macintosh or IBM as the hardware vehicle for their production. The advantage of the general purpose machine lies in offering the user standard business applications and hence contributing to overall office automation strategy. Dedicated word processing systems are nowadays out of vogue since they are too inflexible to meet the demands of the typical office environment.

Developments in local area networks (LANs) and the cost benefits they offer in terms of data storage and peripheral sharing, have generated the need for operating system and hardware compatibility. The task-dedicated PC is generally not able to co-exist in the LAN environment, implies a unique method of operation and very often offers no definitive advantage over the more flexible PC running application-specific software. Since the number of potential users of DTP application software running on (say) the IBM PC is enormous relative to projected users of dedicated machines, the funds available for software development must reflect this massive potential. This enables the creation of software as comprehensive and professional as that available on the PC's dedicated counterpart.

The desktop publishing industry can only benefit from the availability of realistically priced PC based software packages. Not only does this increase the number of users, but in so doing creates a demand for ever-increasing sophistication of layout facilities and output resolution. Had every spreadsheet user been forced to buy a dedicated spreadsheeting machine, we have no doubt that today's proficient level of spreadsheet functionality would not exist. Availability of PC-based application software encourages its own development and increases product competence, to the obvious benefit of the user.

Dedicated systems - the hardware advantage

The advantage of the dedicated system lies in precise hardware design that takes into account the special needs of the task. The dedicated word processing system offered, for example, a large qwerty keyboard with additional function keys, each one being specially assigned and labelled for a specific task. The operator had no need, therefore, to remember commands and key sequences. The screen was generally larger than that supplied with the average PC and boasted excellent ergonomic advantages. The systems were, in effect, treated as an extension of the typewriter.

The same is true of the dedicated DTP system. Specially developed hardware such as A4 or large screens, configured keyboards and laser output devices offer the user optimum benefits as long as work requirements warrant the use of a one-task system. Very few manufacturers have opted for this route. The most notable exception is Xerox's Documenter which combines all the normal hardware requirements of a standard DTP system in a dedicated package.

Xerox never grasped desktop publishing opportunities in the early stages when paradoxically they were most involved. Initially developers of the much vaunted WIMPs environment, implemented on the now obsolete Star workstation, Xerox then lost key staff, frustrated by the lack of commitment to the development of page description languages. These ex-employees in turn formed Adobe systems and went on to refine basic work carried out at Xerox, which resulted in the overwhelmingly successful Postscript PDL.

It has been propounded that Xerox were merely waiting for an application that could make use of their technological developments. Yet the desktop publishing market did not evolve as a result of user demand: it was consciously created, hyped and sold... in the main by a combination of Apple, Adobe and Aldus. We have no reason to assume that Xerox could not have also made it happen; certainly their credibility

Other players in the market

in the area of office equipment and after-sales support could have positioned them in the vanguard of the DTP revolution. Instead they are running to catch up. In purchasing sole distribution rights to Ventura Publisher they are winning back lost ground, but the main thrust comes from their total DTP offering, Documenter.

Rank Xerox Documenter

Documenter represents a mere part of an overall DTP strategy that covers a range of related products including an Ethernet-based LAN, terminal emulation to allow the direct transfer of information from mini and mainframe systems and software specifications for colour laser printing (despite the dearth of available technology).

The Documenter consists of a large (15" or 19") screen, qwerty keyboard with 2 groups of 10 function keys, an optical mouse that unlike the Macintosh variety will only perform when used in conjunction with a special mouse pad, floor standing system unit and a laser printer. Physically it is a relatively large system that implies a little manipulation of the term 'desktop ' given that the main unit sits on the floor.

The system unit is of open architecture design and houses in its current form up to three processors. The main chip, specially designed by Xerox, is the Mesa processor, which is aided by an Intel 80186 to handle input and output tasks. IBM PC emulation can be achieved by installation of a third processor, though Xerox are at pains to point out that they cannot guarantee total compatibility. Just over 1 megabyte of RAM is supplied as standard. This can be increased to 3.7 megabytes. A 10 megabyte hard disk is provided on the base model with the option to expand up to 80. An IBM 'compatible' disk drive is also included as standard.

The large paper white screen features a resolution of 880 X 697 pixels on the 15" version, 1,184 X 925 on the 19". As increasing numbers of PC-based desktop publishers are demanding larger screens to allow a full A4 page to be previewed, it is obviously advantageous to have one available from day one.

The Xerox 4045 Laserprinter supplied with the system is unique in that it doubles as a photocopier. The latter takes the form of a reader mechanism that resides on top of the laser unit. When a document is passed through the reader, the printer accommodatingly performs a copying routine. Apart from this unique feature, the 4045 is relatively inflexible. Typefaces can be selected through the use of fount cartridges that plug directly into the printer or can be sent down in bit-mapped mode. Output is at a standard 300 dpi resolution and fount sizes range from six to 36 point. The real disappointment lies in the fact that despite use of the Interpress page description language, industry standard founts are not supported. In the main typewriter faces are supplied : Gothic, Modern and Pica to mention a few. Times (referred to as Classic) and Helvetica are bastardised versions. Only bold, italic and underline styles are currently supported. Interpress is currently supported by Compugraphic's new laser phototypesetter.

The system's Viewpoint software constitutes a user interface and a series of 20 modules including wordprocessing, spreadsheet, business graphics and freehand drawing. The entire suite is provided with the system on an astounding 54 floppy disks. The user interface is designed along the lines of GEM or Windows yet, although Xerox and WIMPS go back a long way, they appear not to have perfected the environment to the same extent as Apple. The user is confronted with a combination of mouse movements, pull-down menus and keyboard commands. Not only does this detract from overall continuity of approach but until the package is well and truly learnt, the logic assigned to the command structure is unclear. On the other hand, Viewpoint allows a number of windows to be open at any one time so it is very simple to switch from one to another and IBM software (given the addition of an IBM emulation processor) can be operated in conjunction with Viewpoint.

Text entry is performed in the document editor which offers all the facilities associated with a standard WP package, plus certain graphics handling features. Text can either be created and then moved into pre-defined columns (up to 10 per page) or keyed directly into the formatted page.

Every element contained within or created using Viewpoint possesses a property sheet that holds information describing its attributes. Each document therefore has a property sheet that allows changes to be made to columns, line spacing, typefaces, styles, point size, etc. Automatic repagination does not necessarily occur following amendments. In the event that point size is increased, line spacing must be altered accordingly or descenders and ascenders will tend to overlap.

Viewpoint provides a graphic toolbox which allows the creation of simple graphics within the editor. Drawings and charts can be produced

Other players in the market

in a system of graphic frames for subsequent incorporation into the document. The width of graphic frames must conform to either column or page width but cannot for example run accross two columns in a three column page.

In general the lack of flexibility, automatic reformatting of text and sophisticated typographical features puts Viewpoint in a different league from the PageMakers and Venturas of the DTP world. Xerox are quite sensibly planning to implement Ventura on the Documenter, which will enhance its appeal and sophistication considerably. However, while Xerox persist in offering a printer without Postscript or DDL support (or enhance Interpress considerably) one is left high and dry with non industry-standard founts.

Documenter is aimed at the corporate user whom it is assumed is not primarily concerned with adherence to printing/publishing industry standards. While this may hold true today, it is naive to suppose that this attitude will continue to prevail. The appeal of the Xerox solution lies in the credibility of the organisation behind the product, the efficient after sales service and the simplicity of an all-in-one solution. At the risk of overt cynicism, the success of Documenter may also be directly attributable to Xerox's aggressive direct sales policy.

Apricot desktop publishing

Apricot's DTP offering is in fact a collection of constituent parts marketed, like Documenter, as a total solution. It comprises an IBM AT compatible Xen i, based on either the Intel 80286 or 80386 processors, both of which offer fast performance, though the latter would prove the better bet for DTP. Supplied with one megabyte of RAM as standard, the Xen i 386 has the theoretical capacity of 16 megabytes of system memory.

Not surprisingly, the software selected to form the core of the Apricot system is PageMaker, running under Microsoft Windows. Microsoft Word version 3.0 (see chapter 6) and Microsoft Draw are supplied as standard.

In opting for PageMaker as the page make-up software supplied with the system, it was unfortunate that initially the Apricot laser offered no Postscript support. In fact it is a badged version of the single bin Kyocera F1010 laser printer with an output speed of up to 10 pages per minute and the standard 300 dpi resolution. The Kyocera offers a fairly rudimentary page description language, Prescribe, for which there is as yet no supported software. However, Prescribe commands can be embedded in the text to provide the user with greater control over the finished page. The Kyocera offers some pretty impressive facilities. It provides six in-built printer emulations, making it suitable for most software applications, the single bin will accept 250 pages at one time and the printer is supplied complete with 36 built-in founts. Apricot have very recently announced their intention to supply a badged Apple LaserWriter as part of their 'high-end' DTP system.

The addition of a Postscript device will allow the user to benefit from the Apricot's speed of operation and comparatively low price while obtaining output of an acceptable standard.

The Apricot also suppports Prefis' Book Machine, a sophisticated page-composition program (see chapter 6) that was originally developed some years ago with the Apricot in mind.

Apple Alliances

When it became apparent that desktop publishing was more than a mere flash in the pan, many of the established companies in the print, typesetting and associated trades sat up and took notice. Rather than permitting the small-time Apple dealer to benefit, the industry giants took the opportunity not only to grab a piece of the action but also to ensure their own security in a rapidly-changing industry. Almost overnight Apple formed alliances with Linotype, Gestetner and Letraset.

The immediate results were twofold: desktop publishing and the Macintosh in particular had become respectable and Apple was no longer considered a mere manufacturer of home computers and PCs but an innovator in the publishing arena. Apple were naturally delighted, their existing dealers less so. The second repercussion was that after initial feelings of perfidy and betrayal, the Apple dealer base responded by rapidly developing publishing expertise in order to counter any threat from the big boys. The ultimate beneficiaries were the prospective desktop publishers, who were met with an unexpected barrage of expertise from the least-likely sources.

Gestetner

Gestetner Publishing Software is the basic Macintosh DTP software configuration with the addition of a small desktop organising front-end and Gestetner's own forms production software. The former, Gestetner's Integration Manager, presents the user with one on-screen menu for the various software components - PageMaker, MacWrite, FullPaint, MacDraw - and the proprietary package Formation.

Gestetner's rationale in supplying what is in effect the equivalent to Apple's own Mini-Finder is to reinforce their role as system integrators for the range of Macintosh DTP products. Upon booting up, the user is confronted with the main menu entitled Gestetner Publishing Software, under which lies the choice of applications and a help facility. The Mini-Finder supplied with the Macintosh can be set up to perform the same function.

A more significant software contribution to the Macintosh system is Formation, a forms design package that combines the text facilities of MacWrite with the drafting features of MacDraw. While forms can be created simply and effectively using the latter, Formation - available from Gestetner as a stand-alone package - enhances the precision and certain alignment routines.

Gestetner's main marketing drive concentrates on the area of support. Given their printing background, the user will benefit from professional expertise... an advantage that is slowly diminishing as specialist DTP dealers emerge. The system is sold as a 'package' that includes two days on-site user training and a full maintenance agreement on all items of hardware. Free telephone support is also provided.

Letraset

Letraset purchased the sole distribution rights for MacPublisher, marketed as Letrapage. Following a policy decision, Ready Set Go 3 was purchased in addition and now forms the core of the Letraset offering. We are told the Letrapage is still under development.

The Letraset package is based purely and simply on the Macintosh DTP system. In effect, Letraset are attempting to achieve a slice of the market based on similar criteria to Gestetner.

With the advent of viable DOS-based desktop publishing it will be interesting to see how Letraset and Gestetner will react. More and more potential desktop publishers are demanding full demonstrations of both systems (and Documenter as well) prior to making their decision. As always in the PC industry there is a very real fear on the part of the users of being 'left behind'. This manifests itself in protracted buying cycles since the prospective DTP (or other application) candidate is always waiting for the best possible solution.

Apple have generously but realistically conceded that IBM will pick up the lion's share of the DTP market, leaving the Macintosh solution with approximately one third but as the market potential is escalating even a drop in market share will still enable Apple to ship more systems than before. So whilst Gestetner and Letraset can be sure that the Macintosh user base will increase, it is less certain that the business will be channeled through the Macintosh-only solution houses, despite their direct sales set-up. It seems likely that the specialist outlet able to offer a wide range of DTP solutions will win out by providing the user with the comparisons he so badly wants.

Alternatively we may see the so-called industry giants rapidly applying for IBM dealerships!

Digital Equipment Corporation

Significantly, DEC views desktop publishing as part of an overall office automation strategy. This is significant, because so many other manufacturers tend to see DTP as a distinct, stand-alone application. Apple obviously hold the same view as Digital but are travelling a different route. Having their DTP solution firmly in place, they are now concentrating their efforts on desktop communications, networking and total office automation. Either way the end result will be similar, if at very different points on the computing spectrum.

The corporate user, currently dependent on specialist 'print departments' or on buying in external typesetting services will continue to carry on the run-of-the-mill operations that ultimately produce the material that requires typesetting. To subsume the control of document output within the auspices of the total office automation strategy therefore makes perfect sense.

Information could often beneficially be held centrally since it may be required for output in a variety of formats. This could avoid both re-keying and, since file transfer can readily overcome the problem of input duplication, reformatting. All users therefore could access the original file for the purpose of editing, reformatting or placing in a page make-up system.

Digital offers four publishing solutions which, though providing the necessary 'links' from one environment to another, are also targeted at

Other players in the market

discreet applications and specific systems, while all the time maintaining a 'handle' on the overall computing strategy.

DECset. DECset is no newcomer to the publishing market, nor should it justifiably be termed desktop publishing, but we have included it merely to demonstrate the range of DEC's total publishing strategy. DECset is a batch-pagination program that runs on the entire DEC VAX family from the MicroVAX to the 8800. Text from wordprocessors, such as WPS Plus can be input in Standard General Mark-up Language (SGML) format. H&J and pagination are automatically performed throughout the document in a single run. DECset constitutes, in DTP phraseology, a true document-based system and is aimed at the professional typesetter and the corporate publishing department.

Graphics and text integrated can be achieved by incorporating images from a variety of CAD/CAM systems and Autokon scanners. Output is available through a variety of typesetters, standard laserprinters or any Postscript device.

InterLeaf. Interleaf, discussed in the preceding chapter, is available on the entire range of DEC equipment using the Ultrix operating system (DEC's implementation of UNIX) and constitutes part of the total DECset package. Enhancements to Interleaf's CAD file import facilities have been developed internally and serve to extend the graphic options. Input from WPS PLUS enables wordprocessed documents to retain their format. DEC's implementation of Interleaf supports output to Postscript devices.

DECPage. DECPage is offered as an enhancement to DEC's proprietary wordprocessing package WPS-PLUS running under VMS. Graphics can be accepted from DECgraph and DECslide. A standard set of style sheets is provided primarily to assist the office worker with no previous page-layout experience. DECPage outputs to the LN03 laser printer, but does not offer Postscript drivers.

PageMaker. Digital Equipment Corporation will also be supplying PageMaker on the IBM compatible VAXMate as the low-end component of their overall publishing strategy. PageMaker documents can, in keeping with DEC's more sophisticated publishing offerings, import files from WPS-PLUS, which implies an overall compatibilty throughout the range. PageMaker output in Postscript format can be produced on the DEC LPS40 printer.

DEC are committed to expansion in the publishing arena and forging ahead with a total strategy encompassing DTP to professional typesetting systems. In the Digital offerings we could well be witnessing the emergence of a most comprehensive range of electronic publishing tools, a strategy that may well be adopted by other traditional computer manufacturers.

Other players

Wang has recently announced an implementation of PageMaker to operate in both stand-alone and networked office automation environment. Appeal will no doubt be in the established Wang user base.

Canon's complete desktop publishing system, based on the Canon IBM-compatible PC, was available long before the onslaught of specific page make-up systems. Canon have adopted an enhanced version of WordPerfect (see chapter six for clarification) that offers limited integration of text and graphics and decidedly unfriendly forms design. Output is through the standard Canon LBP-A2 Laserprinters, with no facility for PDL support.

Yet another company putting considerable effort into the DTP drive, is Advent Data Products who offer a range of three systems running their own DOS-based Ad-Text, AD-Sketch and AD-Draw software. Two of the systems offer A4 screens, the other operates on a standard IBM PC XT/AT. The systems are limited in their output capabilities, supporting Canon, Hewlett Packard and Kyocera laser printers and can only offer non industry standard founts.

As the desktop publishing 'revolution' gains momentum so the number of players involved will increase.

9
Peripherals and add-ons

Front-end peripherals are those that can be used to accept input into the system; back-end peripherals are used to output copy. There have been a number of developments in both areas.

Front-end peripherals

The most important front-end devices are the keyboard and the mouse. These are implicit in the process of entering data and of manipulation, selection and all the requirements of day-to-day operation.

The most significant recent contribution to desktop publishing is the graphical digitiser.

Graphic digitisers

A graphic digitiser converts an image into digitised information. The personal computer processes this, stores it, displays it on the screen and prints it on a printer.

Once a display has been digitised and displayed on a computer screen as an image, it is then possible to use special graphics software to edit and enhance it. This can include scaling, cropping, editing and adding and deleting sections, often working at pixel level. The image can then be exported into page layout software and placed in the text of the publication.

Image scaling

Image scaling is complicated because scaling images down causes distortion, sometimes rendering them unusable. However with the advent of more sophisticated scanning software so the need for manual scaling (i.e. 'picking up' the corner of a graphic and moving it inwards or outwards in order to enlarge or reduce) is less important. Enhanced scanning software allows the scaling to be specified in the conventional graphic terms of percentage increases or decreases, which avoids the possibility of distortion.

The LaserWriter can enhance the enlargement/reduction facilities since it offers a range of 15% reduction to 100% enlargement at 300 dpi. You may therefore have to use the output device to achieve acceptable hard copy of a scanned image and then resort to manual cut-and-paste. Somewhat tiresome, but a means of achieving precision scaling at the required resolution.

In order to position an image in a publication, be it integrated with text or not, the precise area allocated for that graphic must first be established. Secondly, the size of the scanned original must be measured. Images can then be reduced or enlarged before placing in the composition software. Not all image scanners yet provide software that allows this precise scaling.

Avoiding problems like image distortion depends on the functions provided by the digitising software and the graphics program. It is a standard function of even the most rudimentary digitisers that the software enables the user to alter digitised images, changing their contrast, brightness and grey scale.

Editing scanned images

Once scanned in, images can be immediately transferred into a freehand graphics package for editing. The reason that the lower resolution 'Paint' packages are used rather than their higher resolution 'structured graphics' counterparts lies in the ability to 'blow up' sections of the image. This enables editing at pixel level in order to smooth fuzzy lines, add or delete legends or even make drastic changes. The problem of reduced resolution is nowadays overcome since enhancements to scanning software enable the image, though edited at 72 dpi resolution, to be reinstated at 300 dpi when editing is completed. Quality is increased if images are scanned as large as possible (though you can only currently scan up to A4 on typical DTP devices) and then reduced prior to incorporation into the document.

Generally speaking, scanning in halftones at low resolution is pointless....manual cut-and-paste is necessary here.

There are several types of digitisers that can be used with personal computers. All convert an image into binary information that the computer can process and store. One digitising method uses video cameras to capture an image on the computer. The video camera is connected to a digitiser and the camera is focussed on the subject. Digitisers convert the signal from the camera into a stream of binary information and relay it to the computer where it is stored. The digitiser and the software distinguishes various tones of grey in the video image and reproduces patterns of black and white dots on the screen to define the shade of the image.

Video digitisers

The earliest digitisers available for the Macintosh were those that depended on a video camera as a means of capturing the image. The digitiser is connected to a black and white video camera at one end and to the Macintosh serial port at the other. Once the camera and digitiser are set up, the digitising software is loaded, the lens is focussed on the subject and the digitiser builds up an image on the screen in anything from 0.1 to 5 seconds.

The precision and aesthetic 'look' of the digitised image will depend on several factors, including the standard and type of video lens provided - ideally a 12.5mm to 75mm zoom. The camera and lighting must be set up for each object to be digitised. In the event that line drawings are to be captured, a lighted copystand should be used.

The system allows adjustment to the focus, contrast and brightness of the screen image and requires judgements that call for a specific camera angle or staging. This can only be done with training and practice and a modicum of photographic knowhow.

Results can differ enormously. We have used video digitisers to produce interesting 'halftones' of physical objects (like people !) which we could not have performed with a scanner. On the whole, however, the primary use of digitisers in the DTP environment is to capture line drawings that are too complex or time consuming to recreate. In this area the video method leaves too much room for operator error. Macintosh-based video digitisers include: New Image Technology's Magic (Macintosh Graphics Input Controller) and Microvision's MacViz DTP. The latter, though more costly, offers a superior lens and is supplied complete with illuminated copystand.

A sample of digitised image produced with the Magic video digitiser is shown in illustration 9.

Optical scanners

Optical scanners are a second type of digitiser used with personal computers. These scanners do not use a video camera but run an optical device across a flat image and digitise the information read from it.

Thunderscan is a rudimentary optical scanner that can be used with a Macintosh computer. The scanner cartridge, a light sensitive detector, replaces the ribbon cartridge of Macintosh's ImageWriter printer. The illustration to be digitised is inserted in the printer. When scanning, the scanner head reads back and forth across the image, gathering digitised information as the illustration advances through the printer. As it moves, it points a thin stream of light at the image, reads the lightness or darkness of many small spots and converts the information into numeric values, which are stored in the computer's memory. The digitiser then analyses the binary information and converts it into the dot patterns that become the printed image.

After the optical reader has been inserted, the scanner is connected at the back of the printer and then to the Macintosh printer port. Half tones and line drawings up to an A4 sized sheet can be captured. Thunderscan's software allows adjustment to the contrast and brightness of an image and also limited editing of the captured image, re-drawing, copying and cutting and pasting proportions of the image. An image can be magified up to 400%, provided it is on the standard A4 page, or reduced to 25% of its original size. The digitised image is saved as a MacPaint file for further editing and eventually transferred to the page composition program.

The main drawbacks of Thunderscan are the slow scanning speed and the low resolution produced. Scanning can take up to 15 minutes as the

**Illustration 9.
Digitised image from the Magic video digitiser.**

126

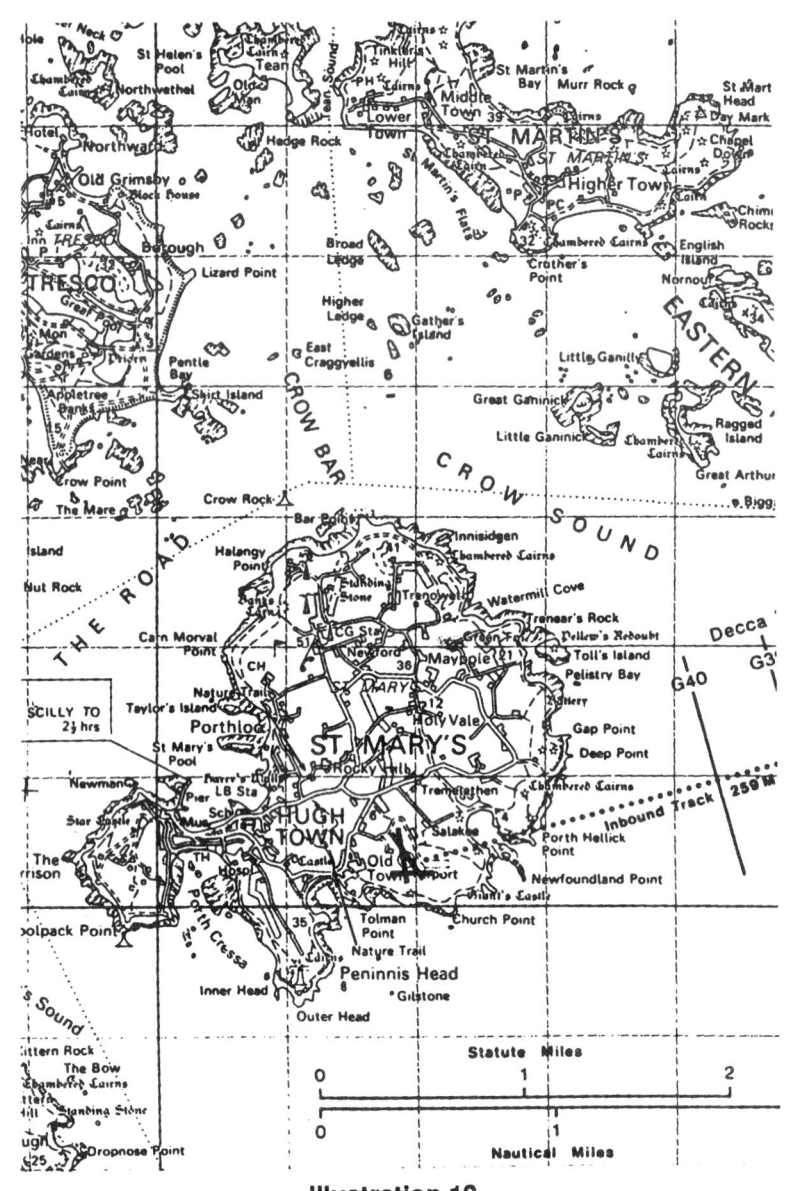

**Illustration 10.
Digitised image from the Microtek MS 300A.**

scanning head moves back and forth across the image in minute increments. The larger the image to be digitised, the longer the scanning takes.

Thunderscan although priced at under £300 is not recommended for the serious DTP user since the amount of pixel editing required to smooth fuzzy edges is excessive. In addition it requires an Imagewriter printer which is of limited DTP use otherwise.

Other types of digitisers

A third type of digitiser scans images using a method similar to the way a photocopier works. A flat image is placed on the scanner and lit with a low frequency light.

The image is reflected from a mirror and focussed through a lens to a bank of electronic elements called Charged Coupled Devices (CCDs), that sense light and dark areas and convert them into binary data. The digitised information is then sent to the computer as an image.

One scanner that uses an array of CCDs is the Microtek Ms 300A (a badged version of the Abaton 300), which works with both the IBM range and compatibles and with the Macintosh. A page is inserted into the scanner and rolls past the light-sensitive element during scanning. It can scan pages up to A4, for which the scanning time can be as little as 20 seconds but this depends entirely on how the graphic is built up. Half tones will take longer than line drawings for example. Versascan and Cscan, the software supplied with the Abaton, allows seven different modes of scanning suited for a mix of text, graphics and pictures with multiple grey levels. Various viewing levels are supported as an aid to the editing function. The scanner is smaller than a typical dot matrix printer and can be conveniently placed on a desktop near the computer. A sample image digitised by the MS-300A appears in illustration 10.

As the name implies, the MS-300A scans in at a resolution of 300dpi - in keeping with the LaserWriter. Another scanner of note is the Canon 1X-12. Originally sold exclusively as part of Canon's total DTP offering, this is now available as a stand-alone unit. Much more compact than the Abaton/Microtek, it offers the same resolution.

Storage of scanned images

It should be noted that most scanned images (produced from scanners of the Abaton type) can be stored in compressed or non-compressed mode.

This is because the image once scanned requires considerable disk space. It is also noteworthy that to accept and process a graphics image of A4 size requires more than one megabyte of RAM. Whilst the Macintosh RAM can be upgraded from one to four megabytes, this is less easy on the IBM PC and compatibles since DOS limits available address space to 640Kbytes. Additional memory boards can overcome this, as outlined in chapter four. An image can be 'uncompressed' for the purposes of editing and printing. Often it is possible to hold images on a library of floppy disks.

The Macintosh's inbuilt Scrapbook proves to be a great benefit for holding re-usable scanned images, such as logos, standard symbols, etc. which are normally small and do not consume too much disk space. By holding images in the Scrapbook rather than in separate files they can be more readily pasted into documents.

Scanning standards

As with so many relatively innovative products in the DTP arena, scanning standards are emerging. Firstly it is recognised that to scan at resolutions less than 300 dpi is not acceptable for anything other than very rudimentary DTP. Secondly, the software provided should allow scanned images to be captured, stored and transferred in Transfer Image File Format (TIFF), the scanning equivalent of ASCII.

The current market leaders in the field of page make-up will accept TIFF format (PageMaker, Harvard Professional Publisher).

High resolution scanners

Because more expensive scanners digitise images in high resolution they may also include data processing devices, such as very large capacity hard disk drives to hold the digitised information. The high end scanner is usually connected to mini-computers and mainframe computer systems. With the advent of the 600 dpi laser printer or the adoption of alternative output technologies such as magnetic or ink-jet based printers, the scanning manufacturers will have to beef up on their input resolution. No doubt they are already doing so.

External scanning services

Scanners are excellent for producing simple graphics but if this is

Peripherals and add-ons 129

inadequate to justify buying, seek out an independent graphic professional who specialises in digital graphics. They will often quote a price on a job-by-job basis and transform illustrations into final art.

Optical character readers

Recent developments include the convergence of technologies in the production of low cost OCRs.

In most circumstances text held on another computer can be transferred via communications software into an environment suitable for DTP. However, should lengthy documents be typewritten, it is laborious, time consuming and costly to rekey all the text and data. Dest's PC-SCAN addresses this problem by providing an image scanner that also recognises certain founts as text and hence allows the creation of editable text files.

Dest - who have been in the scanning market for many years - have produced a product not only smaller but faster than many of its earlier models. PC SCAN operates with IBM PCs and compatibles. It is compact, neat and very small. The entire unit sits between IBM PC monitor and system unit. To date the OCR reads several standard monospaced typefaces at 10 or 12 pitch. Some proportionally-spaced founts are also supported. PC SCAN is also able to read typestyles produced by many of the most widely-used dot matrix printers.

PC SCAN's Text PAC software allows, it is claimed, the input of text at rates up to 30 times faster than the average typist. Obviously in certain cases, particularly when a previously manual system is being computerised and all documentation is typewritten, a product like PC SCAN proves invaluable. Increasingly though, the sophistication of communications software negates the need to read text in when it can be sent down a piece of wire !

Datacopy Corporation's Jetreader, like PC Scan, is a 300 dpi scanner with an optical character recognition program. A specific range of typestyles is supported, with the facility to 'learn' additional founts. Currently available on the IBM PC, a Macintosh version is on the cards.

Graphics tablets

The production of freehand designs can be greatly enhanced by the use of a graphics tablet. The tablet sits in front of the screen and the pen moves across it to simulate the act of drawing on paper. Available in both the DOS and Macintosh environments, a graphic tablet effectively acts as a more precise mouse. A stylus or hairline cursor enables the user to draw and trace with considerable fluency. Macintosh-supported graphics tablets can operate with any and all software since as the mouse port is used the Macintosh treats all movements as if they were mouse driven. Products of note include GTCO's Macintizer, Summagraphic's Mactablet and Softweavers' PenMac.

Back-end peripherals

Back-end peripherals, in the context of desktop publishing are laser devices: page printers or phototypesetters that serve to output the hard copy required for the printing process.

Laser printers

Until recently, laser printers were mainly used in universities and corporate institutions where high volume printing was needed. High capacity laser printers such as the Xerox 9700 or the IBM 66700 are roughly the size of a household deep-freeze and range in price from £50,000 - £250,000. They are controlled by mini-computers and are usually located in computer centres surrounded by technicians and humming equipment that provide dataprocessing services to a multi-terminal computer network. Such laser printers are popular today in organisations that can afford them because they print hundreds of pages per hour over extended time periods and produce documents of a quality that professional and business standards require. Fortunately for desktop publishing, technology has brought laser printing within an affordable price range.

Laser printers like the Apple LaserWriter, Hewlett Packard LaserJet and the ImageGen H/300 are available today at prices ranging from £2000 - £7000.

These printers produce documents of a resolution many dots per inch above the dot matrix commonly used with personal computers. Dot matrix printers produce characters composed of many small dots printed closely together. The more, the closer and the smaller the dots, the finer the look of the character they compose. The Apple ImageWriter, for example, prints characters at a resolution of about 80 dpi. Laser printers

Peripherals and add-ons

like the LaserJet+ and the LaserWriter print more clearly defined characters at a resolution up to 300 dpi. Resolutions of 1000 - 25000 dpi are commonly produced by professional typesetting equipment. The laser printer type founts with a resolution of 300 dpi will resemble the same typesetting fount in size and shape but differ considerably in resolution.

Laser printers output text using a mixture of type sizes and styles and they are able to a greater or lesser extent to integrate text and graphics on a page. No letter-quality or dot matrix printer can mix founts and print graphics as successfully. Changing founts with the letter quality printer usually requires you to stop the printer and replace a print element such as a daisywheel. Some dot matrix printers mix founts and print characters at various sizes. With many laser printers you can print characters of point sizes from 3 up to 255. The range is limited only by your software. Some laser printers produce pages with a mixture of type sizes and styles in one continuous run without stopping to change print control elements.

In most circumstances laser printers are much faster than most letter-quality printers used for personal computers today. Print speeds for letter-quality printers are only as high as 80 or 90 characters per second. Laser printers' speeds vary depending on the amount of text and graphics on the page. With the LaserWriter, for example, setting up a complex image for printing can take several minutes but it can obtain printing speeds of 325 characters per second or roughly eight/ten pages per minute when printing the same page repeatedly.

A further advantage is that such speeds are attained at the noise level of a quiet conversation (approximately 55 decibels), which is remarkably quiet compared with dot matrix and letter quality printers. The latest laser printers fit on a desk, leaving sufficient room for PC, scanner, keyboard and mouse.

It is the ability to output combined text and graphics at relatively high resolution that has made desktop publishing feasible by enabling the production of clean, camera-ready copy from a laser printer or a professional typesetting device. With the considerable economy of laser printers in mind, let us take a closer look at how they work.

Laser printers are comprise two elements: a laser-actuated marking engine, called the print engine and an image processing system. The LaserWriter, LaserJet and Image Gen 8/300 all share the same Canon LBP - CX print engine.

A laser printer engine produces images using a hair-fine beam of laser light. The laser light is directed into a rapidly revolving hexagonal mirror that scans the light in a fine line across a large photosensitive drum. According to image data relayed from the image processor, the laser beam pulses on and off and each pulse of laser light charges a small spot on the rotating drum. As the drum rotates the electronically charged spot on the drum attracts fine toner powder from a toner cartridge. The drum comes in contact with the paper and transfers the toner to it, using a combination of heat and pressure. The many dots fuse to produce a crisp, clear image of text and graphics. The Canon LBP-CX print engine produces 90,000 dots per square inch, 300 dpi x 300 dpi to produce finely defined characters.

Though many laser printers from different manufacturers use the same print engine, the printing capabilities differ because the image processing systems differ. This image processing system is run by a powerful computer built into the printer. The Apple LaserWriter, for example, contains a high speed 68000 processor and 2 megabytes of memory. It has more processing power memory than many personal computers.

The LaserJet uses the same microprocessor, but only has 128 k of memory within the machine.

A great deal of memory is required to hold an image composed of so many small dots and produce it in a variety of styles and sizes. Therefore, differences in memory size and in fount and processing information stored in a printer's memory greatly effect its capabilities.

The Hewlett Packard LaserJet introduced in September 1984 was acclaimed as the first low-cost printer that allowed personal computer users laser performance at an affordable price.

Since then the flood gates have opened, leading to a plethora of products based initially on the Canon LBP-CX print engine, and latterly on the Ricoh 4080, which allows heavier duty usage. Whilst the earlier products provided nothing in the way of support for page description languages and were primarily aimed at the wordprocessing market, we are today witnessing a wealth of new laser printing devices offering improved speeds, paper size, resilience and design which are aimed at the desktop publishing market.

In order to shed some light on the growing range of available printers let us look at four laser printers appropriate to desktop publishing and examine their principal capabilities.There are many more sophisticated laser printers in higher price ranges but the following models are the most financially accessible.

The LaserWriter

The Apple LaserWriter can be said to have made desktop publishing a reality. Its image processing system and large memory (2 megabyte of RAM and ROM combined) enables it to print full pages of text and graphics at 300 dpi resolution. Page size is limited by hardware constraints of the Canon LPB-CX engine, which cannot print full sized metric A4. The printing area is approximately 7mm less on each dimension. Page set-up instructions allow the user to specify A4 (or its close approximation), US legal and B5. One can opt to print in either landscape (wide) or portrait (tall) modes. Scaling can be specified precisely merely by keying in a percentage for enlargement or reduction.

When using the LaserWriter with the Macintosh, the page set-up screen is constant regardless of which software is running (i.e. DTP, WP, spreadsheet, etc) and hence allows the same range of facilities. The reason for this consistent approach to laser printing lies in the fact that the laser printer driver resides in the Macintosh operating system and as such is not application-package specific. All Macintosh software can therefore be printed out at 300 dpi and most packages can access industry standard founts resident in the LaserWriter. One notable exception is MacPaint, Apple's freehand graphics software. Given that MacPaint was designed with the dot matrix Imagewriter in mind, it can only output at 72 dpi. Alternative products such as FullPaint and SuperPaint both output at the acceptable 300 dpi.

The laser printer can mix text and graphics on the page. With the Macintosh, for example, you can use page layout software to format text and images on the screen and then print fully composed pages on the laser printer.

The LaserWriter Plus

Two versions of Apple's laser printer are now available - the LaserWriter and the LaserWriter Plus. In keeping with Apple's commitment to upgradeability, the former can, for little over £600, be modified to plus specification. The operation involves a logic board change and is a simple task (though not one to be performed by the user).

The first difference between the two models is speed - the standard laser outputs at up to eight pages a minute (if repeating the same page) whereas the Plus offers a top speed of ten pages a minute, as indeed do most of its rivals. The second difference lies in the number of ROM-based founts supplied with the printer.

The LaserWriter Plus is provided with the following ROM-based fount families in addition to those supplied with the basic model: Helvetica Narrow, Avant Garde, Palatino, Bookman, Zapf Chancery, New Century School Book, Dingbats. Given that there are obvious limits to the number of type families that can reasonably reside in the LaserWriter's half megabyte of ROM, Apple selected from the Adobe library of Allied and ITC founts those type families that were considered to offer widest appeal to the DTP user.

These may not always prove adequate for the professional user who having already have adopted and implemented a house style wishes to retain continuity by adhering to the selected typeface. The problem is overcome though the use of downloadable founts. These are supplied and licensed by Adobe, as are the resident type families and are disk-based. Founts are loaded through the Macintosh, remain in the printer until it is switched off and to all intents and purposes the process is transparent to the user. The additional fount merely appears as another option on the pull-down menu. Downloadable founts contain the entire type family,i.e. roman, italic, bold. Given that one family will typically use about 40K of RAM, you are limited to downloading only two or three simultaneously but for normal use this is adequate.

The choice of available founts is increasingly rapidly. Adobe released 20 additional downloadable type families in the first three months of 1987 and more are under development.

The LaserWriter comes with three typeface families stored in ROM: Helvetica, Times and Courier.

All available founts support the full European character set, graves, cidillas, umlaut etc. and the Macintosh allows floating accents.

Typefaces can also be printed underlined, shadowed and outlined or any combination of the above. The Macintosh directs the LaserWriter's printing using Postscript.

The LaserWriter can also emulate a Diablo 630 printer and other computers can use it as if they were using the Diablo 630... software that does not output Postscript code can send information to the printer if it has a Diablo 630 printdriver. When the laser printer is emulating a

Peripherals and add-ons 135

Diablo 630 printer you cannot of course access the printer's special features, such as its many typefaces.

The IBM PC and compatibles can take full advantage of the LaserWriter's printing capacities when they run software that transmits data in a Postscript format. You can use the IBM PC with Microsoft Word, Samna and other wordprocessing software as well as graphic programs such as GemDraw.

Phototypesetter output

Using Postscript it is possible to output to Linotype's 100 and 300 series phototypesetters. Macintosh owners can therefore hook up with a professional typesetter to create camera-ready bromide of a document at a high resolution. The LaserWriter might be used as a proofing device with some confidence since with Postscript's use of Linotype founts the output from the LaserWriter will be identical to the Linotronic output in all layout respects.

The desirability of using 'licensed' founts as distinct from 'bastardised' versions is clear. A page laid out on any PC running page layout software and printed out for draft purposes on a laser printer that uses its own aproximations of typefaces will have different H and J parameters due to the different width characteristics of the founts.

More about phototypesetters in chapter ten.

The LaserWriter and any other laser printer using the same Canon engine can accept paper of up to 100gsm in the paper tray. 80 gsm is recommended, but we have used 100 gsm Conqueror. Thicker material such as acetates for the production of overhead slides or coated paper up to 120 gsm should be fed through using the manual feed. Remember incidentally, that weight is not directly related to bulk so avoid the use of high volume pages.

The LaserWriter can print up to eight/ten pages per minute, but this maximum rate is obtained only when repeating a page stored in memory. A single page that includes multiple fount changes, obliquing, underlining and other enhancements can take several minutes to be transmitted and printed. The LaserWriter is designed to print about 3000 pages per month but requires service at 50,000 page intervals.

Do not expect to use the LaserWriter as a printing press. It would be a very expensive way of producing copies, the printing paper tray does not hold more than 100 sheets at a time and the output tray holds only 50 sheets at a time. You must be there to refill and empty page trays. Like desktop copiers, the LaserWriter uses dry toner cartridges for printing. A single cartridge costs roughly £100 and is good for approximately 3000 printed pages, depending on the amount of text and graphics per page. It is generally reckoned that the cost of printing one A4 sheet is about 3p -- comparable with photocopying costs.

AppleTalk network

The LaserWriter is supported by the Apple personal network system. AppleTalk is a low-cost network, orientated primarily towards peripheral sharing. It can theoretically support up to 32 devices, including Macintoshs, Laserwriters, Imagewriter II (with the addition of an internal AppleTalk card) in addition to IBM PCs and compatibles. The latter can be connected via TOPS, a combined hardware and software product that allows coexistence with the Macintosh and by extension use of the LaserWriter as a shared resource. Apple have also announced their own IBM PC compatible AppleTalk card.

The recent entry of IBM DTP software into the arena has created a demand for precisely the solution that TOPS and Apple provide. We anticipate a wealth of similar products in the very near future.

The LaserWriter can be linked serially to the IBM PC and, given software with Postscript drivers, will allow the user access to all its benefits. The device can be shared by a number of PCs networked with any of the standard LAN offerings (Novell, Torus, etc).

Realistically, 31 Macintoshs should not share one LaserWriter. Whilst Appletalk can cover significant distances (1000ft, with the option for bridging two networks together and thus increasing this considerably),there is currently no spooling facility supplied as standard. Whichever user excecutes the print command first will print; all others who attempt to do so will be given a message advising them that user X is printing and offering the option to cancel the print command. Users working in remote offices would find this quite laborious.

Print spoolers

Thankfully print spoolers can be obtained as add-ons to the system and Apple will shortly be supplying their own version. That said the prospective desktop publisher should carefully assess his anticipated print volumes before deciding whether or not to share a printer.

The LaserWriter price tag is from £5,000, the Plus a mere £650 more. The cost of one LaserWriter shared between, say, ten users, gives approximately the same cost as 10 standard dot matrix printers !

AppleTalk at £50 per connection per device, allows for extremely cost-effective peripheral sharing. Laserspoolers are currently in the £100 price bracket. One such example of a spooler is Infosphere's LaserServe, a software-based product that requires neither hard disk (though this is reccommended for all DTP applications) nor dedicated server. A special priority service facility, it allows desperate users to override the normal queueing process for immediate output. Pop-up menus inform the user when the document has been printed.

Fortunately an increasing number of print shops and computer stores charge an hourly or printed page rate for LaserWriter use. You can avoid the expense of buying the LaserWriter by purchasing printing time instead.

Hewlett Packard's LaserJet and LaserJet+

Despite their inherent unsuitability for serious desktop publishing, the Hewlett Packard LaserJet and LaserJet+ warrant consideration for the simple reason that they made laser printing affordable and acceptable at the PC level. Designed around the same Canon engine as the Laser-Writer, they print at the same speeds, with the same low decibel level.

The primary difference between the Hewlett Packard and Apple products lies in the processing power available and in the lack of any page description language. Hence the LaserJet provides a mere 128k of combined RAM and ROM, the LaserJet+ 512K. Consequently typefaces cannot reside in the printer; they are supplied as firmware on fount cartridges and need to be plugged in to the printer as and when required. Each fount cartridge includes not a type family but various limited style and size options. One cartridge might hold, for example, Times Roman 10 and 12 point, Times Oblique 12, Courier 10 Bold. Production of a document requiring several fount size and style changes could necessitate numerous cartridge changes. Not only does this slow down the print processes but it is is cumbersome and decidedly unfriendly ! Fount sizes are limited, as are the choices available.

The restricted memory of the Hewlett Packard laser printers inhibits their value as graphics printers since only a small portion of the page can be taken up with images. That said, the LaserJet has found a definite niche as leader in the PC-based WP arena. At less than £2000 for the basic model, its appeal against traditional daisywheel printers is significant. It has also met with some limited success as the output device for Clue, a page layout system running on the HP Vectra and IBM PC.

What is significant for the purposes of this overview is Hewlett Packard's descision to adopt Imagen's DDL (Document Description Language) for its new generation of laser printers. Announced in August 86, we were still waiting in the spring of 1987 for the new product. The attributes of DDL against Postscript have been discussed elsewhere. Hewlett Packard wisely intends to provide an upgrade path for existing LaserJet users. This will involve swapping the logic board and adding a RIP (Raster Image Processor).

The majority of page layout software packages currently available on the IBM PC are rapidly developing DDL drivers (if they have not already done so), to take advantage of Hewlett Packard's proposed product. In support of this move Imagen have announced a DDL controller in the form of a PC expansion card. This will allow PC users software independence, i.e. the ability to drive the printer regardless of whether DDL drivers are supplied with the software package in use. Already announced in the States, though not yet available in the UK, Imagen's DDL PC card also functions as a network print server/printer controller.

Dataproducts LZR 2665

If today's desktop publisher were to devise a 'wish list' of attributes he would like to see incorporated in a low-cost system, doubtless A3 printing would appear high on the agenda. Yet A3 printing is available and indeed has been for some time... at a price.

Dataproducts were the first to launch a 'low cost' A3 laser device, which not only adhered to the accepted standard of 300dpi, but offered full Postscript support. The Dataproducts LZR 2665 supports AppleTalk in addition to offering parallel, RS232 and RS422 interfaces. Thirteen resident fount families are supplied and others can be downloaded using precisely the same operation as is performed on the Macintosh. Whilst quite bulky, the LZR 2665 is designed for heavier duty use and is able, once the image has been recreated in Postscript, to output at up to 26 pages per minute.

Peripherals and add-ons

Whereas the strength of the LaserWriter lies in its ability to create camera-ready copy and artwork for subsequent printing on other equipment, the Dataproducts device does have the capability of performing significant print runs. The printer's appeal and success has been proportionately greater in the US than here. This reinforces the view that the American market is less picky about its output quality and more likely to use a LZR 2665 to perform the entire task through typesetting and printing rather than turning to professional typesetting equipment. That said, the Dataproducts laser printer certainly has its place here about, given the A3 option and increased throughput speeds. The Dataproducts LZR 2665 A3 costs about. £14,000.

Page description languages

Any discussion of desktop output would be incomplete without drawing attention to the benefits of page description languages. Not only do the majority of successful page layout software packages all support a PDL (and those that do not have very little appeal) but laser manufactures such as Hewlett Packard are in the process of developing a laser device offering a resident PDL.

The demarcation between Postscript (or PDL in general) laser printers and those without a page description language should be understood. This is absolutely fundamental since any system without a PDL will have:

1. severe fount limitations
2. difficulty accessing industry standard founts
3. less flexibility in terms of output devices

More resilient print engines

Ricoh (previously of daisywheel fame) have recently developed the 4080 print engine which offers far greater resilience than the canon. While monthly throughput using the Canon engine was reckoned to be 3000 pages (if the machine were to sustain a three year life), the Ricoh is considered to allow 5000 pages per month over the same period. Sharp have also developed a print engine which is geared to greater resilience, not only to provide for a longer or more productive life, but also to cut down on maintenance charges by extending the period between overhauls.

Xerox are also offering a print engine which has been adopted by both QMS and Imagen, though the latter continue to use the Canon for their low-end devices. Imagen printers support the Impress PDL, whilst QMS have taken the safe route opted for Postscript.

Apple recently announced UK distribution of Laser Connection's PS-Jet, a product that adds Postscript capabilities to Canon-based laser printers. The unit replaces the top cover assembly and is apparently user-installable. It enables the upgraded printer to become fully LaserWriter compatible and includes Times, Helvetica, Symbol and Courier typefaces. Any Postscript software, either DOS or Macintosh based, can be benefit from this enhancement.

Xerox 4045

The Xerox 4045, as supplied with Xerox's Documenter DTP system, is worthy of mention since it is the only laser printer that doubles as a photocopier. A reader resides on top of the unit through which the original copy is run. In offering this option Xerox are cutting down on the use to which the print engine is subject, in addition to freeing up the printer in the event of multiple copy runs. With a standard resolution of 300 dpi, the 4045 uses a combination of 'Bitstream' fount cartridges and the Interpress PDL to build up pages.

Third generation laserprinters

Given the apparent need within the computer industry to categorise everything in terms of generations, it may shed light on past and future developments of PC-based laser devices to follow this example. The first generation encompasses the LaserJet lookalikes, 300dpi printers offering limited fount flexibility and limited graphics output; in short the daisywheel replacements.

The second generation covers those printers also operating at 300dpi but offering page description language support, expanded memory to allow for full page graphics printing and ideally access to industry standard typefaces.

The third generation will reflect the growing trend towards increased resilience, allowing more use of the device for larger print runs. In

Peripherals and add-ons

addition, it seems likely that we will witness a move away from the Motorola 68000 microprocessor adopted by both Apple and Dataproducts. The latter recently set the trend by moving to National Semiconductor's 32000 family in their LZR 2630. The NS 32000 provides more powerful bit manipulation capabilities for graphics output, faster processing and hence less waiting around whilst Postscript or whichever PDL is in use re-creates the page for printing.

Colour laser printing

Colour laser printing, thought by the pundits to be the next major development on the cards, is in reality far out of reach of the desktop publisher. Whilst the technology exists, it is currently too expensive for the broad PC market. Until such time as the more sophisticated DTP systems are able to perform colour separation, the average user will no doubt remain content with monochrome. Coloured toner cartridges are available for laser printers using the standard print engines so multiple pass printing could theoretically achieve at least limited and rudimentary spot colour output.

Increased resolution

Undoubtedly the most dramatic change to emerge in the third generation laser printer is an increase in resolution. Canon and Ricoh already have print engines capable of 400 dpi and 600 dpi output so printers of this resolution will be with us in due course. Undoubtedly the existing and quite distinct, lines of demarcation between professional typesetting and desktop publishing, will become increasingly nebulous and perhaps arbitrary. But as we have explained elsewhere, progress towards high resolution laserprinters involves considerable technical difficulties and may be slower than we wish.

A4 screens

Despite its good resolution the Macintosh nine inch screen has been a cause of considerable criticism. Yet one of the Macintosh's strengths is its small footprint (9" x 9") and the minimum desk space it occupies. The apparent dilemma has been overcome by the availability of add-on big screens which can be simply disconnected when not in use. The success of desktop publishing has made the need for larger screens more pressing in particular screens of true A4 size obviously help the page layout process since far less scrolling is necessary when working on a bigger display.

Competition from Xerox's Documenter, which is supplied with either a 19" or 15" monochrome paper white display has lead to Apple's recent announcement that their new open architecture Macintosh II will incorporate a standard 12" monitor with the option for larger add-on screens. In the meantime existing Macintosh users must content themselves with third party add-on products involving extra expense and rendering the built-in screen redundant.

The first big screen available for the Macintosh was the MegaScreen, a 19" paper white display, allowing for a resolution of up to 1024 x 1024 pixels. Costing around £2500 including graphics display card, the MegaScreen is expensive, but was until relatively recently the only option available. Sadly not all Macintosh software is supported. MacPaint, for example, employs only a portion of the screen and offers no benefit to the user. This is a constraint found in some of the earlier Macintosh software. It is essential, therefore, in considering the purchase of a large screen that the software to be used takes full advantage of the additional size. We found the MegaScreen ideal when using PageMaker and other DTP software.

The Radius screen is true A4 size and priced at £ 2000 offers a practical aid to the dedicated DTP user. As with the MegaScreen not all Macintosh software can benefit from the larger display area. PageMaker, Ready Set Go3 and the majority of page make-up software will, however, make full use of the Radius screen.

The open architecture of the IBM PC lends itself to the addition of specialist screens. Hence the choices facing the IBM DTP user are far wider than those available to the Macintosh fraternity.

Micro Display Systems' Genius full page display offers a resolution of 1008 x 736, or 100 dpi, an improvement over the resolution of IBM's Enhanced Graphics Adaptor.. The screen area measures 10" x 8" and displays 66 lines. The Genius supports the majority of DOS-based DTP, graphics and WP software. Priced at around £1800, the monitor is supplied with its own VHR display adaptor, which is used in place of an EGA or Hercules card.

Wyse have produced a low-cost-high resolution screen with the DTP user in mind. The Wyse 700 produces a resolution of 1280 x 800 when fitted with its own graphics adaptor. Despite being produced with a standard 15" display area, the high resolution and low price - £900 including graphics board - makes the Wyse an attractive proposition.

It has become apparent that future developments in the DTP arena will take into account the desktop publisher's insistence on the large/high-resolution screen. Remember, the higher the screen resolution the more readily you will really see what you are getting and the sooner we can get away from WYSI(almost)WYG.

10
DTP as a typesetting front-end

The single most significant advantage in front ending a phototypesetting with a DTP system is cost; the equally significant disadvantage lies in functionality. It is in finding a balance between the two that the publisher can capitalise on the convergence of the two technologies.

In previous chapters we have concerned ourselves with the concept of desktop publishing within the traditional PC environment. We have considered it as a tool for production of documents from inception to finished output, or at least to the stage of CRC. We have also considered it in the light of perhaps one or two users.

The professional typesetter generally requires a grander approach and in an editorial office the front end must offer easy access for editing. It is undesirable that the entire production process be dependent on the movement of floppy disks, a cumbersome procedure. Thus if desktop publishing is to be of any value to the larger publishing organisation it must provide for distributed operation.

Distributed desktop

A distributed system is one which supports a variety of users, some or all of whom may be performing dicreet tasks in the overall production process. Implicit is the notion of connectivity via a set of communication links operating at both local and remote levels the latter being acheived throught the use of modems and telephone lines.

True flexibility also demands that users with varying roles in the publication process, may not require identical equipment. Copy can be *generated* on any system that has communications links to the composition department although page make-up can only be performed by users of the same system and same application software.

Hard copy can be produced on a laser printer for proofing before being sent down to the typesetter for final output.

Various typesetter manufacturers were quick to respond to the opportunities presented by desktop publishing and set about modifying their equipment to accommodate input from these systems. The PC and application software vendors in turn enhanced their products to accommodate typeset output. Ultimately the latter are moving, albeit slowly, to a position of output device independence throught the use of page description languages and specially developed output drivers. Taking as our starting point the typesetting end, let us examine some of the solutions that are currently available.

Hardware-based solutions

Linotype

Linotype were the first to jump on the DTP bandwagon. Realising the potential of the desktop publishing system as a front-end device they implemented a raster image processor to act as an interface between computer systems and the Linotype fourth generation phototypesetters.

Their RIP is effectively a PC without any direct input facilities. Designed around the Motorola 68000 chip, it includes a 17 megabyte hard disk and three input ports: Centronics (parallel), RS232 (serial) and RS422/AppleTalk. Postscript is resident in prom. The RIP outputs direct-ly to the Linotronic 100 typesetter with a maximum resolution of 1270 dpi or to the Linotronic 300 with a maximum 2540 dpi resolution. 70 typefaces are supported with a range of point sizes from $4^1/2$ - $127^1/2$ in $1/2$ point increments.

Linotype's interest was initially prompted by the success of the Macintosh system and its use of Postscript. The company took on Apple dealership in order to sell complete systems, which the traditional

DTP as a front-end

Apple dealer base was not qualified to do. Given the available output ports supported by Linotype's RIP, any system offering full Postscript support can output to the 100 and 300 typesetters.

We have shown below a configured distributed DTP system based on Linotype (see illustration 11).

Monotype

Monotype's Lasercomp range of typesetters accept input from over 60 front-end systems though few of these would fall into the DTP category. Development carried out in conjunction with the Macintosh has been on the Blaser system.

Blaser is a high-quality, laser-based imagesetter which permits output to bromide or flexible plate. Input ports provided are RS232, RS422 and parallel. Blaser supports a combination of Monotype and Stempel/Mergenthaler typefaces, ranging from 6-96 point in increments of one tenth, one eighth and one quarter. Blaser provides an output resolution of 1000 scan lines per inch. Images can be accepted through the Blaserscan, a 300 dpi scanner, or the Logoscanner Plus, a 200 dpi scanner. Both devices are A4 flatbed CCD scanners based on Ricoh and Burroughs machines respectively.

Blaserdriver is the software that allows the Macintosh to output from many of its standard application packages at high resolution. Macintosh software requires no enhancements or changes to existing operating proceedures.

The Macintosh is connected directly to the RS232 port, and thus cannot operate in conjunction with AppleTalk in a peripheral-sharing capacity.

Laserdriver is the software that enables the Macintosh to output directly to the standard Lasercomp typesetter. In the event that throughput demands increase, the addition of the Lasercomp Input Processor will act as a glorified buffer, allowing the Lasercomp to process the next job as the current one is being exposed. The Lasercomp Input Processor includes a buit-in RIP, 128K RAM and 80 megabytes of disk storage.

Software based solutions

In addition to typesetter vendors modifying their equipment to accommodate a DTP front-end, many software packages are being

**Illustration 11.
Linotype distributed system**

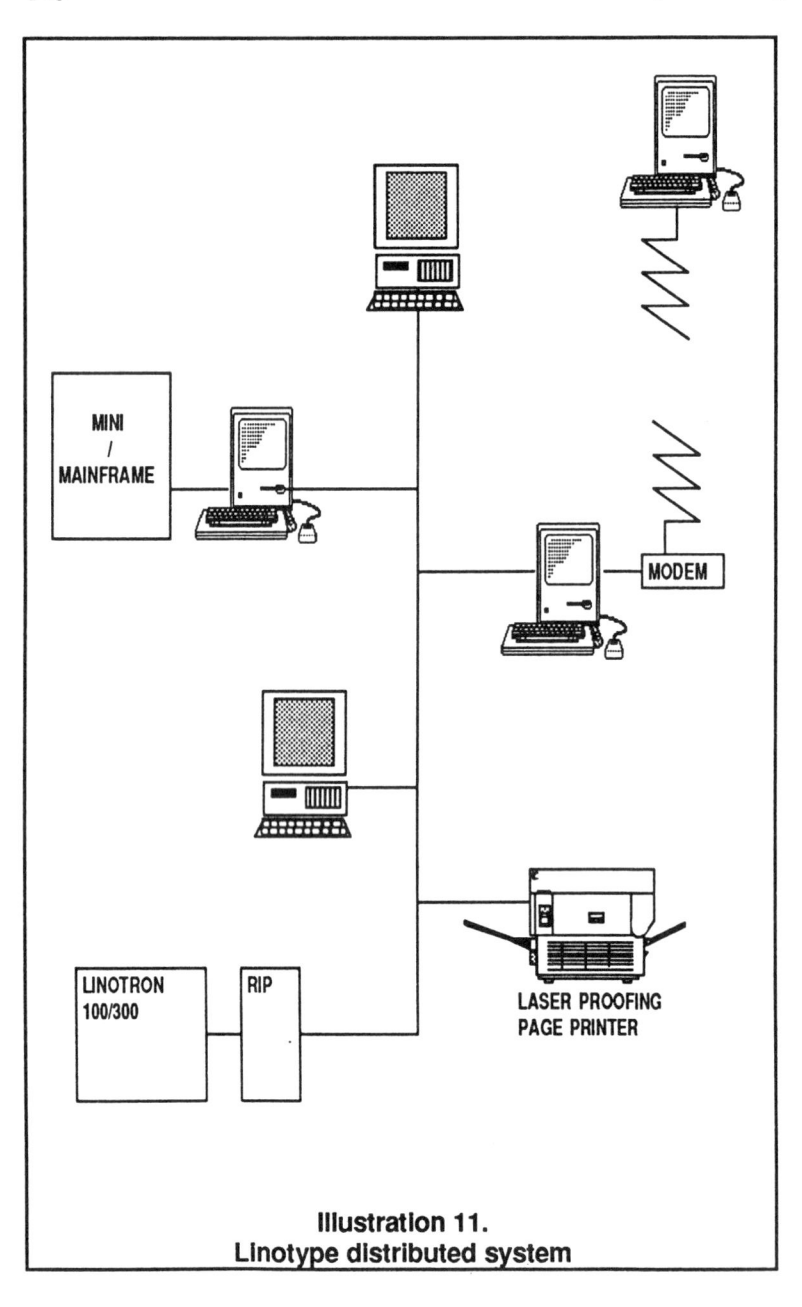

developed to allow typesetter device-independence. That they run on PCs and output to low-cost laserprinters warrants their inclusion in this chapter. In general the cost of such portable software will be considerably higher than the standard PC composition package. Currently the majority of packages are based around a specific typesetter and may well have borrowed the command language of the output device.

MagnaType

MagnaType is a MS DOS-based package, developed for the IBM PC and compatibles that is almost unique in the MS DOS environment in that it allows multitasking. A job can be output while the operator is simultaneously inputting, composing or editing the next.
The package offers comprehensive functionality. A sample of the features is given below:

> 1. Interactive H&J. Five level hyphenation dictionary including user-expandable word dictionary, 99 secondary exception word dictionaries and six foreign language dictionaries. In addition discretionary hyphenation and algorithms are supported.
> 2. Four-level tracking, up to 1500 kern pair combinations per fount.
> 3. Embedded codes define composition, through a simple command structure. User defined codes are supported
> 4 Pagination controls include X-Y coordintaes and nested formatting.

For the purpose of this excersise, the most important attribute of the package lies in the wide choice of output drivers. Not only does Magnatype offer full PostScript and CORA support, the latter allowing output to the third generation Linotron 202, but it also drives Compugraphic, Monotype (Lasercomp and Blaser), AM and Autologic typesetters. Note, however, that it is not a WYSIWYG system but offers high-speed batch pagination to user-defined parameters.

PS Publishing's PS Compose

PS Compose is a Macintosh based composition system that makes use of a typesetting command language based on the Compugraphic MCS system. A WYSIWYG preview facility is supported and, given a large screen, you can view both the coded and the WYSIWYG pages simultaneously.

PS Compose can drive the Compugraphic 8400 typesetter and white spaces are left where graphics should be. The package does provide

Postscript drivers and offers limited graphics support. Images can be accepted from the Macintosh clipboard and scaled and cropped on screen but PS Compose handles graphics interactively and the pagination system does not allow for the pre-definition of positioning of illustrations. Postscript commands can be attatched to a graphic to allow control over contrast, brightness and tints but it cannot be previewed in WYSIWYG mode.

Archetype's Impression

Impression, like PS Compose, is able to output to the Compugraphic 8400, and is aimed as much at the typographer as the desktop publisher. Impression is a WYSIWYG MS DOS package which provides full Postscript support. Graphics are supported through Postscript but cannot be output through the Compugraphic.

As would be expected from software aimed at the typesetting front-end market, Impression offers sophisticated typographical features, over and above those normally found in typical DTP sofware. These include hanging puctuation, skewed and hung indents, H&J using algorithms, exception word dictionary and optimum spaceband values.

Impression is currently aimed at the display advertising and brochure creation market. The software is slow and currently not recommended for long-run documents.

Digital Publishing System's DMS

Display Ad Make-Up system is a Macintosh-based WYSIWYG package and, as the name implies, is aimed at the generation of display advertisments. No embedded coding is required.

DMS operates in much the same way as traditional Macintosh composition software. Rules and boxes in varying widths can be drawn directly on screen, copy is placed and positioned using the mouse. Founts, typeface attributes, point size and leading are specified through the use of the now familiar pull-down menu.

Of particular value is the 'Divide and Conquer' feature which automatically divides the screen into boxes of precise size and alignment as determined by the operator.

DMS offers full Postscript support and drivers for the following typesetters: Compugraphic (8000, 8300, 8400, 8600), Linotype (101,

202 and Postscript devices), Monotype (Blaser and Lasercomp) and Autologic APS Micro 5. No RIP is required, other than with Postscript devices, since DMS drives the typesetter by a direct cable connection. A driver for any of the above is specified at time of purchase, as is a choice of founts to be available.

T$_E$X based systems

As the move towards greater typographic control and precision gains momentum, systems such as T$_E$X are growing in popularity in the DTP arena. T$_E$X is probably the only true standard machine-independent publishing system in existence, having been successfully implemented on mainframes, minis, and PCs. As a typesetting make-up language, T$_E$X is not easy to master.

The results obtained from traditional T$_E$X-based packages (or those closely related) are generally speaking typographically more precise than the standard WYSIWYG software. Furthermore, the traditional typesetter is familiar with systems of this ilk and hence not daunted by the prospect of learning what are, to him, meaningful commands. Most recent T$_E$X products allow for a preview feature. The desktop publisher is therefore not going in blind, but has recourse to a limited WYSIWYG facility.

T$_E$X was developed by a professor of mathematics, Don Knuth, as a vehicle for producing text books. The software provides extensive support for mathematical formulae but does not offer graphics support as standard. White spaces are merely reserved on the print run, to allow traditional cut and paste thereafter.

It must be said that in general this type of software has a long document orientation, and is therefore ideal for publications such as books. As the aestheic standards of the WYSIWYG camp improve we may see a move away from software requiring embedded codes and typesetting make-up languages but for the present they have a part to play.

The following T$_E$X packages are currently available for PC systems:

Addison-Wesley T$_E$Xtures. A Macintosh-based package conforming to standard T$_E$X composition. Non-editable WYSIWYG screen preview facility, including option to view images. The latter cannot be output but the facility allows precise sizing of space allocated for the graphic.

Postscript devices are supported and by extension the entire range of LaserWriter founts in addition to Computer Modern founts.

Addison Wesley MicroT$_E$X. An IBM PC XT or AT version of the Macintosh product. Optional drivers are available for the Hewlett Packard Laserjet. It also offers dot matrix output, which is not really in keeping with a composition system as sophisticated as T$_E$X.

FTL Systems MacT$_E$X. A Macintosh program conforming to standard T$_E$X conventions with a non-editable preview option. Graphics can be entered in the form of Postscript command text, embedded directly into the document. In addition MacPaint images can be included in a document and thereafter cropped, scaled and positioned.

Future of the front end

Throughout 'The Publisher's Guide to Desktop Publishing' we have described the strengths and weaknesses of software and hardware and the disparate facilities available in today's market place. All technologies evolve, of course, but this development of typesetting methodology is in a very real sense a technology in transition.

It is also in some considerable degree a pattern of converging technologies: microcomputer hardware, text processing software, laser developments, electrostatic printing and chemistry, and so on. We appear to have reached a stage where each discreet advance in one area facilitates a move forward in other parts of the system. We expect this exponential growth of technical offerings to continue for some time to come. Limitations are essentially transient in this business in the 1980s; we expect them to disappear one by one.

If you want a WYSIWYG system which can handle all conceivable typographical niceties and can batch paginate at a rate of knots, you'll have it before long. If you want a plain paper output device which can produce an image at an acceptable resolution for ordinary commercial printing purposes, can handle large size sheets and run fast enough to be used as a press... wait a bit and it will be with you.

Meanwhile we all have to earn a living with the tools available to us now. And we think DTP is just about ready for that.

Useful names and addresses

Listed below are some useful contacts, together with their main products and/or services. We have supplied company name, address, product type, product name and operating environment. The code 'PS' denotes Postscript support.

Software Products

Aldus (UK) Ltd
   031 336 1727
   Craigscrook Castle
   Craigscrook Road
   Edinburgh EH4 3UH
   Page Composition S/w
   PageMaker
   Mac/MS DOS/PS

Archetype Inc
   (617) 482 2739
   179 South Street
   Boston
   MA 02111, USA
   Page composition s/w
   First Impression
   MS DOS/PS

Bristol Office Machines
   0272 299201
   Page composition s/w
   Clue
   MS DOS

Cognita Software Ltd
   01 221 7621
   34 Mallard Street
   London SW3 6DU
   Page composition s/w
   Newswriter
   MS DOS

Digital Publishing Systems
   0268 23471
   Acorn House
   Great Oaks
   Basildon
   Essex
   SS14 1AH
   Advertising make-up s/w
   Display Ad Make-up (DMS)
   Mac/PS

Icon Technology
   0533 556268
   Leicester Computer Centre Ltd
   9 Jarrom Street
   Leicester
   LE2 7DH
   WP/Page make-up
   MacAuthor
   Mac/PS

Interleaf Inc
   (617) 577 9800
   Ten Canal Park
   Cambridge
   MA 02141
   USA
   Page composition s/w
   Interleaf WPS/TPS
   Unix/Ultrix

LaserMaker Ltd
  0602 731803
  West Gate
  Long Eaton
  Notts
  NG10 1EF
  Page composition s/w
  LaserMaker
  MS DOS/PS

Lotus Development Corporation
  Consort House
  Victoria Street
  Windsor
  Berkshire
  SL4 1EX
  Technical document processing
  Integrated software
    (business graphics)
  Manuscript
  Jazz, Lotus 1-2-3, Symphony
  Mac/MS DOS/PS

Mac Europe Ltd
  01 904 4313
  9A Lyne Court
  Church Lane
  London NW9
  Page composition s/w
  Just Text
  Mac/PS

MacSerious Company
  041 332 5622
  17 Park Circus
  Glasgow
  G3 6AH
  Mac s/w
  Silicon Beach's SuperPaint
  Mac/PS

Microsoft
  0734 500741
  Excel House
  49 De Montfort Road
  Reading
  RD1 8LP
  User interface
  WP/spreadsheet/graphics
  Windows
  Word, Excel
  Mac/MS DOS/PS

Microspot
  0622 858753
  9 High Street
  Lenham
  Maidstone
  Kent
  Plotter driver
  Imagewriter Colour driver
  MacPlot
  MacPalette
  Mac/PS

Mirrorsoft Ltd
  01 377 4644
  Maxwell House
  74 Worship Street
  London
  EC2A 2EN
  Page composition s/w
  Fleet Street Publisher
  Fleet Street Editor
  MS DOS

Useful names and addresses

Orange Micro Inc,
(714) 779 2772
1400 N Lakeview Avenue
Anaheim
CA 92807
USA
Integrated page processing
(WP, spreadsheet, graphics, make-up)
Ragtime
Mac/PS

Paintbox Computers
0703 760359
Page composition s/w
Studio Software's Frontpage
(DDL, Intepress, PS)
MS DOS/PS

Prefis
0920 5890
Page composition s/w
Book Machine
(supports CORA)
MS DOS

Samna International
01 587 1121
Southbank House
Black Prince Road
London
SE1 7SJ
Enhanced WP
Samna 1V
MS DOS

Software Publishing
01 839 3864
87 Jermyn Street
London
SW1Y 6JD
Page composition s/w
Graphics S/w
Harvard Professional Publisher
Harvard Presentation Graphics
MS DOS/PS

Talbot Computer Ltd
0202 519282
293 Charminster Road
Bournemouth
Dorset
BH8 9QW
Page composition s/w
Dialtext
Mac/PS

Unixsys UK Ltd
0925 827834
The Genesis Centre
Garrett Field
Science Park South
Birchwood
Warrington
Cheshire WA3 7BH
Page composition s/w
Softquad
Unix

WordCraft International
0206 561608
Cowdray Centre House
Cowdray Avenue
Colchester
Essex CO1 1GH
Enhanced WP
Wordcraft
MS DOS

Hardware and software products

Apple Computers UK Ltd
  0442 60244
  Eastman Way
  Hemel Hempstead
  Herts HP2 7HQ
  PC
  Macintosh
  LaserWriter
  Mac
Applied Technology Marketing
  0642 225854
  2g CADCAM Centre
  Middlesbrough
  Cleveland TS2 1RJ
  Scanner
  Abaton scanner, C scan s/w
  Mac/MS DOS
Apricot Computers PLC
  021 456 1234
  Desktop Publishing Division
  Apricot House
  111 Hagley Road
  Edgbaston
  Birmingham B16 8LB
  Total DTP system
  MS DOS
Canon (UK) Ltd
  01 773 3173
  Canon House
  Manor Road
  Wallington
  Surrey SM6 0AJ
  Total DTP system
  Scanner
  Canon Personal Publishing
    System
  Canon IX-12 300 dpi scanner
  MS DOS

Compugraphic (UK) Ltd
  0937 61944
  Sandbeck Way
  Weatherby
  West Yorkshire LS22 4DN
  Typesetter
  Page composition s/w
  Compugraphic Phototypesetters
  MCS, GO Graphic's DeskSet
  Mac/PS
Computers Unlimited
  01 349 2395
  246 Regents Park Road
  London N3 3HP
  Large screen
  MecaScreen
  Mac/PS
Dataproducts Limited
  0734 884777
  Unit 1
  Heron Industrial Estate
  Spencers Wood
  Reading
  Berkshire RG7 1PJ
  Laser Printer A4
  Laser Printer A3
  LZR 2665 A3
  LZR 2665 A4
  PS
Digital Equipment Corporation
  0734 868711
  DEC Park
  Reading RG2 0TR
  Total electronic/Desktop
    publishing
  DecPage, Interleaf, Pagemaker
  MicroVax
  MS DOS/UNIX/PS

Useful names and addresses

Esselte Letraset
 01 379 0323
 3 Bedford Street
 London WC2E
 Total DTP system
 Page composition s/w
 Letraset page & print
 Ready Set Go Three
 Mac/PS
Gestetner Ltd
 01 387 7021
 Desktop Publishing Division
 210 Euston Road
 London NW1 2D
 Forms generation s/w
 Gestetner DTP Sytem
 Formation
 Mac/PS
Heydon & Son
 01 203 5171
 Spectrum house
 Hillview Gardens
 London NW4 2JQ
 Video Digitiser
 Graphics
 Magic, Cricket Graph
 Mac
IBM UK Ltd
 0926 32525
 Engineering, Scientific and
  Industrial Centre
 Birmingham Road
 Warwick CV34 5JL
 Page composition s/w
 PCs, and Unix system
 Interleaf RT Publishing
  Software
 IBM PC, IBM 6150 - PC RT
 MS DOS/UNIX

Lexisystems Ltd
 0373 61446
 Apex House
 West End
 Frome
 Somerset BA11 3AS
 Scanner/Optical Character Reader
 Dest PC Scan
 MS DOS
Linotype Ltd
 0242 518288
 Chelham House
 Bath Road
 Cheltenham
 Gloucestershire GL53 7LR
 Typesetters
 RIP
 Linotronic 100 and 300 Imagesetters
 Mac/MS DOS/PS
McQueen Ltd
 Elliot House
 8-10 Hillside Crescent
 Edinburgh
 EH7 5EA
 Scanner
 A4 Screen
 Founts
 Microtek MS 300A
 Radius A4 Screen
 Adobe (Merganthaler, ITC) Founts
 Mac/MS DOS/PS
Mekom Computer Products Limited
 021 454 2288
 Enfield Hall
 Edgbaston
 Birmingham B15 1QA
 Laser Page Printers (non Postscript)
 Kyocera F1010
 MS DOS/Prescribe

Micro Display Systems
  (800) 328 9524
  A4 Screen
  Genius hi resolution A4 monitor
  MS DOS
Monotype
  01 250 1257
  Electronic Publishing Office
  Clerks Court
  Clerkenwell Green
  18 -20 Farringdon Lane
  London
  EC1R 3AU
  Image/Typesetters
  Typesetter Drivers
  Blaser, LaserComp
  BlaserDriver
  Mac/PS
Rank Xerox (UK) Ltd
  0895 51133
  Bridge House
  Oxford Road
  Uxbridge
  Middlesex
  UB8 1HS
  Total DTP system
  Page composition s/w
  Documentor (Interpress PDL)
  Ventura (Postscript/DDL)
  MS DOS/PS

Summagraphics Ltd
  0635 32257
  Graphics tablet
  Mouse
  Mactablet
  Summa Mouse
  Mac/MS DOS

Symbiotic Computer Systems Ltd
  0344 485611
  Courtnay House
  Waterside Park
  Western Industrial Estate
  Bracknell
  Berkshire RG12 1YZ
  SCSI hard disk
  Tape back-up Unit
  Symbfile, Symbstore
  Mac

Useful names and addresses

Other specialist contacts

Bacchus and Smith Ltd
    0491 576171
    9-11 The Fair Mile
    Henley-Upon-Thames
    Oxon
    The Postscript Language
      -Reference Manual
    The Postscript Langauage
      - Tutorial

CCA Micro Rentals Ltd
    01 731 4310
    Unit 7-8
    Imperial Road
    London SW6 2AG
    Training
    DTP Training in conjunction with
    Alfred Marks Office systems
    Mac/MS DOS

The Desktop Publishing Company Ltd
    0753 684633
    43 Hithermore Road
    Stanwell Moor
    Staines
    Middlesex TW19 6AH
    Desktop Publisher - Newsletter

Macintosh User Group UK
    0865 58027
    55 Linkside Avenue
    Oxford OX2 8JE
    Independent user group
    Mac/PS

Mandarin Publishing
    0233 39776
    The Old House
    Church Road
    Kennington
    Ashford
    Kent
    The Wordsmith

Seybold Publications Inc.
    (215) 565 2480
    PO Box 644
    Media
    PA 19063
    USA
    The Seybold Report on
      Desktop Publishing

161

Glossary

accents Marks added to letters in some languages to indicate stress, eg é (acute e) in French.
access The ability to retrieve data from a computer storage medium or peripheral device.
access time The time taken to retrieve data from a computer storage medium or a peripheral.
add-on device See **peripheral**.
address The character or string of characters identifying a unique storage location in computer memory or backing store.
algorithm An arithmetical computer routine in the form of programmed instructions which performs a recurring task.
align To line-up type, horizontally or vertically, using a typographical criterion, eg **base alignment** (qv).
alphanumeric Relating to the full alphabetic and numeric character set of a machine.
ANSI American National Standards Institute. Standards co-ordinating body similar in constitution to the **British Standards Institution** (qv).
appearing size The physical size of a type, as opposed to its nominal point size. Two type faces of the same point size can have very different appearing sizes.
applications software Programs which are applied to solve specific problems, such as business systems.
arabic figures The numerals 1, 2, 3, 4, etc, as distinguished from the Roman I, II, III, IV. Evolved from Arabic symbols.
archive To store data economically off-line for future use in a computer system.

art See **artwork**.
artwork Original illustrative copy or typesetting ready for reproduction at pre-film stage.
ascender The part of a lower case character which extends above the **x-height** (qv). As in 'b', 'd', 'f', etc. See also **descender**.
ASCII One of the most widely-used codes for representing the character set in a computer.
ASPIC The generic coding system recommended for use by the BPIF.
assembler A computer program which translates a symbolic language into **machine code** (qv). See also **assembly language**.
assembly language A computer language close to **machine code** (qv) which needs an **assembler** (qv) to translate.
asynchronous A mode of data transmission, typically used for interactive communications.
auto-kerning Automatic closing of spaces between characters where ascenders overlap the adjacent **x-height** (qv). Available on many modern photosetting systems.
automatic heading The positioning of a heading on consecutive pages by means of a generic instruction at the start of a project. Common on modern page-make-up systems.
a/w See **artwork**.

background Computer processing mode which can occur concurrently with the main use of the machine, eg hyphenation and justification of a text file while other material is being input.
backing-up See **back-up**.
back up 1. Print the reverse side of a sheet. 2.

Appendix 2

Extra standby equipment, personnel or copies of data. 3. The act of duplicating data for security purposes.
bad break Undesirable end-of-line hyphenation of a word.
base alignment Method of aligning characters of different sizes on the same line. See **base line, align.**
base line Horizontal line on which characters in a line of type appear to stand.
BASIC Beginners All-purpose Symbolic Instruction Code. A widely used high-level computer programming language.
bastard founts Non-industry standard founts.
batch Method of computer processing where input data is collected into batches before processing, as distinct from **real time** (qv).
baud Number of computer bits transmitted per second over a data communications channel.
beta test The stage at which software is tested under real conditions, prior to general release.
bf bold face (qv).
binary Numbering system using the base 2 as opposed to decimal which uses the base 10. The only digits used are 0 and 1. See also **bit.**
bit 'Binary information transfer' or 'binary digit' is the basic information unit in computer systems. Each bit is either 0 or 1. A group of bits is known as a **byte.**
bit-mapping A graphics display technique wherein each pixel (picture element) of the displayed image coresponds to one or more bits of the processor's memory. In a monochrome display the number of bits corresponding to each pixel determines the number of grey scale levels supported.
black and white Single colour black only originals or reproductions as distinguished from multicolour. Sometimes called **mono** or **monochrome.**
black box Colloquial term for an electronic device which converts one type of input into another form of output.
bleed Printed matter running off the cut edge of a page. The bleed allowance beyond the **trimmed size** is usually 3mm or ⅛in. to ensure a clean cut-off.
block Computer term for a group of **bytes** (qv) of information.
blow-up To enlarge photographically; or a print so made.
body Phototypesetting term for the size of the body of type, eg 12pt=a 12pt body.
body matter Text pages as distinct from prelims, index, display etc.
bold Heavier version of a typeface, as distinct from light or medium. Sometimes abbreviated to **bf** (bold face).
boot or **bootstrap** Computer term for necessary instruction structures where programs are loaded and activated prior to operating.
borders Decorative designs usually edging the page or type.
BPIF British Printing Industries Federation.

brackets Pair of marks ( ), [ ], used in text. Also called **parentheses.**
British Standards Institute British national co-ordinating body for technical standards in industry.
bromide Photographic light-sensitive paper used in photographic reproduction or phototypesetting, producing a positive image.
buffer Computer storage used when information needs to be held temporarily en route from one device to another.
bug An error in a program or system.
bullet Phototypesetting term for a large dot used for ornamentation.
bus In computer architecture, an internal path by which signals travel to and from various components on the system. The signals may be of a particular kind, such as 'data bus' or 'address bus'.
byte Computer term for a group of **bits** (qv).

c&sc Capitals and small capitals, ie words which begin with capitals and have the other characters in small caps the height of the lower case body size.
CAD/CAM Computer aided design/computer aided manufacturing.
camera ready artwork or **camera ready copy (CRC)** or **camera ready paste-up (CRPU)** Typematter or type and line artwork pasted up into position ready for photographing.
cap height The height of the capital letters of a fount.
caps Capitals. Upper case letters, eg A, B, C etc. See also **lower case.**
carriage return Keyboard command key which terminates a line of setting and may enter text from a computer screen into memory.
cartridge Holder for toner in a laser printer.
case See **lower case** and **upper case.**
casting off Calculating the number of pages a given amount of copy will make when set in a given type-face and size to a given area.
catch line A temporary heading in a manuscript or proof for identification.
cathode ray tube See **CRT.**
CCD Charged coupled device. A photodiode array which translates areas of dark and light into binary data.
CD-ROM Compact Disc Read-Only Memory. High density storage device.
central processing unit See **CPU.**
centre To position type centrally in a given measure.
chapter head Chapter title and/or number.
character Letter, figure or symbol of type.
character count Total number of characters and spaces in a piece of copy.
character generation Projection of type images on a cathode ray tube.
character printer A printer which prints individual characters as distinct from complete lines. Often capable of reproducing specific typefaces.
character recognition Reading characters by

Glossary of terms

machine, often for digital storage.
character set The full range of characters on a keyboard in memory or available for output from a machine.
chip A small electronic component containing extensive logic circuits, also slang word for microprocessors.
close up Reduce spacing between characters of type or other elements on a proof.
club line First line of a paragraph at the bottom of a page.
code A character string or line of symbolic instructions to a computer.
column balancing Automatic adjustment of columns to create a visual evenness.
command A computer instruction specifying an operation.
communications The electronic transfer of data between different hardware.
comp 1. To **compose** (qv). 2. A **compositor** (qv). 3. A **comprehensive:** a layout showing everything in position.
compact disc See **CD-ROM.**
compatibility A characteristic of computer equipment which permits the interchange of data and programs from one machine to another, without modification.
compiler A computer program which converts programs from one language to a language understandable by the machine.
computer typesetting The use of a computer to store and display typesetting and to perform many other functions such as hyphenation and justification.
condensed type A typeface with narrow characteristics.
configuration The arrangement of peripherals into a computer system.
contrast Wide range of tonal gradations.
converter A computer peripheral which transfers data from one medium to another.
copy Material for publication, especially manuscript for typesetting.
copyboard Holding frame for material being photographed for reproduction.
CPI Characters per inch. Unit of measurement of type in a line or information on a linear storage medium.
CP/M Control Program for microcomputers. A single-user operating system developed by Digital Research.
CPP Characters per pica. Copyfitting method using average number of characters per **pica** (qv).
CPS Characters per second. A measurement of the output speed of a phototypesetter.
CPU Central processing unit. The principal operating part of a computer.
CRC See **camera ready copy.**
crop Cut back part of an illustration to give better effect or achieve better fit.
cross-head A sub-heading ranged centrally over a column.
CRT Cathode ray tube. An electronic display device in which an electronic signal is used to modulate beams of electrons. These beams are directed on a target surface (usually a phosphorescent screen), producing a visible display, such as is used with microcomputers and third generation phototypesetters.
cursor Moveable indicator on a screen to show a location as instructed by the operator.
cut-and-paste 1. Traditional paste-up methods using scalpel and adhesive. 2. Also used for the on-screen version of the manual task. Defining an area of text or graphics, cutting or copying for subsequent insertion (pasting) into another area, page or file.

daisywheel Flat disc with characters on stalks used as the removable printing element of a letter-quality printer. Hence **daisywheel printer.**
data Information in a computer store. **Data base** or **data bank** is a collection of organised information from which categories may be selectively retrieved. **Data processing,** sometimes referred to as **DP,** is the generic term for the use of a computer to carry out business applications. **Data transmission** is the use of communications to transfer information from one machine to another.
debugging The detection and correction of errors in a computer program before it goes into use.
DCA Document content architecture. Standard IBM PC DOS text transfer file format.
DDL Document description language. A proprietary page description language developed by Imagen and recently adopted by Hewlett Packard.
dedicated An item of equipment or electronics used for only one type of application and maybe only running one program.
definition The degree of detail and sharpness in a reproduction.
delimiter Character used to denote the limit of a computer field.
descender The part of a character which descends below the base line or x-height, as in g, y and p.
diacriticals Marks above and below letters, such as accents or the cedilla.
digipad Input device on which drawn images are digitised and displayed on a VDU and/or stored in memory.
digital computer Computer which uses numbers to represent and manipulate data. **Digital fount** is a typeface fount converted to digital form for storage on magnetic medium.
digitise To scan a subject and place the information into computer memory for subsequent regeneration.
digitiser See **digipad.**
direct access Use of a storage medium which can access information without the need for sequential searching, eg a disk as compared with a cassette.
disk 1. Circular glass typefount used in some second generation photosetters. 2. Computer storage device available in various sizes and giving direct access to the information it contains. **Disk drive** is the unit which rotates the disk in use.

discretionary hyphen Hyphen inserted by keyboard and which overrides the hyphenation program in use.

DOS Abbreviated from **MS-DOS**.

dot The individual element from which a halftone reproduction is made up.

double density disk A **floppy disk** (qv) which can store twice as much information as its 'single density' counterpart.

double-sided disks Disks which can store information on both sides.

double spread Print going across two facing pages.

downtime Non-productive computer time resulting from hardware, software or power failure.

dpi Dots per inch. A measurement of resolution, mainly associated with output devices using xerographic techniques.

draft quality output Low-quality high-speed wp printer output from dot-matrix printer. See also **NLQ, letter quality output**.

driver Computer routine or device which handles communication between CPU and peripherals.

drop caps Drop capitals. Letters at the beginning of a paragraph which extend beyond the depth of the rest of the text line. Also called **drop initials**.

dropped heads Chapter headings positioned a few lines below the top of full text pages.

DTP Desktop publishing.

dummy Mock-up of a book or other piece of printing to indicate specifications.

dump Transfer a computer file into or out of storage.

EBCDIC Extended Binary Coded Decimal Information Code. The IBM code.

edit Check, re-arrange and correct data or copy before final presentation.

electronic composition Computer-assisted page make-up.

electronic mail Transfer of documents or messages between computers or word processors using direct links, telecommunications or satellites.

electronic publishing The publication and circulation of information in electronic rather than printed form.

elite Small size of typewriter type: 12 characters per inch.

em 1. Width of the body of the lower case 'm' in any typeface. 2. Standard unit of measurement (also called 'pica'). One em equals 0.166044 inches.

embedded codes Instructions signifying format and typeface criteria, not displayed on-screen.

emulation The imitation of one system's code-set by another such that the two may communicate.

en Half the width of an **em** (qv). Is the width of the average type character, and so is used as the basic unit of measurement for casting off copy.

end-of-line decisions Decisions on hyphenation or justification made either by the operator or automatically by the typesetting system.

ergonomics The study of equipment design in the context of man/machine interface, with the express purpose of reducing operator fatigue and discomfort, and to ensure maximum operating conditions.

escape code Code which signals a change of mode from, say, text to function symbols.

even pages Left-hand, or verso, pages, with even numbers.

exception dictionary Computer store of words which do not hyphenate in accordance with the machine's rules of logic.

execute The function that initiates performance of user-specified operations.

exclusive type area Type area exclusive of headline and folio.

expanded type Typeface with characters wider than the normal roman fount.

extended type See **expanded**.

extent Length of a book in pages.

extract Quoted matter within a text, often set indented and in a smaller type size.

face 1. The printing surface of a piece of type. 2. A style of type, ie typeface.

facing pages Pages which face each other in an open book or magazine.

facsimile 1. Exact reproduction of a document or part of it. 2. Machine which copies and transmits documents by telecommunications. Hence **facsimile transmission**.

family A series of **founts** related to the basic text roman face.

FAX See **facsimile**.

feeder The mechanism on a press or printer which separates and lifts sheets into the printing position.

field A predefined area of a computer record.

figure A line illustration referred to in the text of a book.

file A collection of related computer records.

fill pattern A choice of patterns and shades used to fill objects created under most WYSIWYG graphics packages. Originally a MacDraw/MacPaint feature, now emulated by other software packages.

Finder Macintosh operating system.

firmware Software which is necessary for the general routines of a computer and which cannot be changed by the user. Usually held in **ROM** (qv).

first generation Early photosetters modelled after hot metal machines and largely mechanical in operation.

fit Space between letters which can be reduced or expanded.

fixed space The amount of space between letters and words which cannot be varied for justification needs.

flag An indicator in a program which marks the position of data or signals a condition to the program.

flatbed scanner A scanning device wherein the scanning element is moved over a fixed

Glossary of terms

page. As distinct from the most common method, where the page moves over a fixed scanning element.

floating accents Accents which are not tied to a given character in a type fount and can therefore be positioned over any letter.

floppy disk Small flexible plastic disk widely used for magnetic storage of information on micro computers.

flowchart Diagram showing the sequence of steps in a computer program.

flowing The entering of text into a preformatted page such that it continues to fill out columns and/or pages until a rule or image is encountered, or until text is exhausted.

flush left/right Type aligned with either the left or right-hand margins.

folio Page number at the head or foot of a page of text.

font American spelling of **fount** (qv).

foot Bottom of a book or page.

footer See **foot**.

footnotes Notes explanatory to the main text, set in smaller type at the bottom of the page.

format 1. The physical specification for a page or a book. 2. Frequently occurring set of typographical commands stored as a code on a phototypesetter.

Forth A very compact, flexible programming language, mainly used in the microcomputer environment.

fount A complete set of sorts all of the same type-face and point size.

fourth generation Photosetters using lasers to expose characters.

front end An input/output processor that is used to format and/or process input data, eg the parts of a photosetting system used before input to a slave typesetting or printing machine.

function codes Codes which control the function of a phototypesetter rather than generating characters.

galley 1. Shallow tray used to hold a column of type. 2. Proof pulled from a galley of type. 3. Proof of continuous (unpaged) type.

generic coding Coding the structure of a document rather than its typographical constituents.

gigo Garbage in, garbage out. Programmers' slang to describe bad output caused by faulty data.

global search and replace The facility of a computer program to find all examples of a word or group of words in a file and replace them with an alternative.

glossary Alphabetically arranged list of terms and their meanings.

grainy Photographic film or print with coarse 'grain' visible usually due to high speed of film.

grammage Weight of paper expressed as grams per square metre.

graphic display terminal VDU capable of displaying pictures in line or tone.

graphics Pictures and illustrations in printed work.

graphics insertion Text and pictures photoset in one operation.

graphics tablet Calibrated tablet on which, using a **light-pen** (qv), an operator brings together components of a design and fixes them electronically in their correct positions according to the required layout.

grid Sheet with ruled lines used to ensure square make-up of photocomposed material.

guideline Line on artwork indicating the printing area.

gutter Binding margin of a book.

h&j Hyphenation and justification.

half-tone Illustration created by dots of varying size, resulting in the appearance of 'continuous tone'. Therefore, **half-tone negative** and **half-tone positive**.

handbill Publicity sheet, normally printed on one side only, for delivery by hand.

handout See **handbill**.

hanging indent Typesetting style in which the first line of a paragraph is set full out and the remainder are indented, as in this glossary.

hard copy Copy written, typed or printed as distinct from stored in electronic form.

hardware Computer term for equipment as distinct from programs.

head Top-or top margin-of a page.

header See **headline**.

headline A displayed line or lines at the top of a page or a piece of text. See also **running headline**.

head margin The white space above first line on a page.

heading See **headline**.

host 1. Main central processing unit in a multi-computer system. 2. Holder of an on-line database.

house style See **style of the house**.

hyphenation logic Programming to break words according to grammatical rules where necessary at line ends.

hyphenless justification Justification without breaking words. On narrow measures this creates widely varying spacing characteristics.

icons Meaningful pictorial representations of computer related and everyday items.

impact printer Printer where the printing element strikes the paper through a ribbon, eg daisy wheel or golfball.

indent Set type further in from the left-hand margin than the standard measure of surrounding text.

index Alphabetical list of subjects contained in the text of a work, together with their page numbers.

inferior Small character set below the base line at the foot of another character.

information retrieval Holding text in an electronic file so that it may be accessed by a computer.

initial First letter in text when set in such a way

that it stands out, eg bigger than its normal cap text size.
initialise Run a program which sets up a storage medium such as a floppy disc to be compatible with the system in use.
inkjet printer A non-impact printer using inkjet technology to reproduce text and images.
in-house print department See **in-plant**.
in-plant Printing department within commercial organisation.
input 1. Data going into a CPU. 2. The process of entering data into a processing system or a peripheral device, or the data that is entered.
instruction Order in a program telling a computer to carry out an operation.
interactive Computer system used in real time so that the operator can issue commands which affect the processing.
interface The link between parts of a computer system, varying from a simple cable to an 'intelligent' device which translates protocol.
interlinespacing Leading; space between lines in photocomposition of text.
International Standards Organisation (ISO) The organisation which coordinates the drawing-up of internationally accepted standards.
Interpress Rank Xerox's proprietary page description language. Recently adopted by ICL.
I/O Input/Output Relating to systems which can input and output to and from a computer.
ISO sizes Formerly **DIN sizes** (qv). International range of paper and envelope sizes, comprising **A series, B series** and **C series**.
italic Letters that slope forward.

justification The spacing of words to a predetermined measure, giving 'straight' left and right margins.

K Measure of computer storage. K=1024 computer words but often used loosely as 1000.
kern Part of a typographic character projecting beyond the body.
key Keyboard text.
keyboard The array of keys used to input into a system.
keyboard equivalents Keyboard controls, intended to be used instead of mouse commands. Found in software adhering to the WIMP convention.
keystroke One key depression, often used as a measure of productivity of an operator.

LAN See **local area network**.
landscape Illustration that is wider than it is deep, as distinct from **portrait**.
language Computer communication medium using words which translate into machine code, eg BASIC, COBOL etc.
laser Acronym for light amplification by stimulated emission of radiation. Concentrated light beam with narrow width used in creating images, engraving etc.
layout Sketch of a book or other publication, showing the plan to work to.
leader Row of dots used to lead the eye across a page.
lead-in The introduction in a piece of setting, often in a bold or different face.
leading The spacing between lines of type (strips of lead in metal composition).
leaf Single sheet, comprising two pages.
legend Caption.
legibility The ease with which a page, design or typeface can be read.
Letraset Proprietary name of sheets of transfer lettering.
letter-fit Spacing between characters in a typeface.
letter quality output Slow-speed, good-quality wp printer output, typical of daisy-wheel printers.
letterspace Space between letters.
ligature Two or more letters joined together on one body.
lightface Lighter version of a roman typeface.
line copy Copy which has no gradation of tones, ie comprising solid black lines or shapes. Also **line drawings, line engraving** etc.
line feed Vertical depth creation in photosetting.
line overlay Line work on overlay separate from half-tone.
line printer Output device which prints one line at a time usually with non-letter-quality resolution.
linespacing Space between lines of photoset type.
lining figures Arabic numerals the same height as capitals. As distinct from **non-lining** or **old-style figures** (qv).
Linotron Name for high-speed cathode ray tube phototypesetting machines manufactured by Linotype.
Linotype Linecasting machine manufactured by Linotype.
listing Computer print-out of data or a file.
literal Mistake introduced in keyboarding, often only affecting one or two characters.
local area network A data network implemented with direct links between terminals (PCs) within a restricted geographical area.
long run A high printing number for a job.
lower case Small letters as distinct from capitals. Abbreviated as **lc**.

M abbreviation for 1000.
machine code Primary code used by the computer's processor.
machine language Language understood by a computer without translation. See also **machine code**.
magnetic tape Narrow tape magnetically coated for the storage in serial form of computer data.
mainframe Large computer.

Glossary of terms

make-up Making-up typeset material into pages.
manuscript Abbreviated to **MS**. Typed or handwritten copy for setting.
margins Areas of white space left around printed matter on a page.
mark up Instructions on a layout or copy for the compositor to follow when typesetting or making up pages.
Master page Column grids and format elements that will appear on every page. Different formats can be assigned for verso and recto pages.
MB Abbreviation for **megabyte** (qv).
measure Length of a line of type.
mechanical Camera-ready paste-up.
media converter Device which reads from one medium (normally a disk) and translates its content in order to output to another medium (often a disk). See also **multi-disk reader**.
megabyte One million computer bytes or, more loosely, one million characters.
memory Internal storage of a computer.
menu List of optional procedures displayed at the start of a program.
menu-driven Software program laid out in the initial form of a number of questions to which the operator replies in order to action the program.
merge Combine two or more files into one.
metric system The decimal system of measurement.
microcomputer Small computer, usually without multi-user capabilities.
microprocessor A semiconductor component, or group of components containing extensive circuits and which implement the central processor of the computer.
mini See **minicomputer**.
minicomputer Originally a computer that physically went within a single cabinet. Positioned between the mainframe and micro in terms of speed and processing power. Traditionally dedicated to single tasks, and based around proprietary CPU architecture. Today, it serves the same data processing functions as the micro.
misprint Typographical error.
mock-up A layout or rough of artwork. Also called **visual**.
modem or **M**odulator/**Dem**odulator Device which converts analogue communication (eg telephone transmission) into digital form and vice versa.
modern figures See **lining figures**.
modular Hardware system capable of being expanded by adding on compatible devices.
monitor Screen which displays the operations of a machine in real time.
mono See **black and white**.
monochrome One colour.
monotone Illustrative material in one colour.
Monotype Proprietary name of a 'hot metal' typecasting machine which assembles characters individually rather than line-by-line.

montage Several images assembled into one piece of artwork.
mouse Small electronic puck which may be moved laterally and vertically on a plain flat surface to control the movement of a cursor on a VDU screen.
MS See **manuscript**.
MS-DOS Microsoft's Disk Operating System. The operating system of IBM PC clones. See also **DOS** and **PC-DOS**.
multi-disk reader Machine which reads a variety of disks in different formats and translates their content to output disks.
multiplexor Device enabling communication between central storage and peripherals.
multiprocessing Computer operation of several tasks simultaneously.
multitasking Performing several tasks simultaneously, using a single processor.
multi-user Computer system allowing multiple users access to the same machine, software and data files.

negative Reverse photographic image on film.
newspaper lines per minute Standard measure of photosetter speeds. Specifically, output measured in 8pt lines to an 11em measure.
NLQ Near Letter Quality. Used to describe fair-quality output from higher-density dot-matrix printers. Between **draft quality** and **letter quality** output (qv).
non-lining figures See **old-style figures**.

oblique Slanted roman characters.
OCR Optical Character Recognition The interpretation of typewritten characters by a machine which scans the text and stores it in memory, often for subsequent typesetting.
OCR paper High-quality bond suitable for optical character recognition equipment.
off-line Mode of computer peripheral operation in which equipment is not physically linked to a CPU and must be operated through an intermediate medium.
offset Printing which uses an intermediate medium to transfer the image on to paper, eg a rubber blanket wrapped around a cylinder as in offset litho.
old-style figures Also called **non-lining figures.** Numerals which do not align on the base line but have ascenders and descenders. As distinct from **modern** or **lining figures.**
on-demand publishing The concept of printing books one at a time from computer store 'on demand', rather than tying up capital by printing for stock.
on-line Connected direct to a central processing unit and communicating with it.
operation Result of a computer command.
optical character recognition See **OCR**.
optical letterspacing Space between letters which accommodates their varying shapes and gives the appearance of even space.
orientation Positioning of matter on a page. Choices are **portrait** (tall) or **landscape** (wide).

original Photograph or drawing to be reproduced.
origination All the processes involved in the reproduction of original material, including make-up, up to plate-making stages; and also including typesetting.
outline Typeface comprising only an outline with no 'solid' area.
output Data or any form of communication coming.out of a computer after processing.
outwork Operations put out to another company for reasons of specialism or capacity.

package Set of software bought 'off-the-shelf' rather than specifically written for a purpose.
page One side of a leaf.
page description language Type of computer language used as a mechanism for controlling output. Creates device independence, since any output device supporting a specific page description language can accept composed pages from any software with the corresponding driver and produce precisely the same results (albeit at a different resolution).
page make-up Assembly of the elements in a page into their final design.
page proof Proof of a page before printing.
page view terminal VDU which can display a page in its made-up form.
pagination Page numbering.
paging Scanning text on a VDU page by page.
parameter A variable set to a constant value for a specific operation.
parenthesis A round bracket.
parity bit A check bit added to a series of binary digits to make the total odd or even according to the logic of the system.
pass One run through a machine.
paste-up Dummy or artwork comprising all the elements pasted into position.
PC Personal computer. See **microcomputer.**
PC-DOS Version of Microsoft's Disk Operating System specific to the IBM PC. Slight, mainly insignificant, variations from **MS-DOS.**
PDL See **page description language.**
peculiars Special characters outside a normal fount range.
peripheral Computer input or output device which is not part of the main CPU, eg a printer.
phase encoding Method of representing phase shifts as binary information.
photocomposition Typesetting performed by a photosetter.
photocopy 1. Duplicate of a photograph. 2. Duplicate of a document, etc, produced on a copying machine.
photomechanical transfer Abbreviated to **PMT.** Paper negative which produces a positive print by a process of chemical transfer.
photosetting See **phototypesetting.**
phototypesetting Setting type on to photographic paper or film. **Phototypesetters** employ various techniques to create the image, with computers assisting in the operation logic.

photounit The part of a phototypesetter in which the photographic image is created and exposed.
pi characters Special characters outside the normal alphabetic range and not normally contained in a standard fount, eg special maths symbols.
pica 1. Unit of typographic measurement equal to 12 points or 4.21mm. 2. Size of typewriter face with 10 characters to the inch.
pitch Measurement of the number of characters per horizontal inch in typewriter faces.
place The positioning of text and/or images on the page with the use of a mouse.
plate 1. Printed illustration separated from text matter and often on different paper. 2. A one-piece printing surface (as distinct from assembled type).
plotter Device which draws graphics from computer instructions.
PMT See **photomechanical transfer.**
point system The main system of typographic measurement. 1pt=.013837" or 0.351mm. See also **Didot, em, pica.**
port An input and/or output connection to or from a computer.
portrait The shape of an image or page with the shorter dimensions at the head and foot.
positive An image on film or paper in which the dark and light values are the same as the original, as distinct from **negative.**
Postscript Adobe system's proprietary PDL. Achieved prominence through adoption by Apple, currently the most widely used PDL.
ppi Pages per inch. American method of specifying the thickness of paper.
prelims Abbreviation of **preliminary matter.** The matter in a book which precedes the text.
pre-press proofs Proofs made by techniques other than printing.
print A photograph.
print-out The text printed out by a computer printer.
process camera Camera designed for the various photographic processes involved in printing, as distinct from original photography.
program The complete set of instructions which control a computer in the performance of a task.
PROM Programmable Read Only Memory Stores programs which cannot be altered by the user. See also **firmware.**
proof A trial printed sheet or copy, made before the production run, for the purpose of checking.
proof-reading Checking typeset proofs for accuracy.
protocol A formal set of conventions governing the orderly exhange of information between communicating devices.
pull down menus Also referred to as 'pop up menus'. Options are revealed only when a menu type is accessed, usually by a pointing and dragging action with a mouse. Once the option has been selected the menu disappears leaving the screen free.

Glossary of terms

quad left, right or centre To set lines flush left, right or centre.
quarto A page one quarter of the traditional sheet size, eg Crown Quarto.
quotes Inverted commas.
qwerty Standard typewriter keyboard layout, QWERTY being the arrangement of keys on the top left hand row of the board.

ragged right Text with irregular line lengths, ie with an even left margin but an uneven right margin.
RAM Random access memory.
random access Method of directly accessing a specific address on a computer file without the need for a sequential process. **Random access memory** is often abbreviated to **RAM.**
range Align (type, etc).
raster Device which scans lines to generate an image.
raster image processor Device used in advanced area make-up systems which first processes the digital information it has been given relating to individual lots of type and images, then arranges and outputs type and images together in their correct positions. Abbreviated to **RIP.**
raw data Data before processing or preparation.
reader 1. Device which can 'read' from magnetic media or in the case of OCR, from typescript. 2. Person who checks proofs for accuracy.
read-write head The component which reads from and writes to a magnetic disk or tape.
real time Method of computing in which operations are performed on data simultaneously with input and output.
recall Calling a computer file from backing store into memory.
record A block of computer data.
recto A right-hand page.
reformatting Setting new typographical parameters for a previously set piece of copy.
refresh rate Rate at which an image is flashed on a VDT, eg 60 times a second, etc.
reprint New impression of previously printed work. See **offprint.**
response time The time required for the system to respond to a command in supplying stored data or completing a processing cycle..
reversal Creation of white text or images on black background. Sometimes referred to as WOB (white on black). See **reverse out.**
reverse out Type printing white out of another colour.
revise A revised proof for subsequent reading.
RIP 1. Rest In Position. An instruction to allow all the other pieces in a batch of artwork to undergo the same enlargement or reduction as one piece marked. 2. See **raster image processor.**
river Undesirable formation of word spaces into a vertical 'river' of white in the text.
rivering See **river.**
ROM or **Read Only Memory** Computer memory which cannot be altered by the user.
roman figures Roman numerals such as iii, xviii, xxv, etc.
roman type 'Upright' letters as distinct from **italic** (qv).
rough A sketch or layout.
rough proof Proof for identification rather than reading.
routine A computer program with a selective task.
RS 232 A standard interface protocol for the serial transmission of data between computers and peripherals.
RS 422 A more robust version of the RS 232, specifically designed for integrated technology. As used for the AppleTalk LAN.
rule A line (of specified thickness).
rules Printing lines, measured in points.
run The activation of a computer program.
run-around Type set around a picture or other element of design. Also referred to as picture wrap.
run on Continue copy on same line.
running head A title repeated at the top of each page. Also known as **running headline.**

sans serif A typeface with no **serifs** (qv).
scaling Calculating or marking the enlargement or reduction of an original for reproduction.
scanner 1. Electronic equipment which reads the relative densities of copy to make colour separations. 2. An electronic reading device for capturing black and white text and graphics. Converts image into binary data.
screen The dot formation in **half-tones** (qv).
scrolling Moving text vertically into and out of the display area of a VDU.
SCSI Small computer systems interface, an interfacing standard.
search routine Computer routine for finding specified words or groups of words in text.
second-generation Photosetters using electro-mechanical means of exposing typefounts.
sequential access Reading items in computer memory in sequence rather than by **random access** (qv).
series A complete range of sizes in the same type-face.
serifs The short cross lines on the ends of ascenders, descenders and strokes of letters in certain typefaces.
set 1. To typeset. 2. The width of a character.
set width See **set.**
SGML Standard Generalized Mark-up Language. A complex generic coding scheme published after many years of research in late 1986, and adopted as both an ISO International Standard and as a BSI British Standards Institution standard.
shift A key which, when depressed, gives a different designation to all the other keys, eg turns a lower case letter into upper case.
sizing See **scaling.**
small caps Abbreviated **sc.** Capitals the same size as the x-height of the normal lower case.

Appendix 2

SmallTalk Xerox's proprietary operating system, which formed the basis of the WIMP environment.
snap to guides Permits exact fit when placing text or graphics on a page, approximately positioned content will snap to a grid. Grid can be turned off if more precise placing is required.
soft copy Non-paper version of text, eg on a VDU.
software Term coined to contrast computer programs with the hardware of the computer system. A stored set of instructions which govern the operation of a computer system and cause the hardware to operate.
solid 1. Type set with no leading between the lines. 2. Printed area with 100 per cent ink coverage.
sort 1. A single character of type. 2. To order data into a given sequence, eg alphabetical.
spec Specification.
specimen Sample page set to show the typography.
spread Pair of facing pages.
spreadsheet A business modelling tool composed of rows and columns, allowing for the dynamic analysis of numerical data.
square serif Typeface with serifs heavier than the strokes.
s/s Abbreviation for 'same size' in reproduction specifications.
stand-alone A self-contained hardware system which needs no other machine assistance to function.
stet Proofreader's instruction meaning 'ignore marked correction', ie let it stand as it was.
storage Computer memory or a magnetic medium which can store information, eg a floppy disc.
straight matter Straightforward text setting.
strike-through Too heavy an impression in letterpress printing which leads to the printed image bleeding through to the underside of the sheet.
string A sequence of alphabetic or numeric characters in a computer program.
style of the house Typographic and linguistic rules of a publishing house. Also **house style**.
subscript Inferior character. Small character printed below the base line as part of mathematical equation.
superior Small character set above the line, especially used in mathematical statements (eg 10^2) or to indicate footnotes.
superscript See **superior**.

tabular material Typeset tables or columns of figures.
tag A format definition specifying a combination of attributes such as fount, fount size, indents and columns. Tags are named and can be applied to words, lines or paragraphs. Specific to certain DTP page composition software.
teletypesetter Abbreviated to **TTS**. Linecasting system driven by six-channel paper tape generated on separate keyboards.
terminal Keyboard and/or screen for computer communication or text generation.
text The body typesetting in a book as distinct from headings and display type.
text editing Any rearrangement or change performed upon textual material, such as correcting, adding and deleting, as distinct from alterations.
text pages The principal matter in a book as distinct from the prelims, index etc.
text type Body type of a printed work. Loosely, type smaller than about 12pt.
thermographic printing Relief effect created by heating special powder or ink on a sheet to give 'raised' typesetting.
third generation Phototypesetters using cathode ray tubes to generate the typographical images.
thumbnails Small sketches.
TIFF Transfer image file format. Emerging standard for all scanning software. Scanned images are more easily accepted by page composition software if converted into TIFF.
time-sharing Concurrent processing of several jobs or programs on a computer.
title page Page of a book carrying the title, author's name and publisher's name. Always recto.
tone Colour variation or shade of grey.
toner Chemical used to create image in photocopying processes.
tracking Automatic reduction of spacing between characters and words in the line.
transducer Electronic device which converts input signals of one type into output of a different nature.
transparency Full-colour photographic positive on transparent film for viewing by transmitted light. Suitable as copy for separation.
transpose Abbreviated **trs.** Exchange the position of words, letters or lines, especially on a proof. Hence **transposition.**
Troff Typesetter run-off, a UNIX utility allowing text to be output to a typesetting device.
TS Abbreviation for typescript.
type area Area occupied by text on a page.
typecasting Setting type in metal by a machine such as a Linotype.
typeface A specifically designated style of type, eg Times or Helvetica.
type family Roman, italic, bold and all other versions of one typeface.
type gauge A rule calibrated in picas for measuring type.
type scale See **type gauge.**
type series All the sizes available in one typeface.
typesetter Person (or company) who sets type.
typographer Designer of printed material.

u and lc also **u/lc** Abbreviation for upper and lower case. Instruction to follow copy for caps and lower case.
Ultrix Digital Equipment Corporation's

Glossary of terms

proprietary version of UNIX.
underline Caption (USA).
unit Division of the em measurement into smaller sections, varying with the manufacturer's system.
unit value The number of units in a character. See **unit**.
UNIX A multi-user operating system allowing several operators to use the same computer simultaneously.
unjustified Typesetting with even spacing, therefore having a ragged right edge.
update Edit a file by adding current data.
upper case Capital letters.

variable space Space between words used to justify a line.
VDU/VDT See **visual display unit/terminal**.
verso Left-hand page with even number.
vertical justification Spacing a column of type to fit a set depth. Automatic process on some typesetting systems.
visual A layout or rough of artwork.
visual display unit/terminal Cathode ray tube screen and keyboard for input and correction of copy to a computer or photosetter.

weight In typography, the degree of boldness of a type-face style (eg light, medium etc).
white out See **reverse out**.
white space Unfilled space on a composed page. May result from excessive rivering.
widow Short last line of a paragraph at the top of a page. Considered undesirable.
WIMP Window, icon, mouse and pull-down menus. An environment first adopted by Apple and emulated by Microsoft Windows and Digital Research GEM. A user friendly interface.

window Portion of the screen dedicated to a particular file/document. Several windows can be open on screen at one time, allowing the user to jump from one to another rapidly. Ideal operating conditions for on-screen cut and paste.
word break Division of a word at a line ending.
word processing The act of composing, inputting and editing text through the medium of a dedicated **word processor** or specific word processing software.
word processor Machine using computer logic to accept, store and retrieve documents for subsequent editing and output in typewriter style.
wordspace The variable space between words which may be increased or decreased to justify a line.
word wrap The automatic wrapping of text onto the next line when a line end is encountered.
workstation Part of a computer typesetting system manned by an operator, eg an editing terminal.
WP See **word processing**.
write To record or output electronic data.
wysiwyg what you see is what you get Acronym used to describe a visual display showing an exact replica of its output.

x-height Height of body of lower-case letters, exclusive of ascenders and descenders, ie height of the letter x.
x-line Alignment along the tops of lower-case letters.

zoom Feature allowing a preview of the entire page, or the ability to enlarge sections of the page.

Index

APL front end, 10
Apple ImageWriter, 130
AppleTalk card, 60
AppleTalk local area network, 14, 136
Apricot desktop publishing, 115

Back-end of desktop systems, 6
Book Machine (Prefis), 98

Canon LP-CX print engine, 131

Daisywheel printer, 17
Dataproducts LZR 2665, 138
DCA, 72
DDE, 72
DEC desktop publishing, 118
Dedicated system, advantages of, 112
Desktop, front-end of, 6
Desktop publisher, decisions facing the, 24
Desktop publishing
  advantages, 20
  and laser printer, 18
  and networks, 101
  and UNIX, 101
  attractions of, 7
  birth of, 35
  distributed, 145
  forces responsible, 13, 18, 35
  system, minimum software components of a Macintosh system, 29
  the term, 31
  three main elements, 15
  under DOS, 73-83
Diacritical mark, 96
Digitisers, types of, 127
Documenter (Xerox), 112, 113, 142

DOS vs WIMP environment, 64
DOS, limitations of, 68

Eddie Shah's publishing environment, 103
Editing
  at pixel level, 22
  scanned images, 122
Electronic mail, 105
Excel, 44

File
  text and graphics, 11
  in DOS, 65
Filing system, hierarchical, 66
Fleet Street Editor, 82
Front-end
  future of, 152
  of desktop system, 6
  peripherals, 121
Front page, 82
Founts, 37

GEM, 29, 69
  draw, 70
  graph, 700
  paint, 69
  what is, 69
  WordChart, 70
Gestetner, 116
Graphic digitisers, 121
Graphics
  business, 44, 109
  freehand, 42
  scanned image support, 49, 77
  scanned input, 81
  structured, 40

Graphics—cont.
  tablets, 129

Harvard Professional Publishers, 79

IBM PC, 57
IBM PC, importance of, 59
Icons, concept of, 32
Image scaling, 122
ImageWriter, 130
Ink-jet printer, 17
Interleaf workstation, 108

Jazz (Lotus), 44
Just Text, 52

Laser printers, 130, 140
LaserJet, 137-138
LaserWriter, 133-135
Letraset, 117
Linotype, 60, 146, 148
Local area networks 102, 111
Lotus 123, 17, 34

MacAuthor, 93
MacBottom, 36
Macintosh, 3, 34
  as a DTP tool, 36
MacPaint, 42
MacPublisher, 55, 117
MacWrite, 39
MagnaType, 149
Manuscript (Lotus), 94
Menus, pop-up or pull-down, 32
Microsoft Word, 40
Monotype Lasercomp, 3, 147
Multi-user system, reasons for, 103

Networking, 58
NLQ printer, 17

Operating system
  Macintosh, 34
  MS-DOS, 59, 63
Optical scanners, 124
Ouput
  phototypesetter, 135
  quality of, 6
  size, 7
  speed, 7

Page Description Language (PDL), 10, 18, 23, 49, 139
Page
layout, 15, 25
make-up, 10, 45
production, the constituent parts of, 39
PageMaker, 3, 10, 11, 38, 47, 74
PC SCAN (Dest), 129
Peripherals
  back-end, 130
  front-end, 121
Personal computer, 14, 16, 59, 60, 64, 68
Pixel
  and IBM PC, 28
  editing, 22
Postscript was the brain child of, 23
Prefis (Book Machine), 73
Printers, 17
  laser, 130
PS Compose, 149

Ragtime (Orange Micro), 55
Raster image processor (RIP), 3, 14
Ready Set Go, 50
Ricoh 4080, 132, 139
RTF, 72

Scanned images, storage of, 127
Scanners, high resolution, 128
Scanning
  services, 128
  standards, 128
Seybold Conference, 74
SCSI interface, 36
SoftQuad, 106

Tex, 99, 151
Text composition functions, 25
Thermal printer, 17
TIFF format, 29, 96
Troff, 106
Typesetter co-existing with DTP, 21
Typesetting, micro involvement in, 14
Typography
  images, 5
  standards of, 5

UNIX, 105, 107

Ventura Publisher, 76
Video digitiser, 123

Windows, 71
WIMPS, 18, 49, 83
Wordprocessing, 8, 17
  and WYSIWYG, 9, 85

concept of, 85
  enhanced, 88
Wordprocessors, 75, 76
Word (Microsoft), 40, 92
WordStar, 9, 75, 86
WYSIWYG, 18, 26, 34, 53, 80, 83, 96

WYUTIWIB, 27, 60

Xerox, 32
  Documenter, 112, 142
  part played in desktop publishing, 19
Xyvision, 38

Index of Advertisers

Advanced Graphic Communications *facing page 73*
Mirrorsoft Ltd *facing page 72*
Scientex Ltd *back cover*
Studio Box *facing page 73*
Supermac Technology *inside front cover*
Unitex Systems *facing title page*